MARINE AND SHORELAND RESOURCES MANAGEMENT

by
JOSEPH M. HEIKOFF

ANN ARBOR SCIENCE
PUBLISHERS INC / THE BUTTERWORTH GROUP

Second Printing, 1981

Copyright © 1980 by Ann Arbor Science Publishers, Inc.
230 Collingwood, P. O. Box 1425, Ann Arbor, Michigan 48106

Library of Congress Catalog Card No. 79-89720
ISBN 0-250-40338-2

Manufactured in the United States of America
All Rights Reserved

Butterworths, Ltd., Borough Green, Sevenoaks, Kent TN15 8PH, England

PREFACE

Since 1972, when Congress passed the Coastal Zone Management Act, considerable literature has appeared which deals with various coastal resources management concerns. Some of this literature reflects the continuing interest environmental scientists have had in learning about coastal habitats and the plant and animal species that inhabit them. Other scientists are learning more about the effect of wind, waves and other climate factors on shorelines. Another branch of the literature is being produced by engineers and applied scientists who are seeking more effective ways for coping with shore erosion and pollution, and improving fisheries productivity and aquaculture. Still another group of investigators is primarily concerned with the legal, institutional and fiscal aspects of coastal resources management.

Why, then, another book in the field? The objective of this one is not to suggest solutions to management problems, but rather to introduce students and the interested public to some of the major coastal management programs that state and local governments have been engaged in for years, long before the federal government recognized the importance to the nation of proper husbandry of its coastal resources. This book will attempt to answer questions about what these public agencies do and how they do it. New York State has pioneered in many aspects of coastal resources management, and a description of some of its programs may indicate what other states are doing.

This is the third in a series of studies that have been supported by the New York Sea Grant Institute and the Office of Sea Grant in the National Oceanic and Atmospheric Administration. I am grateful for the opportunity they offered to learn about coastal management programs. Special thanks are due to Dr. Donald F. Squires, Director of the New York Sea Grant Institute for his continuing interest and support. I am grateful also to Edward E. Lewis, President of Ann Arbor Science Publishers, for his willingness to undertake once again the risks involved in expanding into a new field of publication. Robert C. Hansen, Coastal Program Manager in the New York Department of State, was unfailingly cooperative in responding to requests for information about the New York program in spite of the heavy pressure of administrative responsibility. Without the remarkable patience and diligence of Maxine H. Morman and her secretarial helpmates, Addie Napolitano, Ada Bradley and

Crystal Smith, the manuscript would never have been deciphered and prepared for publication. Thanks to Christina Bych, Managing Editor, and the staff at Ann Arbor Science for bringing this volume to fruition and for invaluable help in index preparation.

Joseph M. Heikoff

Joseph M. Heikoff has been involved in public planning and land use at the corporate, government and academic levels throughout his academic and professional career. He studied at the Harvard graduate schools of design and public administration, then earned a PhD in Planning from the University of Chicago. After serving as a landscape architect for New York firms, he became land planning engineer for the Federal Housing Administration in New York. Subsequently, he was involved in city planning, industrial development and urban renewal in Puerto Rico. For 10 years he directed the Bureau of Community Planning at the University of Illinois in Urbana and since 1969 has been Professor of Public Administration at the State University of New York at Albany.

Professor Heikoff is author of three other books published by Ann Arbor Science—*Politics of Shore Erosion: Westhampton Beach*; *Management of Industrial Particulates: Corporate, Government, Citizen Action*; *and Coastal Resources Management: Institutions and Programs.*

To

The New York Sea Grant Institute

LIST OF FIGURES

LIST OF TABLES

CONTENTS

INTRODUCTION

The United States coastline is extensive and biologically and physically varied. States have different legal foundations and institutions for managing their coastal resources. Their approaches to this task vary according to the social values and economic interests of those who contend for political dominance in the state legislatures. Population increase, economic growth and urbanization have been most marked along the nation's shores, including the Great Lakes. Competition for coastal land and water resources has caused their depletion, environmental damage, occupation of hazardous areas and loss of recreational opportunities. In 1972 Congress declared that management of coastal resources was a national concern. It passed the Coastal Zone Management Act and offered financial assistance for planning coastal resources management programs and carrying them out.

Coastal resources management is complex because the environmental, economic and political characteristics of the nation's coastal states vary from Maine to Alaska and Hawaii. The management process is also complicated by these constraints: scientific uncertainty about biological resources and their land and water environments; pressure for economic growth and increased employment opportunity; and political constraints on the manner in which governments may intervene in private investment decisions and the operation of markets for goods and services.

These variables make difficult a comprehensive understanding of the concepts, activities and attitudes that are elements of the developing process called coastal resources management. An appreciation of what is involved in attempting to carry out this endeavor may be obtained, however, from a sampling of efforts. This account is based upon an examination of some New York State management programs, many of which were started years before Congress established the national coastal program in 1972. In order that this investigation might be of manageable size, it has been confined mostly to that part of New York State's marine coast included in Nassau and Suffolk counties on Long Island. It is by no means an exhaustive analysis and description of coastal resources management even for this area. It may, however, offer an introduction to the technical and governmental factors that interact in the coastal management process.

It would be difficult and not very useful to describe in detail every action that every local, state or federal agency has taken that has affected the Long Island coast. This study will therefore examine only the major programs, with the objective of illustrating the complexity of the institutional arrangements for coastal resources management. Each level of government established its own agencies to carry out various management functions. Duplicating or parallel agencies may even have been set up deliberately to protect local, state or national interests or because the legislative bodies concerned did not have confidence in each other's programs.

The resulting institutional pattern is unstructured and confusing, difficult to describe and understand. It has produced duplication of effort and sometimes conflicts in policy and action. Nevertheless, an informal network of communication and coordination has evolved that connects technical staffs and decision-makers in the various agencies. As might be expected, the results of their negotiations vary according to the views of those who hold elective or appointive office.

Management activities by agencies at all levels of government already cover the entire coastal area of Long Island. All of the land areas are zoned, and local regulations cover wetlands and waterways as well. State regulations also govern marine and freshwater wetlands, wildlife and commercial and recreational taking of fish, shellfish and crustaceans. Water pollution, dredging and filling of wetlands and waterways, and navigation are regulated by state and federal agencies. Local governments own and manage most of the lands under water in the great bays behind the barrier islands. The bottom lands out to the state boundary in Long Island Sound and the Atlantic Ocean bottom to the three mile limit are controlled by New York State. Extensive local, county and state parks and other recreation facilities are located on the shore, and large areas of wetlands and other undeveloped reservations are owned and managed by public agencies. The federal government also has facilities and reservations in the Long Island coastal zone.

Although all the land and water areas of the coastal zone of Long Island towns are under public regulation or ownership, this does not mean that there are no environmental problems or conflicts between resources conservation and expanding urbanization. Federal, state and local legal foundations and institutional mechanisms are already available to deal with these problems, but technical knowledge, professional and technical personnel and financial resources are admitted to be serious constraints on current management effectiveness. The federal Coastal Zone Management Act offers additional resources and the requirement that the state must prepare a comprehensive coastal zone management program.

It is appropriate in this introduction to offer a definition of the phrase "coastal zone management" or, as it may be rephrased, "coastal resources management," for these terms will be used frequently in this report. This definition has two parts: (1) managment objectives and the values they imply and (2) management methods.

The coastal resources management objective is to conserve, protect, restore and, where appropriate, to exploit economically the land, water and biological resources of the coastal zone. This objective is based on the understanding that society values the natural ecology of habitats and their plant and animal species, the aesthetic and recreational values of shorelands and waters, productive fisheries and shellfish beds and protection of upland areas from storm and flood damage. Resources management, however, must balance these environmental values against the economic values that may be gained only by obliterating the natural features of shorelands to provide sites for urban expansion, transportation terminals, fuel production and power generation; by changing the bottom configuration for sand and gravel mining and navigation; and by degrading water quality by disposing of the liquid and solid wastes produced by industry and consumers.

The actual process of management begins with inventory and analysis of the state of coastal zone resources, designation of areas of particular environmental concern and determination of the carrying capacity of various shoreline reaches for economic use. Management programs that are planned and carried out by governments at all levels are of two kinds: (1) public acquisition of shorelands and underwater lands for direct public action to conserve environmental resources and to provide services and facilities for the public and to support the private economy; and (2) public regulation of private economic activity to guide its location, density and compatibility with environmental quality standards.

The New York State Department of State is the lead agency for preparing the coastal management program in accordance with the federal Coastal Zone Management Act. As part of this effort, it has to propose a formal coastal zone management structure, which is expected to rationalize existing organizational and functional relationships without further complicating them.

There is another difficulty in the way of attempting to describe coastal management organizations and programs. This is the problem of going beyond identifying the various agencies and their program responsibilities to measuring their performance. Some programs may be inactive, underfunded or poorly managed. Successive political administrations may adopt policies that change program emphasis, reallocate budget resources and reassign management personnel. It is beyond the scope of this study to evaluate performance. In any case, at the time this report is being prepared, the New York State coastal zone management program is in the development stage.

Formal approval by the federal Office of Coastal Zone Management in the Department of Commerce is not expected until some time in 1979. Evaluation of the program will have to wait until it has been given a chance to demonstrate its effectiveness.

The entire New York State marine coast has long been covered by an overlapping array of federal, state and local management programs. What, then, might be expected from a new, federally aided, statewide program? At least three possible advantages may be suggested. One has already been noted. It is the rationalization of the institutional structure of federal-state-local communication, decision-making and program coordination. Political conflict, interagency competition and interest group lobbying will not be eliminated by new institutional designs, but these may help to smooth intergovernmental and interagency relations and help the state coastal managers meet their responsibility to implement a coherent program for conserving and protecting coastal resources and at the same time encouraging economic development by making use of them.

The second advantageous consequence of a statewide coastal program would be the improvement of county and local coastal management performance so that the less effective local efforts would approach the level of the more effective governments. Long Island has excellent regional, county and municipal resources management programs. State coastal program guidelines and requirements may produce more effective management in other areas of the state.

The third contribution of a statewide coastal program could be protection of the interests of people in communities that may be chosen as sites for facilities that serve regional or national interests. Airports, power plants and offshore petroleum exploitation facilities are examples. Such facilities have severe impacts on the communities in which they are located. Coastal managers in state governments may be able to plan for the amelioration of adverse impacts and maximizing the possible economic advantages these developments may bring.

In order to explore these possibilities, this study will first describe the approach to coastal resources management taken by the federal government. It will then describe New York state and local programs already in existence. Finally, it will describe the state program developed under the aegis of the Coastal Zone Management Act and the influence it is expected to have on earlier state and local efforts.

CHAPTER 1

THE FEDERAL COASTAL MANAGEMENT PROGRAM

In its most general sense the phrase "coastal zone management" could signify the public interest in managing anything and everything that goes on in the coastal zone, however that area may be defined. In these terms coastal zone management overlaps and includes everything that all governments already do or will do in the area. This most comprehensive definition of the phrase is too broad to give it operational meaning, particularly as it may be applied to public policies and programs. A narrower definition, which focuses on environmental resources in the coastal zone, is given in the federal Coastal Zone Management Act of 1972, as amended in 1976. This law in effect defines coastal zone management for the states that have elected to participate in the federal program.

ENVIRONMENTAL CONCERNS

Some of the language in the Coastal Zone Management Act focuses on Congressional concern for environmental values. Among the Congressional findings in Sec. 302 of the act are these statements:

The coastal zone is rich in a variety of natural, commercial, recreational, ecological, industrial, and esthetic resources of immediate and potential value to the present and future well-being of the nation;

The increasing and competing demands upon the lands and waters of our coastal zone occasioned by population growth and economic development . . . have resulted in the loss of living marine resources, wildlife, nutrient-rich areas, permanent and adverse changes to ecological systems, decreasing open space for public use, and shoreline erosion;

The coastal zone, and the fish, shellfish, other living marine resources, and wildlife therein, are ecologically fragile and consequently extremely vulnerable to destruction by man's alterations;

5

In light of competing demands and the urgent need to protect and to give high priority to natural systems in the coastal zone, present state and local institutional arrangements . . . are inadequate;

The key to more effective protection and use of land and water resources of the coastal zone is to encourage the states to exercise their full authority.

Following up on these findings, with their primary concern for environmental resources in the coastal zone, Sec. 303 of the Coastal Zone Management Act contains this statement:

The Congress finds and declares that it is the national policy (a) to preserve, protect, develop, and where possible, to restore or enhance, the resources of the nation's coastal zone for this and succeeding generations (b) to encourage and assist the states to exercise effectively their responsibilities in the coastal zone through the development and implementation of management programs to achieve wise use of the land and water resources of the coastal zone . . .

ECONOMIC CONCERNS

Consideration and protection of the natural environment is not the exclusive concern of the Coastal Zone Management Act. Congress recognized also that much of the nation's economic activity has concentrated along the marine and Great Lakes coasts. Increasing the prosperity and potential for growth of the national economy is also an objective of coastal management. The statement from Sec. 302 quoted above notes the existence of commercial and industrial resources in the coastal zone that contribute to national well-being.

The congressional declaration of policy in Sec. 303 of the act favors the promotion of both environmental and economic values. Coastal programs for the wise use of land and water resources are to give "full consideration to ecological, cultural, historic, and esthetic values as well as to needs for economic development." The 1976 amendments to the act also emphasize economic considerations. The coastal energy impact program, which will be described later on, was motivated by the national demand for growth in energy resources and the need to cope with the economic, as well as the environmental, consequences of petroleum exploration on the outer continental shelf. Nevertheless, balancing economic and environmental values in state coastal management programs will be a difficult and politically sensitive task.

COMPONENTS OF STATE COASTAL
MANAGEMENT PROGRAMS

Section 305 of the Coastal Zone Management Act of 1972, as amended, authorizes the Secretary of Commerce to make grants available to coastal states to prepare management programs. The following technical components of a state coastal zone management program are listed in this section of the act:

1. identification of the boundaries of the coastal zone,
2. definition of permissible land and water uses in the coastal zone that have a direct and significant impact on coastal waters,
3. inventory and designation of areas of particular concern,
4. broad guidelines on priorities of uses in particular areas, including uses of lowest priority,
5. definition of the term "beach" and a planning process for the protection of, and access to, public beaches and other coastal areas,
6. planning process for energy facilities that may be located in or significantly affect the coastal zone, including managing the impacts of such facilities, and
7. planning process for assessing the effects of shoreline erosion and for studying ways to control such erosion and restore areas adversely affected by it.

The administrative components of state coastal zone management programs are to include:

1. identification of the means by which the state proposes to exert control over land and water uses, including relevant constitutional provisions, laws, regulations, and judicial decisions, and
2. description of the organizational structure proposed to implement the management program.

To assist the coastal states, the Secretary of Commerce is authorized to make annual grants to cover up to 80% of the cost of preparing coastal management programs. Sec. 305 of the federal act provides that states may normally receive only four program development grants, but under specific conditions, the Secretary may make additional funds available to help the states qualify for administrative grants under Sec. 306. These are grants to help implement coastal resources management, but the state must qualify by having a management program approved by the Secretary. The authority to make program development grants will expire on Sepember 30, 1979.

An important provision of Sec. 305 is that, with the approval of the Secretary of Commerce, coastal states may allocate part of their federal grants to local governments, regional agencies or interstate agencies to support their participation in preparing the state coastal management program. New York State has taken advantage of this provision to make contracts with counties and regional planning agencies for this purpose.

The Coastal Energy Impact Program

A long new Sec. 308 has been added to the Coastal Zone Management Act by the 1976 amendments. It describes the kinds of financial assistance the federal government will give to state and local governments to deal with the impacts of energy development. Financial assistance may take these forms:

1. grants to coastal states to plan and carry out projects and programs to deal with the impacts of energy development,
2. grants to coastal states to plan for measures to deal with economic, social or environmental consequences of location, construction, expansion or operation of new or expanded energy facilities,
3. loans to coastal states and local governments to assist them to provide new or improved public facilities or services required as a result of coastal energy activities,
4. guarantees of bonds or other indebtedness issues by coastal states or local governments to provide new or improved public facilities or services required as a result of coastal energy activities,
5. grants or other assistance to coastal states and local governments to enable them to meet obligations under loans and guarantees (under 4 above), which they are unable to meet as they mature, and
6. grants to coastal states that have suffered or may suffer unavoidable loss of a valuable environment or recreational resource as the result of coastal energy activities.

Interstate Grants

Another new section contained in the amendments of 1976 may have considerable future interest for New York State coastal management. Section 309 of the amended act is concerned with interstate grants. It provides that the Secretary of Commerce may make annual grants of up to 90% of the cost of carrying out interstate coordination, study, planning or implementation of coastal management programs according to approved interstate compacts or agreements. Negotiation of such agreements with neighboring states may be of great benefit to New York State. The coastal resource problems of Long Island Sound and the New York Bight cannot adequately be attacked without cooperative action with Connecticut and New Jersey. Water pollution, shore erosion, fisheries management and development of offshore petroleum resources are only among the more obvious of such problems.

Estuarine Sanctuaries and Beach Access

Although the emphasis of this study is on coastal zone management as defined in Sections 305 and 306 of the federal Coastal Zone Management Act, brief mention should also be made of Section 315. This section of the act provides for a program of financial assistance to states to acquire estuarine sanctuaries and lands to provide access to beaches and other areas. This program may be operated either independently of or in conjunction with the coastal zone management program. The act simply states that the Secretary of Commerce may make grants for this purpose to any coastal state that conforms its application to the rules and regulations promulgated by him.

Federal grants may be made for these specific purposes: (1) to acquire, develop or operate estuarine sanctuaries, or (2) to acquire lands to provide access to public beaches and other public coastal areas of environmental, recreational, historic, esthetic, ecological or cultural value and for the preservation of islands. These grants may cover up to 50% of the cost of the project, but there is a $2 million limit to the federal share of acquiring an estuarine sanctuary.

Criteria for Federal Approval of State Coastal Management Programs

The Secretary of Commerce may make annual grants to coastal states to cover up to 80% of the cost of carrying out coastal management programs. The Secretary must first find, however, that the state's management program conforms to the detailed requirements of Sec. 306 of the Coastal Zone Management Act as amended. These are the criteria for approval set forth in Sec. 306:

1. The state coastal management program has been developed and adopted in accordance with the rules and regulations promulgated by the Secretary of Commerce. There must also have been opportunity for full participation by relevant federal agencies, state agencies, local governments, regional organizations, port authorities and other interested parties, public and private.
2. The state coastal management program has been coordinated with local, areawide and interstate plans applicable to areas within the coastal zone. The state coastal management agency must also have an effective mechanism for continuing consultation and coordination with local governments, interstate agencies, regional agencies and areawide agencies to assure their full participation in the coastal mangement program.
3. The state has held public hearings in the development of the management program.
4. The coastal management program has been approved by the governor.

5. The governor has designated a single agency to receive and administer federal grants for implementing the coastal mangement program.
6. The state is organized to implement the management program.
7. The management program provides for adequate provision of the national interest in facilities, including energy facilities, which are necessary to meet requirements which are other than local in nature.
8. The management program provides for the designation of areas for the purpose of preserving or restoring them for their conservation, recreational, ecological or esthetic values.
9. The state, its various agencies, its various area-wide, regional and interstate agencies, and its local governments have the authority and power to implement the coastal management program, including:
    a. Power to administer land and water use regulation, control development and resolve conflicts among competing uses.
    b. Power to acquire fee simple and less than fee simple interests in lands, waters and other property through condemnation or other means.
10. The management program provides for at least one of these general techniques for control of land and water uses in the coastal zone.
    a. State criteria and standards for local implementation, subject to state administrative review and enforcement of compliance.
    b. Direct state land and water use planning and regulation.
    c. State administrative review for consistency with the management program of all development plans, projects or land and water use regulations proposed by any state or local authority or private developer, with power to approve or disapprove after public notice and an opportunity for hearings.
11. The management program provides a method of assuring that local land and water use regulations within the coastal zone do not unreasonably restrict or exclude land and water uses of regional benefit.

If the Secretary of Commerce finds that all of these criteria have been met, he may approve the state coastal management program. Federal implementation grants may then be made available to the state. With the approval of the Secretary, the state may in turn allocate portions of these grants to local governments or to areawide, regional or interstate agencies. States do not have to submit management programs that cover their entire coastal zones at once. With the approval of the Secretary, the state may also submit a management program for a segment of the coastal zone. The state must provide, however, for the ultimate coordination of the various segments into a single unified coastal management program.

Section 307 of the federal act describes how federal agencies and the states must cooperate and coordinate program development and implementation. The Secretary of Commerce is to coordinate his department's activities with other interested federal agencies. This would include submitting state coastal programs to these federal agencies for review. They would also be expected to comment during the environmental impact statement review procedures.

After the Secretary has approved a state coastal management program, federal agencies conducting activities or undertaking development projects in the coastal zone must do so in a manner consistent with the approved management program to the "maximum extent practicable." It may be expected that the latter part of this provision may lead to some disputes between state and federal agencies as to what is indeed practicable.

Any plan for exploration, development or production of petroleum resources from outer continental shelf leases granted by the Department of Interior must carry the certification by the state that the activities will be carried out in compliance with the state coastal management plan. State and local governments submitting applications to federal agencies for financial assistance under various federal programs must also show that these activities will be consistent with the state coastal management program.

The track record for federal government approval of state programs resembles a race among tortoises. Neither Congress nor the federal Office of Coastal Zone Management (OCZM) appear to have anticipated the technical problems that would arise in state attempts to prepare management programs or the problems of intergovernmental relations and internal state and local politics that have hampered progress in some states. OCZM itself has been dissatisfied with program development in some areas and has been slow to accept state proposals.

State coastal program managers find themselves in the difficult position of trying to satisfy and placate a great variety of government officials, politicians, business interests and citizen organizations that have divergent views about what they want from coastal resources management—or if they want it at all. Program planning, therefore, appears to be less concerned with program consequences for resources management than with preparing a document containing the right words to please the Office of Coastal Zone Management, all the local governments whose autonomy with respect to development regulation may have been reduced and all the property owners and lobby groups whose interests may have been affected.

COASTAL MANAGEMENT PROGRAMMING AND OPERATIONS

State coastal resources management efforts fall into two broad categories: (1) the preparation of management programs and (2) carrying them out. As people in coastal states became aware of the value of their coastal resources, state legislatures enacted laws to establish resources management policies and programs and assigned responsibility for them to various state agencies. Many states already have a history of programs for managing wetlands, flood plains, pollution, fish and shellfish, wildlife and land and water uses in the coastal zone. Congress has laudably provided federal financial aid to encourage and assist states in furthering their efforts to conserve and protect their coastal resources. Nevertheless, as with other federal programs, the Office of Coastal Zone Management in the Department of Commerce exacts a toll of bureaucratic rules and procedures in exchange for federal financial aid.

It is natural for federal agencies to be concerned that state and local government recipients of federal grants use the money for the purposes for which it was appropriated and without waste. But in fulfilling their responsibilities, federal agencies tend to proliferate bureaucracies to write ever more stringent rules and lean over the shoulders of state and local officials, watching every move they make, to enforce the rules. Every document prepared at the state and local level, be it an application to initiate a program, a preliminary or final program plan, a progress report or a technical study is reviewed in careful detail to see that the rules have been obeyed.

The result of this relationship between federal bureaucrats and their state and local opposite numbers is a game. For the local people the object of the game is to find out exactly what the federal people want to hear, then tell them what they want to hear, in the words they want to hear it. The major objective of state and local agencies is to produce correct documents for the federal agency. Only after they have put down the right words may they be certified to go ahead and do what needs to be done to bring the benefits of the program to their people. Meanwhile, great costs have been incurred to prepare revision after revision of the required documents and have them subjected to review after review by the federal people.

In the case of coastal zone management, the superposition of the federal program over the ongoing state and local efforts required enactment by Congress of the Coastal Zone Management Act of 1972; promulgation by the Secretary of Commerce of draft and final regulations separately for Sec. 305, Sec. 306 and Sec. 312 of the Act; and preparation by the Office of Coastal Zone Management of two versions of "Threshold Papers" to refine and strengthen the rules and regulations. Congress then enacted the Coastal Zone Management Act Amendments of 1976, precipitating another round of rule making and requiring expansion of the federal OCZM to make sure the requirements of the expanded federal rule book are obeyed.

The proliferation of rules, procedures and bureaucrats at the federal level can only be regarded as evidence of a profound distrust by people in federal agencies of state and local elected officials and public servants. It would appear that the reason for imposing minutely detailed instructions on how to prepare elements of state coastal resources management programs is the federal assumption that state resources managers are ignorant, incompetent, or both. It may be assumed, however, that professional and technical personnel in state and local government have the same qualifications of education and experience as their opposite numbers in the federal agency. It is true that the federal employees seem to have a wider scope and greater power than state and local civil servants, but they are far removed from responsibility for program operations and achieving results and from the local values and political environments in which program decisions must be made.

State coastal resources managers have full responsibility for devising and implementing programs to conserve and protect state environmental resources. They are charged to do this by state as well as federal laws. They include not only the managers, planners, scientists and engineers in the state planning and resources conservation agencies, but also similarly qualified personnel in cooperating public and private universities in the state. Federal agencies urge on the state people speed and efficiency in preparing resources management programs; then they sometimes change the rules right in the middle of state efforts to comply with earlier rules and instructions. Is there no alternative to the federal agency role as taskmaster and overseer? It would appear that the role of leader and technical advisor would be more appropriate. The great expenditures used to produce tons of paper for bureaucrats to review could also be put to more productive use.

RESOURCES MANAGEMENT

The Coastal Zone Management Act, the regulations, the OCZM threshold papers and state and local coastal management programs use the term "management" without really defining it. The federal act defines "management programs" as a "comprehensive statement . . . setting forth objectives, policies, and standards to guide public and private uses of lands and waters in the coastal zone" [Sec. 304 (g)] . The management program, then, is supposed to be a document, and the various coastal states are enjoined by OCZM to present an acceptable one that expresses in the "right" words the state's intentions for managing coastal resources.

This "administrative" definition of management could be usefully supplemented by an operational definition that describes management action or behavior rather than a document. There are two aspects to public management of coastal resources that could be included in such a definition. One is direct operational management of publicly-owned or controlled resources. The other is regulation of privately-owned coastal resources.

In the operational aspects of management, public agencies are directly responsible for attaining the management objectives for the various resource areas. For example, parks and other recreation areas are managed to offer maximum public access to the facilities that are constructed and maintained by the public agency. Wetlands and other areas with fragile ecosystems, however, may be managed to conserve the plant, fish and wildlife habitats and offer only limited public access.

The other aspect of resources management involves governmental regulation of the private use of the resources. Zoning and subdivision regulations are examples of land use controls. Under other laws or ordinances, building construction, fishing and shellfishing, dredging, sand and gravel mining, petroleum extraction, and transportation and other private activities are regulated. The regulatory process includes setting standards, acting on permit applications and hearing appeals from regulatory decisions.

In the context of the coastal zone program, management refers to *natural resources* management. Such resources are the lands, waters and plant and animal life that inhabit the lands and waters. Some lands and waters have already been changed from their natural condition by development for a variety of economic and other uses. This development is generally characterized as urbanization or use for transportation, recreation and energy or fuel production facilities. Other "natural resource areas" may have been degraded by excessive pollution, dredging or draining, or dumping of dredge spoil or municipal wastes. The resources management process, then, may be conceived as having these aspects.

1. Identifying and determining a policy on remaining "natural resources areas":
   a. how much to be retained in "pristine" natural state (preservation)
   b. how much to be restored to "pristine" state (restoration)
   c. how much to be converted to economic, recreational or other permissible uses
2. Determining management policies for each of the above classes of resources areas:
   a. public acquisition of fee ownership or easement rights in land and waters (preservation and restoration)
   b. public acquisition for recreation or other public use (permissible uses)
   c. regulation of private use and development (permissible uses)
3. Devising programs to implement the above policies:
   a. for preservation areas:
      (1) regulating access—if any
      (2) infrastructure construction (paths, roads, toilets, etc.) if any
      (3) regulating permissible uses by private owners
   b. For restoration areas:
      (1) removal of dumped wastes, structures or other manmade features
      (2) restoration of physical configuration of lands
      (3) replanting and restocking with animal life
      (4) regulating access and providing facilities for public use
      (5) regulating permissible uses by private owners
   c. For conservation areas:
      (1) regulation of permissible public and private uses according to legal standards and criteria

d. For urbanized or otherwise developed areas or areas in other economic use (e.g., agriculture, forestry, mining, fishing):
   (1) reconsideration of regulations to achieve legally adopted standards of environmental quality
   (2) enforcement of standards and implementation of permitting procedures
   (3) determination of the extent and nature of future development

CHAPTER 2

COASTAL LAND USE REGULATION

Perhaps the most significant element in a coastal resources management program is regulation of land use. Authority for land use and building regulation has traditionally been delegated by states to local units of general government. New York State has defined this municipal authority in its constitution and in statutes that define local government structure and functions. Local zoning has been the traditional regulator of permissible uses and development priorities within specifically defined zones. Development standards are contained in subdivision regulations and building codes.

Among the components of state coastal management programs that are required by the federal Coastal Zone Management Act, these are particularly concerned with land use:

Definition of permissible land and water uses in the coastal zone that have a direct and significant impact on coastal waters.

Inventory and designation of geographic areas of particular environmental concern.

Broad guidelines on priority of uses in particular areas, including identification of uses of lowest priority.

Preparation of these management program elements would take into account three broad categories of public and private lands. Publicly owned lands are already subject to governmental management. They may be used for open space, recreation, various institutions and public services, and for transportation—including extensive facilities such as highways, seaports and airports. Public lands within the designated coastal zone may readily be managed to meet state criteria for their impact on coastal water, land and air resources.

Privately owned lands may be either developed or undeveloped. These are the areas of regulatory concern for coastal management. Developed areas are already in use for residence, commerce, industry, agriculture, recreation and institutions. The location and construction of facilities for these uses were presumably regulated in most municipalities by local land use regulations and building codes. Zoning and other codes may not be applied retroactively, but emission of air and water pollutants may be regulated in already developed areas in New York State by the Department of Environmental Conservation. Privately developed areas may be designated in coastal management programs as being of particular concern for their economic rather than environmental values and for meeting air and water quality standards.

It is on private undeveloped land that coastal management may make its most important impact. Zoning and other land use regulations are available, and they may be required to meet state criteria of management effectiveness in coastal areas. As will be noted later on, the federal government may also establish criteria for local land use regulations in the Fire Island National Seashore. Private undeveloped lands that have unique environmental values may be designated as geographic areas of particular concern, but they pose management problems. As private lands, their owners may not legally be forbidden to make any economic use of them at all. Coastal managers may solicit voluntary cooperation with the state coastal management program; but failing to succeed, they may have to purchase development or full property rights in these lands in order to preserve or restore their environmental values.

LEGAL FOUNDATION FOR MUNICIPAL REGULATORY POWERS

The federal Coastal Zone Management Act requires that states demonstrate that they have legal authority to manage the coastal zone, including these powers:

1. to administer land and water use regulations, control development in order to ensure compliance with the management program, and to resolve conflicts among competing uses; and
2. to acquire fee simple and less than fee simple interests in lands, waters, and other property through condemnation or other means when necessary to achieve conformance with the management program [1].

The first of these is the police power by which governments may use their coercive authority to protect public health, safety and general welfare. This power inherently resides in the states, but they may delegate it to municipalities. This is the authority for local zoning and other land use controls. The second power is called eminent domain, and it authorizes governments to take private property for public purposes upon payment of reasonable compensation. This power may also be delegated by states to municipalities.

In New York, these powers are granted to local governments by the state constitution and special statutes. Article IX of the constitution concerns local governments. It states that "local governments shall have power to take by eminent domain private property within their boundaries for public use" and also that "every local government shall have power to adopt and amend local laws . . . relating to . . . the government, protection, order, conduct, safety, health and well-being of persons or property therein" [2].

This is the basic legal authority by which local governments may exercise for coastal resources management the police power to regulate land and water uses and the power of eminent domain to acquire ownership or rights in property. The state constitution further provides that the state legislature "shall enact . . . a statute of local governments granting to local governments powers including but not limited to those of local legislation and administration" [3]. This statute defines "local government" as a county, city, town or village and grants them these powers, among others:

1. The power to adopt, amend and repeal ordinances, resolutions and rules and regulations in the exercise of its functions, powers and duties.
2. The power to acquire real and personal property or any interest therein for its purposes.
3. In the case of a city, village, or town . . . the power to adopt, amend and repeal zoning regulations.
4. The power to perform comprehensive or other planning work relating to its jurisdiction [4].

Note that counties do not have zoning power, but they do have power under the General Municipal Law to review local zoning decisions in certain areas.

Municipalities have not only the power of eminent domain and the zoning authority aspect of the police power, but also the other powers listed above for planning and regulating land use as a means for coastal resources management. A more general grant of the police power is delegated to counties, cities, villages and towns under the state Municipal Home Rule Law, which reaffirms their constitutional power to adopt local laws relating to "the government, protection, order, conduct, safety, health and well-being of persons or property therein" [5].

REGULATORY MEASURES

Zoning

New York State statutes enable cities, towns and villages to establish the necessary boards or commissions and carry out planning and zoning [6]. These are related functions, for the state laws require zoning to be carried out in accordance with a comprehensive plan. The term "comprehensive plan" has not been defined in the statutes, but in deciding zoning controversies, the state courts require evidence that local zoning action conforms either to a written plan or to some framework of documents and actions that reflect a planning process.

Zoning ordinances regulate or restrict the size and bulk of buildings, lot coverage and setbacks from property lines, and residential population density. They also specify the use of structures and land for commerce, industry, residence and other purposes. Zoning is an important tool for land resources management, for it has the stated objective of relating the kind and intensity of land uses permitted in particular zones to the design of infrastructure networks to serve those uses. Facilities for transportation, water supply, sewage collection and treatment, education, recreation and public safety should be located and scaled in size to serve particular residential populations, industrial areas, retail centers and other private and public land uses. Land use regulation may thus help communities achieve efficiency and economy in providing services to residents and business firms.

The Coastal Zone Management Act mandates the inclusion of a program element in the state coastal management plan that specifies permissible land and water uses within the coastal zone boundaries. The New York State program will therefore have to relate the state determination of permissible uses along specific reaches of the coast to local plans and regulations.

Zoning regulations inevitably affect land values, for they restrict the free market in real estate. Some properties may be devoted only to uses that bring low economic returns to the owners; others may yield high returns. Restricting the amount of land that may be devoted to high value uses reduces the availability of such parcels and raises their price. Although zoning may reduce the value of a person's property, he is not entitled to compensation for the loss under the police power. Nevertheless, zoning may not be so restrictive as to prevent any reasonable use at all, for this would amount to confiscation or "taking" of the property by government without compensation. For example, it would presumably be illegal for a local government to prevent any use whatever of a privately owned wetland in order to preserve its ecological values.

Drafters of a zoning ordinance cannot anticipate the problems that it might cause for every property owner in every zone. Property owners who are denied a building or alteration permit on the ground that the proposed use or structure would violate the zoning law may apply to the appeals board for a variance. The New York zoning enabling laws provide that a zoning board of appeals may "vary or modify" the application of a zoning ordinance when there are practical difficulties in complying with the strict letter of its requirements or unnecessary hardships for the owner. The "practical difficulty" test is supposed to be used when the lot size, shape, topography or other physical condition makes reasonable use of the property impossible because of the coverage or setback requirements of the ordinance. The "unnecessary hardship" test may be applied when a property owner claims that he cannot obtain a reasonable return from the use permitted by the ordinance and that his proposed use will not alter the character of the neighborhood. If an appeal in either case is denied by a zoning board, the property owner may continue his appeal in the New York State Supreme Court.

Land use plans and zoning have been designed traditionally to accommodate forecasted population and economic growth in the community. Assignment of use priorities has not usually been related to the ecological or environmental characteristics of the land to be included in the various use zones. For example, before the environmental value of wetlands was recognized, they were often included in zones designated for residential, industrial and other uses. They were drained and filled for development regardless of their ecological characteristics or even economic value as fish spawning and nursery areas. Waterfront lands are in great demand and will be developed where zoning ordinances permit it. One of the important tasks of state coastal management programs, therefore, will be to review local zoning ordinances and require that they be revised to conform to the program's resources management objectives.

Subdivision Control

This type of land development regulation complements zoning, but New York law does not require that they be used together. Communities may choose to enact one or the other, both or neither. Subdivision regulations specify the standards for the development of large parcels that are to be divided into smaller lots. Where access to the new lots must be provided, the regulations specify street widths, type of paving, block lengths, sidewalks and street lighting requirements. Standards for surface drainage and storm sewers, earth moving and retention of mature trees may also be included. Water supply and sanitary waste disposal systems must also be approved, for which permits from county or state health departments and the State Department of Environmental Conservation may have to be obtained. Land developers may also be required to set aside park and playground areas.

The New York State General City Law, Town Law and Village Law authorize municipal legislative bodies to grant to planning boards the power to draw up subdivision regulations and to review and approve subdivision plats. Without such approval and the necessary water supply and sanitary waste disposal permits, plats may not be filed with the county clerk. Official filing of subdivision plats is a practical condition for putting the lots up for sale.

The Official Map. The purpose of the official map is to help implement community plans by reserving rights-of-way for future streets and highways and sites for recreation and drainage facilities. By using the police power, development of such mapped lands may be prevented without actually buying them. If building were to be permitted on these lands, the cost of the facilities would be increased because the improvements would have to be bought and demolished. The method used to keep the land open is the legal prohibition on the issuance of building permits within the mapped areas. Municipalities may refuse to issue building permits only for sites within the mapped rights-of-way of future streets. Counties may also adopt official maps that show lands reserved for county roads and drainage systems, as well as for other proposed transportation networks and county, state and federally approved public works. In the case of county official maps, the granting of building permits is prohibited for *any* mapped land. As with zoning, however, hardship cases may be brought before local appeals boards from either municipal or county decisions.

The Role of the Counties

Counties may establish planning boards, and they may engage technical staffs to prepare a county development plan. Once adopted by the county legislature, the plan acquires considerable legal status.

> When . . . approved in whole or in part by the board of supervisors in any county or counties such approved county plan or part thereof shall be deemed to be binding upon the board of supervisors of the county and the several county departments thereof, and no expenditure of public funds by such county for the acquisition of land . . . or for any [county] public improvements shown on such county plan shall be made except in accordance with such county plan, and no expenditure of public funds by the county shall be made for any other [county] public improvements . . . not shown on any such county plan or on the acquisition of land therefor, which would necessitate the modification of such county plan, until the county plan has been amended [7].

Although county governments have not been granted zoning powers by state law, they have important review powers over municipal land use actions. Article 12-B of the New York General Municipal is the source of these powers. This law declares that it is in the public interest that certain classes of local zoning and planning actions be reviewed by county planning agencies, or by metropolitan or regional planning agencies where there are no county planning bodies. The objective of this review is to improve the coordination of planning and zoning actions among municipalities by bringing intercommunity and countywide considerations to their attention. Before taking final action to adopt or amend zoning regulations, issue special permits, or grant variances, local governments must refer such matters to the county planning agency if they fall into these categories:

> (a) Any municipal zoning regulation, or any amendment thereof, which would change the district classification of the regulations applying to real property lying within a distance of five hundred feet from the boundary of any city, village, or town, or from the boundary of any existing or proposed county or state park or other recreation area, or from the right-of-way of any existing or proposed county or state parkway, thruway, expressway, road, or highway, or drainage channel owned by the county, . . . or from the existing or proposed boundary of any county or state owned land on which a public building or institution is situated; and (b) any special permit or variance affecting such real property within such distance of five hundred feet [8].

The county or regional planning agency has 30 days in which to review the proposed local action. If it disapproves the proposal or recommends modification, the local government may not take the action "except by a vote of a majority plus one of all the members" of the local board or legislative body concerned. These bodies must also adopt a resolution setting forth their reasons for disregarding the disapproval or recommendation of the county planning agency.

The New York General Municipal Law also authorizes county or regional planning boards to exercise subdivision control powers within towns outside the limits of any incorporated village or city. The county or regional planning board would assume town powers and act in accordance with the New York Town Law. Where a town planning board is in existence, but presumably not exercising subdivision control powers, the town board must first adopt a resolution consenting to county or regional planning board assumption of this responsibility.

In order to take on subdivision control powers, the county or regional planning board designates specific subdivision control areas. It then adopts subdivision regulations and submits them to the town board for approval. After such approval, no subdivision map or plat may be filed or recorded in the office of the county clerk unless it has been approved by the county or regional planning board.

Other municipalities may also ask county or regional planning boards to exercise their subdivision review powers. The law provides that:

... the common council of any city or the board of trustees of any village or
town ... within any county or region for which ... a planning board has been
established, may assign to such planning board the authority herein set forth in
relation to subdivisions ... in the same manner and with the same force and
effect as though such authority has been assigned to a duly established city,
village or town planning agency [9].

Approval of a subdivision plat by a county or regional planning board, however, does not bind any city, town or village to accept for dedication any
street, highway, park or other area shown on the plat. The municipal governing body must do so by its own resolution.

LOCAL LAND USE PLANNING
AND REGULATION

The comparatively recent national visibility given to coastal resources
management by passage of the Coastal Zone Management Act in 1972 tends
to obscure two of its important features. One is that coastal states, including
New York, practiced some aspects of coastal management long before 1972.
The other is that although the federal act mandates that the states shall take
primary responsibility for coastal management programs, local communities
will determine how much popular support will be given to them. For this
reason, investigation of what is actually happening in coastal management
must start with local governments.

It would not be feasible to examine in detail the land use planning and
regulatory activities of all the municipalities on Long Island. A complete inventory of agencies and programs would produce only a confusing mass of
detail. What may emerge from this sample, however, is an appreciation of the
institutional complexity, data uncertainties, technical difficulties and manpower and money constraints that characterize local participation in coastal
resources management.

The important point to be kept in mind is that the entire Long Island
coastal zone is covered by town and village land use planning and regulation.
All of the land areas are zoned, and local regulations cover wetlands and
waterways as well. Municipal governments also own and manage extensive
waterfront park and recreation areas and nature preserves. The Long Island
Counties, Suffolk County in particular, have active programs of planning,
review of local regulatory decision, waterfront recreation and environmental
management (Figure 1).

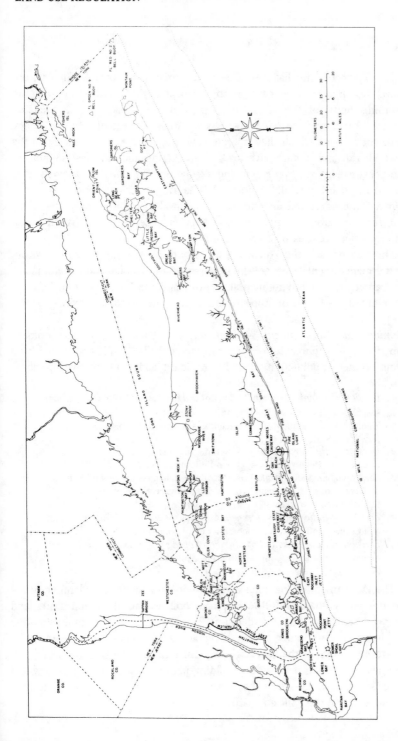

FIGURE 1 Map of Long Island showing county and town boundaries.

The Town of Islip

The Town of Islip has several agencies directly responsible for environmental resources management. It should be recognized, however, that the governing body of the town, the Town Board, created these agencies, endowed them with specific powers and duties and established the policy framework within which they operate. These agencies report directly to the Town Board, and it must give legislative sanction and financial support to resources management programs and regulations. In the final analysis, it is the Town Board that determines whether or not coastal resources in the town will be conserved and protected by local effort. It is only after environmental management policies have been considered by the Town Board that operating agencies are created and funded.

Three agencies in the Town of Islip have major responsibility for environmental management. They are the Department of Planning and Development, the Department of Environmental Control and the Environmental Council. There are also a Board of Appeals and an informal Wetlands Hearing Board.

Planning and Development Department. The Planning and Development Department was reorganized by a town law in 1974 [10]. It is headed by a Commissioner appointed by the Town Board and contains five divisions:

1. *Division of Planning* prepares and maintains the Town of Islip Comprehensive Plan, carries out studies for the Town Board and serves as staff to the Planning Board, a body of seven members established separately under the New York State Town Law.
2. *Division of Building* administers building codes and zoning laws. The superintendent of the division is the town Building Inspector.
3. *Division of Engineering and Contracts* division head is the Town Engineer, who is responsible for engineering design and supervision of construction for town public works.
4. *Division of Industrial Development* develops programs to promote industry and business in the town and compiles employment statistics
5. *Division of Administration of Board of Appeals* maintains the records and manages the procedures of the Board of Appeals.

The Department of Planning and Development advises the Planning Board and the Town Board about development policies and plans, and drafts land use regulations for legislative decision. The Department also administers the permitting process under the building and zoning codes. Development by private enterprise in the town is really managed by the Building Inspector, who has jurisdiction over issuing building permits. Once building, zoning and subdivision regulations have been established, permits are issued routinely for projects that meet the standards.

The Planning Board is related to but separate from the Department of Planning and Development. The Planning Board was established under provisions of the New York State Town Law [11]. It is has no direct control over the Department, for the Commissioner is responsible only to the Town Board. The Planning Board requests technical assistance from the Department, and the Commissioner may sometimes refer controversial or inconclusive matters to the Planning Board for determination [12]. Nevertheless, the Planning Board does not make general policy for the Department. The Town Board does this.

One important power is vested in the Planning Board by Town Law. Land subdivisions must be approved by the Board before they may be filed with Suffolk County and deeds recorded for parcels that are sold. Planning Board approval is also required for street openings and closings.

The Town of Islip Comprehensive Plan. Although community planning had once been oriented mainly to land use and public facilities concerns, it was one of the forerunners of the environmental movement. Planning was itself an attempt to manage community land resources to provide for population and economic growth and at the same time to conserve environmental values, open space, and sites for parks and other recreation facilities. Recent popular recognition of the need for environmental protection and resources management has supported extension of the environmental aspect of community planning.

The Town of Islip Comprehensive Plan contains a broad statement of policy about environmental resources. The plan Summary volume sets out the major planning objectives for the Town of Islip and guidelines for achieving them. These are the goals most relevant to coastal resources management:

> To protect the natural resources and environment of Islip.
>
> To provide recreational services of all kinds in adequate supply and easily accessible to all the Town's people.
>
> To promote only those commercial and industrial developments that are compatible with local employment needs and surrounding environments.
>
> To promote attractive environments that enhance the value of life with aesthetically pleasing surroundings [13].

The concept of carrying capacity has been incorporated into the environmental objectives of the Comprehensive Plan.

The air, water, and land resources of Islip can support only a finite number
of people. Recognizing this fact, care must be taken to insure that the future
population growth of Islip does not exceed the capacities of the Town's
natural resources, with particular emphasis on water resources [14].

The movement of New York metropolitan area population to its suburbs
has been particularly marked on Long Island. Nassau County is almost completely urbanized, and western Suffolk County towns now feel the same pressure of population growth. In just 20 years, from 1950 to 1970, population
in the town of Islip quadrupled from 71,500 to 278,800. People who move
to the suburbs seek relief from the high densities of central cities, but sprawling single family subdivisions and strip commercial development along arterial
highways destroy the original natural setting. Development pressure is most
keenly felt at the coastal edge. Fire Island dunes and Great South Bay wetlands in the Town of Islip have been sacrificed to home seekers who want to
be right on the water.

The Comprehensive Plan advocates strong locally operated environmental
protection programs. They should take account of regional environmental
frameworks, and for this reason, the town government should become deeply
involved in regional planning for the coastal zone, water quality management,
and disposal of liquid and solid wastes.

Through locally controlled land use policies, the town can do much to preserve sensitive open space, wetlands areas and drainage ways. It can guide
and concentrate development into areas suited for higher density because
of adequate sewers and water supplies and other elements which will miti-
gate environmental damage [15].

Town of Islip Zoning Ordinance. In many ways, the Zoning Ordinance of the
Town of Islip is similar to zoning in other communities. The zoning map
shows the boundaries of the various districts, and the text of the ordinance
specifies the uses and physical characteristics of structures permitted in each
district. The Town of Islip ordinance has special features, however, to regulate development in its coastal areas on Great South Bay and Fire Island.

On August 1, 1972, an Ocean Front Dune District was added to the zoning
ordinance. This district was defined as extending along the entire Atlantic
Ocean front of that part of Fire Island situated between the Islip Town
boundaries. It extends inland from mean high water to a line 40 feet inland
from the 15-foot contour line closest to the mean high water line. This 15-
foot contour line above mean high water would be on the primary dunes. If
any ocean front property has a dune crest less than 15 feet above mean high
water, it may be raised to this elevation by proper sand fill. Within this Dune
District permitted uses are severely restricted.

No structure shall be erected or used or occupied except as stair, lookout platform or fence designed to hold or increase the dune. The purpose of this restriction is to preserve the ecology of the dunes and grasses and to safeguard life and property on the barrier beach known as "Fire Island" [16].

Because the sea level is rising and the shoreline of Fire Island is being eroded, many lots that were once back from the water's edge are now either under water or so reduced in area that no building site remains outside the restricted Dune District. The owners of such properties may apply to the Town Board for a special permit to build. The application is first reviewed by the Planning Board, which may ask the Islip Town Environmental Council for an advisory opinion. The Town Board must then hold a public hearing, after which it may render its decision. A dissatisfied property owner may appeal an adverse decision to the New York Supreme Court. If the Court finds that Town prohibition of construction on the lot constitutes a "taking," the zoning ordinance provides that the Town Board may condemn the property and acquire it at fair market value [17].

The Town Board of Islip foresaw actual events when it amended the zoning ordinance to include the Ocean Front Dune District. On April 20, 1977, the New York Supreme Court in Suffolk County decided the case of *Lempe v. Town Board, Town of Islip* in favor of the property owner. The Court first considered the reasonableness of the ordinance and took notice of the fragility of the ecology of Fire Island. The property owner, however, established that the resulting hardship deprived him of any use of the property to which it is reasonably adapted and destroyed the greater part of its value. The property was purchased for the construction of a dwelling, which had already been started; and the Town had not shown that the land was not suitable for that purpose. Restricting use of the property to a stair, lookout platform, or fence was deemed by the Court to be unreasonable and a violation of the Due Process Clause of the Constitution. It therefore found that the zoning ordinance was an invalid exercise of the police power.

The Court decision may be interpreted to mean that the primary dune line is suitable for the construction of dwellings regardless of the fact that the construction itself may destroy the dune. The dwelling may be destroyed by the next storm that undermines the dune, and the adjacent dwellings may also be damaged by destruction of the primary dune. Even though these consequences are probable, nothing in state law prevents a person from considering unstable primary dunes to be real estate and from buying property on them. The police power is not properly used to prevent the property owner from possible loss of his own investment and possible damage to his neighbor's property. The Court therefore found that the zoning ordinance encroached on private property rights without having a substantial relation to a legitimate public purpose.

The Town of Islip was not surprised by this decision. It was willing to be sued by the property owner because this would forestall further construction of the dwelling until the National Park Service could find the money to buy the property [18]. The role of the National Park Service and the Fire Island National Seashore in land use regulation will be described later on in this chapter.

The Town of Islip Zoning Ordinance also designates and regulates construction in Flood Hazard Districts. This is an important zoning tool, for coastal management for practically all of Fire Island and the town shore on Great South Bay are often flooded. Article XL was added to the Zoning Ordinance on November 11, 1974, to cover flood hazard districts and also to comply with the requirements of the federal flood insurance program. Four flood hazard districts are mapped to conform to the relevant Flood Hazard Boundary Maps prepared by the Federal Insurance Administration. For these districts, the ordinance prescribes standards for construction of water supply and sewerage systems and for buildings. First floor elevations must be above the 100-year flood level; heating systems, other utilities and basements below this level must be water tight and flood proof. Regulation of flood hazard areas will be discussed in greater detail in the chapter on management of shore erosion and flood hazards.

Development proposals that do not meet zoning requirements, or where the developer disagrees with the Building Inspector's ruling on the permit application may be forwarded to the Board of Appeals with an application for a variance. Variance applications are sent for review and comment to the Planning Department, the Department of Environmental Control and the Environmental Council. The jurisdiction of these agencies over development and environmental management is townwide. No policy planning or administrative distinction is made between a coastal zone and the remainder of the town. No legal coastal zone boundary, according to which properties on one or the other side of the line are to be treated differently, has been established by the town. Coastal management concerns have been incorporated into the townwide development guidance and resources management process.

Suffolk County in Coastal Land Management

Suffolk County has committed itself to concern for environmental management in its Charter. Coastal resources are not singled out for special attention, but they are included in the full range of County environmental programs. Suffolk County has 600 miles of shoreline that are prized as an important economic, recreational and aesthetic resource. Much of its population and economic enterprises are located near the shore, and tourism is one of its basic industries. The shore of the Atlantic Ocean, Long Island Sound and the

Great Peconic and Gardiners Bays between the North and South Forks afford a magnificent and unique environment for boating, water sports and recreational fishing. Commercial fishing and the harvesting of shellfish and crustaceans are also important to its economic base. Much of the interior of Suffolk County is still devoted to very productive agriculture, including field crops and poultry.

The Suffolk County commitment to environmental conservation is expressed in Article I of its Charter, The Environmental Bill of Rights.

> The policy of Suffolk County shall be to conserve and protect its natural resources, including its wetlands and shorelines, and the quality of its environment and natural scenic beauty, and to encourage the conservation of its agricultural lands. In implementing this policy, the county legislature shall make adequate provision for the abatement of air, water, and soil pollution . . . the protection of wetlands and shorelines, and the conservation and regulation of water resources. The county legislature shall also make suitable provision for the acquisition of land and waters for the county nature preserve or historic trust. To the fullest extent feasible, the projects and activities of the agencies of county government shall be carried out and administered in accordance with the policies set forth in this article [19].

This is a strong statement of policy and objectives. How successfully they are achieved depends largely on the will of the county executive, legislature and agency heads and the amount of financial resources that are made available.

The County Executive. The Environmental Bill of Rights gives the county executive and his office specific responsibilities for environmental management. The county executive must assume responsibility for coordinating the efforts of all county agencies to perform their functions in accordance with the stated environmental policy.

Specific implementation measures to carry out the policy statement are required of the county executive. The Charter requires him to submit at the same time as the annual capital program, an annual report on the environmental quality of Suffolk County. He must tie these two documents together by indicating how the proposed capital program implements the recommendations made in the report on environmental quality. In addition, the report should:

> Review the ecological status of the county, including the air, aquatic and terrestrial environments.

> Describe current and foreseeable trends in the quality, management and use of those environments . . .

> Summarize the programs and activities of federal, state, county and local governments having an impact on the environment

Assess the adequacy of the county's available natural resources, including its water supplies, in relation to its expected population

Set forth the county executive's program, including any recommendations for legislation, for remedying deficiencies concerning environmental matters

Indicate for each legislative recommendation made in the preceding year's report on environmental quality the extent to which the recommendation was implemented

Make recommendations as to what county owned properties should be dedicated to the county nature preserve or historic trust and what properties not owned by the county should be acquired for purposes of dedication [20].

The County Legislature. Although the county executive has responsibility for coordinating the programs of county agencies that would have an impact on the environment, preparing the capital budget and report on environmental quality and recommending legislation, the county legislature has the last word by enacting the laws and appropriating the funds requested. The legislature has the power over environmental policies and programs as an element of its general powers as the governing body of Suffolk County. The Charter also gives it a specific responsibility that could commit the county to particular actions in the coastal area as well as in the rest of the county. This is the duty to adopt and maintain an official map of the county. The county executive must approve the resolution adopting the official map as he does with all other legislative acts.

The county Charter specifies the information to be presented on the official map:

All existing rights-of-way for county, state, and federal highways, roads, parkways, and expressways

All county, state, and federally-owned land within the county, including parks and sites for government buildings

All water courses and major drainage structures within the county

As appropriate, all projects itemized in the capital program

All state capital projects for which boundaries have been established in accordance with state law

All federal capital projects for which boundaries have been established in accordance with federal law [21].

The official map of the county is different from the general comprehensive plan. The latter is an advisory guide to the direction of future land use allocation and the public works that should be provided to support future economic and population growth. Actual zoning by municipalities may not necessarily follow the plan, and even county public works may be located and timed differently. The official map, however, is a firm commitment by the county to carry out particular projects in particular locations. The official map and the capital program are complementary documents, for the Charter requires the legislature to enact simultaneously a resolution amending the official map to conform it to adoption or amendment of a capital program. Municipalities are to be asked for comments on any proposed official map changes that may affect them, but the county legislature is not bound by these comments.

The significance of the official map for coastal resources management is that it is one of the implementation tools by which county projects are approved, located and funded. This includes roads and other transportation facilities; water and sewer projects; sites for facilities to provide the full range of county services; and properties in the nature or historic preserve trusts. Any of these projects may be located in the coastal area. By its approval of the capital program, the official map, and the county budget. The county legislature gives final approval to all county activities that may take place in or affect the lands and waters of the Suffolk County coastal zone. Before it makes its decisions, however, it has available information and recommendations from the County Planning Board and the Council on Environmental Quality. The Departments of Environmental Control, Public Works, Health Services and Parks are among the implementing agencies.

Planning Commission and Department of Planning. The County Planning Commission heads the Department of Planning. The Commission consists of 15 members appointed by the county executive with the approval of the county legislature. Three members are from the county at large; the others are from each of the towns and villages in the county. The commission appoints the employees and consultants who carry out the work of the Planning Department. The primary functions of the commission are to prepare and keep up to date a comprehensive plan for Suffolk County, to carry out special planning studies, to provide planning services to municipalities and to review certain proposed municipal zoning actions and applications for variances, special permits and subdivision plats.

It is by the last of these functions, review of town and village zoning and subdivision actions, that the Planning Commission may influence land use in Suffolk County. The county does not have zoning powers, but the state General Municipal Law authorizes county review of certain important zoning and variance decisions [22]. The Suffolk County Charter uses this state authorization to require the referral of these municipal zoning actions to the county Planning Commission:

> Each town and village in Suffolk County having jurisdiction to adopt or amend zoning regulations shall, before taking final action, refer to the planning commission any zoning regulation or any amendment thereof . . . which would change the district classification of, or the regulations applying to, real property lying within one mile of a nuclear power plant or airport, or within a distance of 500 feet from:
> (1) The boundary of any village or town; or
> (2) The boundary of any existing or proposed county, state, or federal park or other recreation area; or
> (3) The right-of-way of any existing or proposed county or state parkway, thruway, expressway, road; or
> (4) The existing or proposed right-of-way of any stream or drainage channel owned by the county or for which the county has established channel lines; or
> (5) The existing or proposed boundary of any other county, state or federally owned land; or
> (6) The Atlantic Ocean, Long Island Sound, any bay in Suffolk County or estuary of any of the foregoing bodies of water.

There is not much land in the coastal area of Suffolk County that is not subject to county Planning Commission review of municipal zoning, especially since it includes the 500-ft strip of land along the shore. This is a wider area than the officially designated coastal zones of Maine (250 ft.) and the State of Washington (200 ft.).

If the county Planning Commission disapproves a proposed zoning action or recommends changes, the municipality may enact its original proposal only by a vote of a majority plus one of all the members of the referring town or village board [23]. Similar review authority is given to the county Planning Commission over applications by property owners for special permits, exceptions or variances under municipal zoning procedures, or applications for approval of land subdivision plats.

In certain cases, the county Charter goes even further and gives the county Planning Commission actual veto power over municipal zoning decisions, after proper public notice and hearing. In one class of cases, a state agency having the requisite statutory responsibility may file with the county Planning Commission an objection to any proposed zoning action on the ground that it is likely to produce water or air pollution or destroy estuarine values. In such cases, the town or village may not adopt the proposed zoning action at all if the county Planning Commission disapproves; or the action may be adopted only with the changes required by the Planning Commission [24].

The second class of cases where the county Planning Commission may veto a proposed municipal zoning action involves areas within 500 feet of town or village boundaries. A municipality has 45 days within which to file an objection with the county to a proposed zoning action by an adjacent municipality that it believes would adversely affect property within its own borders. If after a public hearing the county Planning Commission resolves by a two-thirds vote to disapprove the zoning proposal, the town or village concerned may not adopt it [25].

These are extraordinary grants of power to Suffolk County that go beyond the authority given to counties by the General Municipal law. No other county in the state has these powers. Suffolk County has them because they were incorporated into its Charter by separate referendums held in the incorporated villages and in the unincorporated areas of the towns. The New York Court of Appeals has upheld the Charter in a case involving a proposed zoning change within 500 feet of a town boundary.

Land Use in the Fire Island National Seashore—
The Federal Role

Most of Fire Island is within the Town of Brookhaven. Several miles of the western end are in the Town of Islip, which contains two incorporated villages, Saltaire and Ocean Beach. Incorporated municipalities and unincorporated settlements on Fire Island take the form of strips of land of varying width that extend across the island from bay to ocean. These 17 "exempt communities" alternate with undeveloped areas that are federally owned as part of the national seashore. A unique feature of the Congressional Act creating the national seashore is that the Secretary of the Interior is given authority over private land use and development. Local governments have traditionally had exclusive zoning and other land development regulatory powers given to them by New York State laws. Federal legislation overriding this traditional local authority has aroused considerable controversy.

The 1977 General Management Plan for the national seashore notes that in the past, local governments had been reluctant to enforce their zoning ordinances [26]. Hundreds of variances had been granted by the Town of Brookhaven and the Village of Ocean Beach zoning authorities that changed the physical and social character of the communities. New commercial and high-density residential uses were permitted and more houses occupied by "groupers," large groups of unrelated persons who occupy single-family residences [27].

The 17 exempt communities in the Towns of Islip and Brookhaven and the Villages of Saltaire and Ocean Beach have been included in the national seashore plan as comprising the "development district." The Fire Island

National Seashore Act of 1964 did not intend to prohibit further development in these communities, but only to assure that it was consistent with
environmental conservation and preservation objectives. This was to be done
by requiring further development should conform to local zoning ordinances
that adhered to federal regulations and were approved by the Secretary of
the Interior.

By the time the 1977 Fire Island plan was published only the Town of
Islip and the Village of Saltaire had submitted zoning ordinances for review
by the Secretary. The Town of Islip had a conservationist approach to its
part of Fire Island and wanted to stop further development. It had not been
successful, however, in prohibiting construction on privately owned lots,
even those located on the primary dune line. The Town is therefore relying
on the National Park Service to stop further development in the national seashore "dune district" by acquiring these lots.

Although the Fire Island National Seashore Act gave the Secretary of the
Interior authority to approve local zoning ordinances, he was given no legal
power to compel local zoning authorities to submit zoning ordinances for
review. Apparently it is the political climate on Long Island that makes possible local disregard of national seashore conservation objectives. The system
of indirect federal control of private property has been relatively more effective in other national seashores such as the one on Cape Cod [28].

Unfortunately, the legal basis for the National Park Service to enforce its
presumed zoning review authority and enjoin local governments from granting variances has not been clarified. The Department of the Interior has apparently been unwilling to become involved in litigation to test these provisions of the federal law. The Park Service does have authority to acquire
private property by condemnation in communities where zoning ordinances
do not conform to federal standards and have not been approved by the
Secretary of the Interior. Nevertheless, acquisition funds are insufficient to
stop substandard development in all critical areas.

According to New York State law, property owners may build on substandard lots that do not meet minimum area requirements if they were held
in separate ownership before a zoning ordinance was enacted. Local zoning
authorities may approve building permits for such properties without going
through the variance procedure. This is possible because New York court
decisions have held that enforcement of zoning retroactively would be an
unconstitutional taking of property without just compensation [29]. Given
these constraints on its authority, the National Park Service finds that

> Continuation of the present land use control system will probably result in
> development of nearly all lots, including substandard ones, dune properties,
> and wetlands. . . . A greater danger with the present system is that no effec-
> tive method will exist to resist pressures that would permit higher densities

on already developed lots, including multiple-family dwellings and additional commercialization. Illegal conversion of single-family dwellings to multiple-family dwellings would continue. High density uses and additional commercialization would be in contradiction to the conservation and preservation mandate of the Fire Island National Seashore Act [30].

Land Classification Within the National Seashore. Determination of permissible land uses in the coastal zone is illustrated by the land classification scheme presented in the 1977 Fire Island General Management Plan. Land classification was based on intensive land suitability analysis. Data about the natural, cultural, economic and social environments were compiled, mapped and analyzed. A 1971 inventory of resources included information about climate, biota, geology, coastal processes and estuarine water quality. The inventory was expanded in 1974 to include information about land use and ownership, carrying capacity for particular uses, topography, soils, ground water hydrology, historic uses and other categories. On the basis of these analyses, all lands and waters within the national seashore were evaluated to determine their suitability for broad classes of land use. The entire area was then zoned according to these use categories:

Class I - Natural Zone
   IA. *Environmental Protection/Primitive Zone.* Lands and waters possessing particular value as wildlife habitat and/or research areas with outstanding physical and biological characteristics. Limited hiking, surf fishing and hunting would be permitted.
   IB. *Outstanding Natural Feature Zone.* Geological and biological features possessing intrinsic value or uniqueness; for hiking, natural history and environmental education.
   IC. *Natural Environment Zone.* Lands that require protection of the natural environment but can accommodate environmentally compatible activities; for limited public day-use recreation, natural history and environmental education.
Class II - Historic Zone. Areas to be managed to preserve and interpret significant historic structures, and include lands containing resources listed on or eligible for the National Register of Historic Places.
Class III - General Outdoor Recreation Zone. Lands and waters where visitor use has altered or may moderately alter the natural environment. Facilities provide medium-density recreational opportunities for day-use recreation, hiking, camping, picnicking.
Class IV. Special Use Zones.
   IVA. *Community Development Zone.* Private lands within the 17 communities located within the boundary of the national seashore. Federal

control within the communities is limited by existing legislation to certain zoning standards. Uses limited to single-family residences and necessary commercial facilities that conform to local zoning ordinances approved by the Secretary of the Interior.

IVB. *Major Park Development Zone.* Large scale facilities, bath houses, and parking lots located within Smith Point County Park; for high-intensity beach recreation.

IVC. *Dune District.* Extends landward 40 feet from a line representing the primary high dune crest, as determined from a 1976 aerial survey, and seaward to the mean high water mark. All recreational and construction activity will be prohibited on the dunes. Access across the dunes will be limited to specified pedestrian and vehicular dune crossings [31].

Land Use Regulation in the Community Development Zone. It has been noted that the National Park Service was critical of local zoning enforcement and also of Department of the Interior failure to clarify the Secretary's authority to approve local zoning ordinances. The 1977 Fire Island General Management Plan proposes to remedy this situation by formulating a model zoning ordinance for the 17 communities in the development zone. The proposed standards would be incorporated in the zoning ordinances of the villages of Saltaire and Ocean Beach on Fire Island and in special Fire Island districts in the zoning ordinances of the Towns of Islip and Brookhaven.

The model zoning ordinance would limit residences to single-family houses on lots of a half acre or more. New multiple-family dwellings or conversion of single-family houses to apartments would be prohibited. Standards would be included for lot grading, clearing of vegetation, sign limitations, lot coverage, height restrictions, and density. Secondary standards to take account of local differences would be developed in cooperation with each community [32].

REFERENCES

1. Coastal Zone Management Act of 1972 (P.L. 92-583) as amended 1976 (P.L. 94-370), Sec. 306 (d)(1) and (2).
2. Constitution of the State of New York, Article IX, Sec. 1e and Sec. 2(c) (10).
3. Ibid., Sec. 2(b)(1).
4. New York Statute of Local Governments, March 29, 1964, Chapter 58-A of the Consolidated Laws, Article 2, Sec. 10(1), (2), (6), (7).
5. New York Municipal Home Rule Law, April 30, 1963, Chapter 36-a of the Consolidated Laws, Article 2, Sec. 10-1(a)(10).

6. New York General City Law, Town Law, Village Law.
7. New York General Municipal Law, Art. 12-B, Sec. 239-d(2).
8. Ibid., Sec. 239-m.
9. Ibid., Sec. 239-d(7).
10. Town of Islip, Local Law No. 17, 1974, Chapter 39A of the Town Code.
11. New York Town Law, Sec. 271-275.
12. Interview with Stephen Jones, Town of Islip Planning Board, September 14, 1977.
13. Town of Islip, Comprehensive Plan Summary, undated, p. 5.
14. Ibid., p. 13.
15. Ibid., p. 14.
16. Town of Islip Code, Art VA, Sec. 68-59.1 - Sec. 68-59.2.
17. Ibid., Sec. 68-59.3.
18. Interview with Stephen Jones, Town of Islip Planning Board, September 14, 1977.
19. Suffolk County Charter, Article I, Sec. 101, 1974.
20. Ibid., Sec. 109.
21. Ibid., Sec. 225.
22. New York General Municipal Law, Art. 12.5, Sec. 239-m.
23. Ibid.
24. Suffolk County Charter, Sec. 1327.
25. Ibid., Sec. 1330.
26. U.S. Department of the Interior, National Park Service, *Fire Island National Sea Shore, General Management Plan,* Patchogue, N.Y., September 1977, p. 10.
27. Ibid., p. 102.
28. Ibid., p. 101.
29. Ibid., p. 102.
30. Ibid.
31. Ibid., pp. 45-48.
32. Ibid., pp. 102-103.

CHAPTER 3

MANAGEMENT OF SHORE EROSION AND FLOOD HAZARDS

Coastal areas are particularly susceptible to material hazards. Beach and bluff erosion, hurricanes and flooding, and changes in Great Lakes water levels are the major hazards that have a high probability of affecting the New York State shoreline. Other states must also prepare for tornados, landslides, earthquakes, tsunamis and even volcanic eruptions. Shore erosion is a continuous process that may be hardly noticeable in the short run. But erosion, floods and wind damage become severe as the result of hurricanes and other major storms, which are not rare events in New York State. For this reason, the full array of coastal management tools must be used to cope with these hazards.

Extreme events in nature that impact on sparsely populated areas cause little property damage or loss of life. As coastal areas have become relatively more attractive to our shifting population and business enterprises, however, the consequences of these events become very costly. Several elements of coastal management programs following federal guidelines contribute to preparing for and dealing with the consequences of foreseeable hazards.

Geographic Areas of Particular Concern. Areas designated as being of particular environmental concern include those that have a high probability of hazards from storms, floods, slides and erosion.

Permissible Land and Water Uses. Identifying and establishing priorities for permissible land and water uses is an effective way of minimizing damage and losses from natural disasters. Coastal management programs may use local zoning and other regulatory authorities to limit the uses and density of occupation of hazardous areas. Decisions about uses, densities and priorities come out of an assessment and balancing of the potential benefits from the economic development of these areas against the risks of loss. Avoidance of catastrophic losses of life, property and economic value has greater social benefit than the speculative gains that may accrue to relatively few land owners and developers.

41

Citizen Participation. Residents, property owners and business managers make location decisions on the basis of information they have about the advantages and disadvantages of particular sites for what they want to do. Coastal managers have the responsibility to warn potential developers in hazardous areas of the risks to which they may be exposed. They also have the obligation to tailor zoning, subdivision regulations and building codes to limit development to acceptable losses, should catastrophes occur, and to avoid encouraging more intensive development. Regulations are an effective means of communicating the risks of development and thereby contribute to informed decision making by citizens. Another important aspect of citizen participation is their involvement in assessing potential hazards and drawing up land use regulations.

SHORE EROSION

Among the prominent features of the Long Island shoreline are bluffs and beaches. The glacial moraine that formed Long Island left bluffs along the north shore and also along the northern rim of the South Fork out to Montauk. The north shore, especially along the western half of Long Island, is indented by deep, picturesque bays separated by prominent headlands. The south shore is also irregular, but relatively flat and separated from the Atlantic Ocean by a continuous line of barrier islands from Southampton to the Rockaways. Between the barrier islands and the mainland shore lie Jamaica Bay, Great South Bay, Moriches Bay and Shinnecock Bay. These are richly endowed with salt marsh islands and highly productive fisheries, including shellfish and crustaceans. These shores will be described in greater detail later on.

Bluff Erosion and Beach Nourishment

The bluffs and beaches of the outer rim of the Long Island shore, both on Long Island Sound and the Atlantic Ocean, work together in an unstable system of perpetual erosion. The continually eroding bluffs are a source of sand to nourish the beaches. If it were possible to check the erosion of the bluffs, the beaches would be starved of sand and erode in their turn. Another important feature in the shore configuration is the formation of dunes from the dry beach sand blown landward (Figure 2).

The agents of bluff erosion are rain runoff, discharge of underground springs and storm tides. The steeper the face of the bluff, the less vegetation it has, and the narrower the beach at its foot, the greater the rate of erosion. Gradually sloping bluffs that have good vegetative cover and wide protective

FIGURE 2 Bluff erosion. This is the source of sand, which is carried by shore currents, that helps to maintain beaches.

beaches below them are more stable. Regardless of whether erosion is fast or slow, it is a continuous process that is aggravated by heavy rains and high storm tidal surges. Without this source of sand, gravel and even large stones, there would be no beaches.

The closer the beaches are to the source of supply, the coarser is the sand, gravel, or even cobbles that lie on them. The finer materials are carried further by the shore current. Beach material is moved in two directions. Movement on and off shore at right angles to the beach is caused by the waves and turbulent surf that expend their energy against the land. The stronger the force of the waves and the higher the tides, especially during winter storms, the more sand is removed from the beach and deposited in the winter bar parallel to the land. The waves may even undermine the dunes behind the beach. The gentler waves of summer tend to carry sand back from the winter bar to rebuild the beach.

There is also sand movement parallel to the beach caused by shore currents. When waves strike the beach at an angle, there is a resultant movement of water parallel to the beach, which is called the shore or littoral current. The direction of the current depends on the way the winds drive the waves on to the beach, and the shore current carries sand with it in that direction.

Littoral currents along the north shore usually flow east on the eastern side of headlands and westward on that side. Where there are relatively straight stretches of shore line, such as along the eastern half of Suffolk County, the net flow is eastward. Beaches on the north shore have coarser materials than those on the south shore barrier islands, for they are closer to the headlands and bluffs that supply them. The clay and fine silt materials tend to be washed out into Long Island Sound.

Along the south shore barrier islands, the prevailing winds drive the shore current and its sand burden from east to west. Sand is therefore carried from the Montauk bluffs westward to Westhampton Beach, Fire Island, Jones Beach and the Rockaway Beaches. Without the eroding bluffs, the westerly beaches would receive no sand. What is worse, if the shore current does not have a full burden of sand to carry, it will pick up sand and cause the beaches to erode.

Where the shore current is interrupted, it slows down and drops part of its load of sand. When it picks up speed again downdrift, it will also pick up sand and erode the beach there. Obstacles in the form of jetties or groins are deliberately placed to interrupt the shore current and make it drop most of its sand. The south shore barrier islands are separated by inlets that provide navigation access between the Atlantic Ocean and the back bays. Without protection, these inlets would tend to silt up and close or migrate. Stone jetties have been built on one or both sides of these inlets. They are kept open to some extent because the jetty on the upstream side stops the sand from crossing the inlet. The beach widens here, but the beach on the downstream side of the inlet erodes. Aerial views of these inlets show the characteristic arcs of deposition and erosion.

Groins are similar to jetties, but they are built out right from the beach. Their purpose is to deliberately trap sand from the shore current to widen the beach and prevent erosion. They do this very effectively for the sections of beach between the groins, but the unprotected beaches downstream erode away. This happened at Westhampton Beach, and the groin project there offers an interesting case of beach erosion management, which will be described later on in this chapter.

EROSION CONTROL METHODS

Although waterfront property is highly valued for residential development and is necessary for such enterprises as ports, marinas and beach resorts, it may be hazardous for the occupants. Bluffs are subject to erosion, so houses built too close to the edge may be undermined. Beaches also erode, and on the south shore barrier islands hurricanes and severe storms have breached the dunes, swept entirely across them, and caused extensive wave and flood damage to houses. The storms may also cause flooding of waterfront areas on the mainland shore behind the back bays. Breaching of the barrier islands may contribute to flooding by permitting tidal and storm surges to rise higher in these bays. A variety of measures may be taken to manage shore erosion and its associated hazards. They may offer only temporary delaying action, however, or may even aggravate the problem.

Bluffs

These may be protected by maintaining good natural vegetative cover on their tops and faces. Terracing reduces the slopes of bluffs and helps support vegetation. Local ordinances may establish bluff hazard zones that prohibit building construction within specified distances from the bluff edge. Climbing on the bluff face should also be discouraged. Bulkheads at the bluff base may prevent undermining by waves, and seawalls or breakwaters may also be constructed to absorb wave energy and reduce their destructive force. It should be remembered, however, that widespread bluff stabilization will have a counterproductive effect on beaches. Loss of sediment to nourish the beaches could cause them to erode; narrower beaches would, in turn, absorb less wave energy, thus contributing to further upland erosion.

Jetties and Groins

These may be constructed of wood, concrete or stone. It has already been noted that these structures trap sand on their upstream side of the shore current, but they also accelerate erosion on the downstream side. These structural measures to combat beach erosion are very costly as well as possibly dysfunctional. They should therefore be used only where their effects on the entire shore can be accurately forecast and the consequences found acceptable to all riparian interests.

Beach Nourishment

A nonstructural method of coping with beach erosion is to artificially nourish the beach by filling it with sand dredged from other areas. The back bays between the barrier islands and the mainland are the usual sources of supply, and the sand is moved by hydraulic dredging. Unfortunately thousands of cubic yards of sand added to beaches one year may be washed away the next. Artificial beach nourishment must be a continual process, and even though it benefits the owners and users of beaches, there are costs to be borne by others. These are the fishermen and harvesters of shellfish and crustaceans. Dredging disturbs the bay bottom, increasing turbidity, and deepens the water. Dredging, therefore, has negative effects on all the organisms in the food chain, from the phytoplankton deprived of sunlight by turbidity to other small and large sea creatures that feed on them and are also themselves directly affected by changes in habitat caused by dredging.

Land Use Regulation

This is a nonstructural approach that does not attack the problem of shore erosion directly, but rather is intended to reduce the amount of damage that results from natural processes by limiting development in hazardous areas. Avoiding dense development of expensive homes reduces demands by property owners for costly structural measures against inevitable erosion and storm damage. Regulations may also prohibit building on the dunes and require structures to be built on piles so that flood waters may flow under them without obstruction. Because the dunes are the first line of defense against storm surge overwash and flooding, their integrity and vegetative cover may be protected by prohibiting random walking and vehicle riding on them. Pedestrians and vehicles may legally be restricted to boardwalks over the dunes or specific vehicle access points.

Wetlands Conservation

Tidal wetlands are found on the Long Island north shore inside the bays and harbors. On the south shore, they rim the back bays along the bay shores of the barrier islands and along the mainland shore. Wetlands are part of the natural storm protection system that includes wide beaches and high dunes. Wetlands absorb wave energy, store tidal flood waters and help to stabilize upland banks. Land use regulations may therefore protect wetlands from filling and development. It is also feasible to create artificial wetlands by planting appropriate vegetation on dredge spoil banks or islands.

Flood Insurance

The federal government supports low cost flood insurance to property owners if their communities will enact ordinances to limit further construction in flood hazard areas and regulate land use and construction in flood plains. The program is operated by the Department of Housing and Urban Development. It is an additional approach to supplement those noted above to avoid flood damage and costly structural erosion and flood control measures that may do more harm than good in the long run [1].

Emergency Preparedness Planning

The term civil defense is no longer prominent in the vocabulary of government programs. Nevertheless, civil defense organizations still exist to prepare for natural disasters and cope with them when they occur. Warning systems, preparedness plans and relief and rehabilitation assistance are elements of civil defense. If, after adequate warning and dissemination of information about the risks involved, people still decide to locate their residences and businesses in hazardous areas, the effects of natural catastrophes may be mitigated by the rapid mobilization of public and private assistance. The justification of public expenditures to bail out property owners who have chosen to locate in hazardous areas is that these people are presumed to provide an important social benefit by assuming the risks of developing otherwise unused resources.

EROSION STUDIES OF THE NEW YORK MARINE COAST

Policymaking and planning to cope with shore erosion, hurricane damage and flood plains are difficult because scientists and engineers are aware of the limitations of their knowledge about weather patterns and erosion and flood processes. It is not yet possible, therefore, to design erosion and flood control measures for which the results may be accurately predicted. Experience with structural measures such as revetments, bulkheads and groins has shown that they may fail to solve the problems for which they were designed and may even aggravate shore problems in other places. Nevertheless, technical studies of the shoreline must be carried foreward and erosion and flood control measures devised on the basis of the best available knowledge.

The entire marine coastline of New York State has been surveyed extensively by the federal government, and state and local agencies as well as university scientists and engineers have made detailed studies in special areas [2]. This coastline has been divided into the following reaches for survey and planning (Fig. 1).

The Atlantic Shore
1. Staten Island
2. South Brooklyn, including Coney Island (to Rockaway Inlet)
3. The Rockaway beaches and Jamaica Bay (between Rockaway and East Rockaway Inlets)
4. Long Beach (between East Rockaway and Jones Inlets)
5. Jones Beach (between Jones and Fire Island Inlets)
6. Fire Island (between Fire Island and Moriches Inlets)
7. Westhampton Beach (between Moriches and Shinnecock Inlets)

8. Shinnecock Inlet to Beach Hampton
9. Beach Hampton to Montauk Point
Long Island Sound
  1. Westchester County and part of Bronx County
  2. Nassau County
  3. Suffolk County
Eastern Forks
  Gardiners Bay and Great Peconic Bay

The entire Atlantic shore of New York State from Staten Island to Montauk Point on Long Island is subject to shore erosion from wave attack and tidal flooding during severe storms. Part of the Staten Island shore and the Montauk area have high bluffs, but most of the coastline is flat and fronted by beaches. Even the bluffs have narrow beaches at their base. About 70 miles of the central part of the Long Island shore consists of four narrow barrier islands, Long Beach, Jones Beach, Fire Island and Westhampton Beach. East and west of these islands are narrow peninsulas that resemble barrier islands. Behind these islands and peninsulas are extensive bays; the largest are Jamaica, Great South, Moriches and Shinnecock Bays.

The shore of Long Island Sound is quite different. Westchester and Bronx County shores are rocky and generally elevated. Erosion is not a problem, but there is occasional flooding from storm tides in the Sound and from tributary streams. The Long Island north shore offers a marked contrast to the Atlantic south shore. The Nassau County reach is very irregular with deep bays alternating with high bluffed headlands. The bluffs are subject to severe erosion from both surface runoff and wave attack at the base. Tidal flooding occurs where the bay shores are relatively flat, but the flood plains are generally narrow. The western shoreline of Suffolk County is also very irregular, with several deep bays separated by rather narrow peninsulas, or necks. The peninsulas are characterized mostly by bluffs fronted by narrow beaches. The eastern shoreline of the county is quite regular with occasional marshes and beaches in the depressions that interrupt the almost continuous high bluffs. Bluff erosion is serious all along the north shore of Long Island. Tidal flooding is minor compared to the south shore, but it causes extensive damage to low areas.

Between the north and south forks at the eastern end of Long Island lie Gardiner's Bay and Great Peconic Bay. Shelter Island separates these bays. The shoreline is irregular and, including the islands, is 168 miles long. The bluffs are threatened by serious erosion, but flooding is a limited problem. Shelter Island protects most of the shore between the forks from Atlantic Ocean tidal surges.

Shoreline Erosion and Hurricane Protection Studies

The entire marine coast of New York fronting on the Atlantic Ocean and Long Island Sound has been mapped, its erosion and flood problems analyzed, and remedial measures identified. Major studies have been conducted by the U.S. Army Corps of Engineers, the Federal Insurance Administration, the Marine Sciences Study Center of SUNY at Stony Brook and the Marine Resources Council of the Nassau-Suffolk Regional Planning Board. These shores were also examined by the Corps of Engineers as part of the National Shoreline Study, which was published in 1971 [3]. Since 1955 the Corps has been making very detailed studies of most of the reaches of the New York marine coast. These studies and the status of their proposals are tabulated in Table I.

This table demonstrates that concern for shore erosion and flood hazards was an effective component of coastal management long before Congress voted to encourage coastal states to develop comprehensive coastal management programs through the Coastal Zone Management Act of 1972. Flood plain mapping and flood insurance were also begun before this act was passed. Programs for fish and wildlife management and recreation have had important coastal elements. These will be described in other chapters of this study. It is appropriate to point out here, however, that large areas of the New York marine coast on Staten Island, Jamaica Bay and Fire Island have been designated as great national parks.

WESTHAMPTON BEACH, A CASE STUDY

Westhampton Beach is one of the chain of barrier islands that stretches westward from Southampton along the south shore of Long Island. All of these beaches have experienced periodic severe erosion, and property owners have suffered extensive damage and even destruction of their homes. New York State and the county governments on Long Island had tried to cope with this problem, and eventually the U.S. Army Corps of Engineers became involved.

The Corps of Engineers in Shore Erosion Control

In 1930, Congress authorized the Corps of Engineers to carry out studies for shore protection measures in cooperation with state and local governments. In 1946 the Corps was authorized to participate in construction projects to protect state and locally owned shores. In that year the Corps completed a study of the Long Island south shore from Jones Inlet to Montauk Point. A detailed Survey Report on the shore from Fire Island Inlet to Montauk was published in 1958. It provided the technical basis for a groin construction project at Westhampton Beach. After the barrier island had been

TABLE I Shore Erosion and Flood Protection Studies: New York State Marine Coast

Reach	Corps of Engineers Shoreline Study	Congressional Authorization	Implementation
Staten Island	Cooperative Beach Erosion Control and Interim Hurricane Study, Fort Wadsworth to Arthurkill, 1971	1975	Design studies for beach and dune fill; I-wall and pump stations
South Brooklyn	Cooperative Beach Erosion Control and Interim Hurricane Study, Atlantic Coast of New York City from Rockaway Inlet to Norton Point (Coney Island Area 1973 & 1974)	None	Design studies for restoration of recreational beaches, protective beaches, terminal groins
Rockaways	Cooperative Beach Erosion Control and Interim Hurricane Study, Atlantic Coast of New York City from East Rockaway Inlet to Rockaway Inlet and Jamaica Bay, 1964	1965	4 million cubic yards of beach fill and periodic nourishment along 6.2 miles of shoreline; 4.2 miles completed
Long Beach	Report on Beach Erosion Control and Interim Hurricane Study of the Atlantic Coast of Long Island, Jones Inlet to East Rockaway Inlet, 1973	None	Planning work terminated because of local opposition to recommended structural measures
Jones Beach	Beach Erosion Control Report on Cooperative Study (Survey), Atlantic Coast of Long Island, Fire Island Inlet and Shore Westerly to Jones Inlet, 1955	1958	2 million cubic yards of beach fill placed and diking of gorge channel in Fire Island Inlet. Plan for nourishment of feeder beach with 1.2 million cubic yards of sand biennially
Jones Beach	Review Report on Beach Erosion Control Cooperative Study, Fire Island Inlet and the Shore Westerly to Jones Inlet, 1965	None	

Location	Report	Year	Remarks
Long Beach and part of Jones Beach	Tidal Flood Plain Information South Shore of Nassau County, Long Island, June 1971	None	
Jones Beach to Montauk	Interim Hurricane Study of the Atlantic Coast of Long Island, Jones Inlet to Montauk Point (Remaining Areas), 1967	None	
Fire Island to Montauk	Cooperative Beach Erosion Control and Interim Hurricane Study, Atlantic Coast of Long Island, Fire Island Inlet to Montauk Point, 1958	1960	Project design between Fire Island and Moriches Inlets delayed by establishment of Fire Island National Seashore and determination of cost apportionment. Between Moriches and Shinnecock Inlets 15 groins were built between 1966 and 1970. Design studies for beach and dune fill and periodic nourishment
Westchester County	Westchester County, Along Long Island Sound, Interim Hurricane Study, 1965	None	Design studies
Nassau County	Tidal Flood Plain Information Report, North Shore of Nassau County, 1972	None	Design studies
Suffolk County	North Shore of Long Island, Suffolk County, Beach Erosion Control and Interim Hurricane Study, 1969	None	Design studies
Nassau and Suffolk Counties	(Not by Corps of Engineers) Erosion of the North Shore of Long Island, Technical Report No. 18, Davies, Axelrod and O'Connor, Marine Sciences Research Center, SUNY at Stony Brook, 1973	None	

breached by a severe storm in 1962, 11 groins were constructed midway between Moriches and Shinnecock Inlets. This project was completed in 1966, but further erosion and storm damage spurred the construction of four additional groins west of the first field. This stage was completed in 1970, but the erosion problem was not solved. To the west of the last groin, the beach continued to erode, and in 1972 a public beach of the Town of Southampton was completely washed over by a storm (Figure 3).

FIGURE 3 Storm breaching of a barrier island. Eastward view of breach at Westhampton Beach caused by coastal storm of March 6 to 8, 1962 (Photo by U.S. Corps of Engineers).

Erosion, storms, and floods are related phenomena. Erosion does take place slowly at all times, but one storm may cause more erosion than does a year of temperate weather. The Corps of Engineers does not separate shore erosion control and hurricane protection either programmatically or organizationally. Wide beaches and strong, stabilized dunes are natural protection against flood damage from hurricane and other storm surges. The barrier islands also protect the mainland from the full destructive force of waves and tides.

The South Shore from Fire Island to Montauk Point. This shoreline is about 83 miles long. Fire Island is 30 miles long and is separated from Westhampton

Beach by Moriches Inlet. Westhampton Beach is 15 miles long and is separated from the next barrier beach by Shinnecock Inlet. The barrier islands are
generally less than 0.5 mile wide. Behind the beach on the ocean side are
irregular dunes that may reach 30 feet in height. In some places, the dunes
have been leveled or partially removed, and residences, beach clubs, and resorts have been built on the dune line.

The barrier islands are separated from the Long Island mainland by inter-
connected tidal bays that vary in width from about 500 feet, where peninsulas from the mainland separate the bays, to 5 miles. Fire Island inlet connects the Atlantic Ocean with the Great South Bay, 100 square miles in area;
Moriches Inlet leads to Moriches Bay of 20 square miles; Shinnecock Inlet
leads from the ocean to Shinnecock Bay of 15 square miles.

The 33 miles east of Southampton is part of the mainland of Long Island.
It faces the Atlantic Ocean, and is fronted by a relatively narrow beach. The
easterly 10 miles of shoreline from Southampton to Montauk has a series of
headland bluffs that rise more than 50 feet above the ocean level.

Early Efforts at Beach and Hurricane Protection. Before 1946, beach and
hurricane protection work was carried out by the Long Island counties,
municipalities, and private interests. It consisted mostly of sand fence barriers to build up the dunes, a seawall and a few groins and bulkheads in iso-
lated areas. After the 1938 hurricane, Suffolk County placed dune fill, grass
planting and sand fences along 68 miles of barrier beach. New York State
began to share the cost of these works after 1946. Between 1947 and 1954
the state and local governments built jetties and revetments at Moriches and
Shinnecock Inlets. These works helped to stabilize the inlets, which would
otherwise have silted closed. But by trapping sand brought by the shore current on the upstream side of the jetties, the beaches downstream (to the
west) were deprived of sand. Intermittent surveys indicated a net erosion
loss of sand from barrier island beaches of about 300,000 cubic yards annually. The Corps of Engineers estimated that the beach west of Shinnecock
Inlet had receded 500 feet between 1940 and 1960. Hurricane losses along
the south shore are caused mainly by hurricane tides, the action of storm
waves, flooding by the heavy rains and the powerful winds. Since 1935, the
area was hit by 126 storms, about half of them causing severe or moderate
damage. The maximum hurricane tide of record occurred in September
1938, when 45 lives were lost [4].

The Corps of Engineers' Plan. On the basis of extensive surveys and engineering studies, the Chief of Engineers in 1960 recommended to the Secretary of
the Army a $18.7 million project for the Atlantic Ocean shore of Long
Island from Fire Island Inlet to Montauk Point.

The District Engineer finds that the most practicable plan for protecting the
area against shore erosion and hurricane damages would involve widening the
beach along developed areas . . . to a minimum width of 100 feet at 14 feet
above mean sea level, and raising the dunes to an elevation of 20 feet above
mean sea level. . . . Grass would be planted on the dunes. . . . Fifty groins
would be constructed along the shore *if and when experience indicates their
need.* Placement of about 34 million cubic yards of suitable sand would be
involved initially. Maintenance of the stability of the shore would require
periodic placement of about 480,000 cubic yards of suitable sand annually.
. . . The District Engineer believes that the best results would be accomplished
if the entire plan, *except the groins,* were constructed as a unit [5] (emphasis
added).

It is important to note that the proposal was to provide beach and hurricane
protection by massive fill to build up the beaches and dunes. Groins were to
be built only if necessary, and their main purpose would be to stabilize the
fill.

Plan Implementation. The Secretary of the Army accepted the proposal of
the Chief of Engineers, and Congress authorized the project in the River and
Harbor Act of 1960. Because costs were to be shared 50% by the federal
government, 25% by New York State and 25% by Suffolk County, all three
governments had to agree on project design. For several years after Congressional approval, Suffolk County failed to appropriate its share of the project
cost. It was not until 1966 that the first stage of the shore and hurricane protection project was completed at Westhampton Beach. And at Suffolk
County's insistence on cutting costs, the project was not carried out according to the Corps of Engineers original design.

Eleven groins were constructed midway between Moriches and Shinnecock
Inlets, but no beach or dune fill was placed in the groin field. The results were
predictable. Only eight months after the groins had been built, they had
trapped enough sand from the shore current to deprive the beach immediately to the west and cause serious erosion. A storm in April 1967 actually
breached the barrier island just west of the groin field. In a letter to the
Superintendent of the New York State Department of Public Works, an offi-
cer in the Corps of Engineers wrote:

The performance of the existing experimental groin system at Westhampton
Beach demonstrates that groins alone will not fully provide the beach erosion
control and probably none of the hurricane protection authorized under the
existing Federal project, and that dune and beach fill is critically required at
this time to supplement the completed groins [6].

In response to this letter, the DPW Superintendent asked the Corps of
Engineers to build four additional groins west of the first field, place beach

and dune fill at both fields, and place fill in a 2000-ft. feeder beach immediately west of the new groin field. Again Suffolk County officials said they could not pay their full share of project costs. In the face of the disastrous experience with the first groin field, the Corps of Engineers again agreed to eliminate the beach and dune fill at the groins and also the feeder beach.

The results were again unfortunate. Serious erosion occurred west of the new groin field after it was finished in 1970. By 1973 the beach had become so narrow that a severe storm washed over the barrier island in this area. The Town of Southampton Neighborhood Recreation Center beach was completely destroyed and houses in the area were damaged.

Property owners complained to the Governor and filed lawsuits against the federal government and Suffolk County. Consequently, the Corps of Engineers and New York State agreed to support the construction of 6 more groins west of the existing field of 15. By this time, 1973, the funding formula had changed to 70% federal, 21% state, and 9% county. Although its share would have been only a few hundred thousand dollars, the County failed to support the project. This time the reason was not simply that the County did not have the money. There was also an ideological difference between the County Executive and the County Legislature. There had been a change in administration, and the new Executive was adamantly against further groin construction. He vetoed several capital budget items and appropriation resolutions for the project. He did this on the grounds that more groins would only cause further erosion and that all the taxpayers in Suffolk County should not have to support the property values of a few wealthy summer residents on Westhampton Beach. His views prevailed, and the project for a new six-groin field was abandoned. The Corps, the State, and Suffolk County agreed to repair future erosion and storm damage by continually pumping beach fill from the Atlantic Ocean [7].

This case demonstrates some of the uncertainties that plague attempts to cope with the problem of shore erosion. There are technical uncertainties, for there are still many gaps in scientific knowledge about beach dynamics and the causes of various kinds of shore erosion. Technical solutions and engineering works are not always effective. They may solve the problem in one area and aggravate it in others. There are also political uncertainties. Governments and agencies at all levels are involved in negotiations and decision making. There are many executive and legislative hurdles that must be overcome before a shore erosion control project is approved by all parties. The politics of project approval is supplemented by budgetary politics, for shore erosion must compete for attention and funds with other national and local needs. Furthermore, technical uncertainties must be eliminated by additional scientific and engineering research. It may be anticipated that shore erosion will remain a serious problem. After all, it is the natural result of the enormous energies of sun, wind and waves exerted on our shorelines. Human efforts to contain them are likely to be palliative at best.

Local Governments in Beach and Dune Protection

It has been noted that before the Corps of Engineers was authorized to take a leading role in shore erosion control, New York State was already engaged on its own program. It was authorized by Chapter 535 of the Laws of 1945, which defined state and local responsibilities and cost sharing formulas. This program has been in abeyance during the period of state and local financial stringency, and shore erosion control efforts are limited to those supported by the Corps.

Even federally aided projects require local cost sharing. Suffolk County has adopted the position that shore protection benefits are not distributed equally among all taxpayers, because the owners of property on the barrier beaches benefit most. It has therefore sought a method of distributing the County share of projects between these property owners and all other taxpayers. The state legislature amended the County Law, Article 5-B, Sec. 280, to authorize Suffolk County to create a special county district for shore erosion control. The law also contained the formula for assessing the County share of project costs on properties inside and outside the special district boundaries. A county hurricane protection and erosion control district is being created to include that part of Fire Island between Robert Moses State Park and the Fire Island National Seashore property.

Because of Suffolk County and some local government opposition to further groin construction, future shore erosion projects will avoid structural solutions. The policy is no longer to try to *control* erosion, but rather to repair beach and dune losses caused by storms and long-term shore changes. This will be done by hudraulically obtaining sand fill offshore in the Atlantic Ocean. The productive bay bottoms would not be disturbed to provide the fill, since the technology for obtaining sand from the ocean bottom is available. This method will also be used for beach nourishment to create wide beaches to protect the dunes. It would be anticipated that much of this beach fill might be washed away during storms; but having been there to take the brunt of the wave action, this would probably not significantly have eroded the dunes. Intact dunes would protect the properties behind them, barrier island washovers would be avoided, and backbay tidal surges destructive to the mainland would be reduced.

Suffolk County was a participant in the federal shore erosion control and hurricane protection program, but town and village governments on the Long Island south shore were not. Nevertheless, municipal governments have ordinances that contribute to preserving beaches and dunes as an aspect of coastal management.

Town of Southampton. The Town of Southampton Master Plan, published in 1970, recommended this policy:

> Both dune land and ocean beaches should be protected from any improvement or use that would tend to limit their effectiveness as natural barriers to ocean wave overruns. No development or improvement, other than an approved beach protection measure or an approved walk over the dune area, shall be constructed closer than 40 feet inland of the natural crest of the foreward dune [8].

To implement this policy, the Town Board on May 2, 1972, revised its Building Zone Ordinance No. 26 to include a Tidal Wetland and Beach Overlay District. An overlay district makes more restrictive the uses and construction standards in the regular zoning districts within the boundaries of the overlay district.

In the Town of Southampton, the Tidal Wetland and Beach Overlay District prohibited building on the public beach except on approval by public agencies, and then only to protect the natural environment or for some other public purpose. Owners of private lands are prohibited from excavating, re-grading, or disturbing the natural crest of the dune, "except in accordance with a beach protection policy or protective works program approved by the Town" [9]. Unrestricted walking on the dunes contributes to erosion by disturbing the vegetation and dune profile. Therefore:

> A private landowner shall not construct any building or structure on the ocean beach except that one (1) access walkway shall be constructed over the crest of the dune provided that it be established at an elevation of at least two (2) feet above the undisturbed natural crest where grasses exist or directly on the grade without any space between where no grasses exist [10].

Beach Protection Ordinance No. 8, adopted in 1939, prohibits disturbance to any "revetment, fence, work, installation of any part thereof, or any beach grass," which has the purpose of aiding in the restoration of the dunes or natural sand barrier on the south beach of the town. Ordinance No. 14, or 1945, prohibits the removal of any grass or natural growth, except poison ivy, from beaches and dunes in the town except by permit. Autos, dune buggies and other vehicles are prohibited from the dunes by Ordinance No. 22, passed in 1953.

Town of Easthampton. The Town of Easthampton Zoning Ordinance was amended March 21, 1975, to require that buildings must be set back from the primary dunes. In the western part of the town all structures on lots fronting on the Atlantic Ocean, except pedestrial walkways, must be located at least

100 feet inland of the contour line 15 feet above mean sea level. If the primary dunes have a lower elevation, they must be raised to the 15-ft. level across the entire ocean front of the lot for a depth of 50 feet by the addition of beach sand. The required fill may not be taken from the beach in front of the dune, however. Beach grass must also be planted and fencing installed in accordance with the provisions of the "Removal of Beach Grass Ordinance" of the Town.

The configuration of the Atlantic Ocean shoreline of the eastern part of the Town of Southampton changes to narrow stony beaches and bluffs. Along this stretch of ocean frontage, structures must be located behind a setback line of 100 feet from the mean high water line [11] .

FLOOD HAZARDS AND INSURANCE

River estuaries and shorelines along the coast are vulnerable to flooding during spring thaws, hurricanes, severe storms and high tidal surges. Flood plains along river banks have been recognized as serving the important function of storing floodwaters, but shorelands must also play a protective role under high water conditions. Devoting river bottom lands to agriculture and other extensive uses and leaving wetlands and beach and dune systems in their natural state permitted them to store or protect against floodwaters, and there was no significant damage to works of man. The advantages of waterfront locations, however, attracted real estate developers to respond there to demands for houses, business and industrial properties and public service facilities such as power station and ports. Flood damage is naturally more extensive in heavily developed flood plains.

The Federal Program

An early federal government response to disastrous floods was the 1936 Flood Control Act, which supported the construction of dams and floodwater storage reservoirs, levee systems, channel improvements and beach and dune restoration. These were perceived to be structural *solutions* to the problem of flooding. They encouraged more intensive development of flood hazard areas, however, and thereby increased the potential for property damage and loss of life. Flood hazard area management, therefore, should combine structural measures with development regulation so that land uses and structures are compatible with occasional flooding and property damage is minimized. Agriculture and recreation are examples of this kind of development.

More recent federal legislation, beginning with the National Flood Insurance Act of 1968, encouraged rational flood hazard area management by offering subsidized flood insurance to property owners in communities that would regulate development in these areas. Responsibility for the national flood insurance program was lodged in the Federal Insurance Administration of the Department of Housing and Urban Development. In 1969 the Act was amended to include insurance against damage from mudslides. The Flood Disaster Protection Act of 1973 further broadened the program by including protection against losses from flood-related erosion. The 1973 act also required that property owners must purchase flood insurance as a condition for their receiving any form of direct or indirect federal financial assistance or mortgage loans to buy properties or build in an identified special flood, mudslide or flood-related erosion hazard area. Furthermore, without this insurance, property owners might not be able to receive federal disaster assistance or rehabilitation loans if they were affected by such disasters. Insurance may be purchased through local insurance brokers from private insurance companies that have pooled resources as the National Flood Insurers Association under agreement with the Federal Insurance Administration (FIA). First, however, the community must participate in the national program by enacting flood hazard area zoning, subdivision controls, and building regulations that meet federal criteria.

The federal agency finances flood insurance studies to provide communities with information about flood hazard areas. The Flood Hazard Boundary Map (FHBM) is officially issued by the FIA to show the hazard area zones. The FIA also prepares a Flood Insurance Rate Map (FIRM) for each community, which shows the special hazard areas and the risk premium zones. The "base flood" is one having a 1% chance of being equalled or exceeded in any given year; it is also frequently referred to as the 100-year flood. Areas subject to such floods are designated as "areas of special flood hazard." The maps also designate "coastal high hazard areas," which are subject to high velocity waters, including hurricane wave wash. There are also designated "areas of special flood-related erosion hazard." In order that property owners may obtain flood insurance in these zones, the community must receive FIA approval for its flood plain management regulations, which are defined as:

> Zoning ordinances, subdivision regulations, building codes, health regulations, special purpose ordinances (such as a flood plain ordinance, grading ordinance and erosion control ordinance) and other applications of police power. The term describes such state or local regulations, in any combination thereof, which provide standards for the purpose of flood damage prevention and reduction [12].

The New York State Department of Environmental Conservation (DEC) helps communities to apply to FIA for participation in the national program. It provides information about the program and supplies model flood hazard area regulations. The state has gone further and now *requires* local participation.

State and Local Programs

On September 1, 1974, a state law went into effect that mandated local participation in the federal flood insurance program. It was incorporated as Article 36–Participation in Flood Insurance Programs in the New York State Environmental Conservation Law. The law declares that flood plain management is a matter of state concern because floods cause serious threats to the health and safety of the people of the state and their livelihood. The purposes of the state program are: (1) to reduce flood hazards and losses (2) to prevent the termination of federal financial assistance to flood victims, (3) to ensure that all communities with flood hazards adopt programs that will qualify them for participation in the national flood insurance programs [13].

Communities may qualify for participation by adopting land use controls and enforcement measures. Federal standards for such controls that qualify the community for participation in the national flood insurance program have been promulgated by the Department of Housing and Urban Development.

Local governments are formally notified by HUD if they are considered flood prone. The state law requires such communities to notify the Commissioner of DEC of this designation within ten working days. DEC and the NY Department of State are then to provide technical assistance to the local governments to qualify them for the national flood insurance program. Under this New York law, local governments do not have the option to choose whether or not they will participate in the federal program. If they fail to adopt acceptable flood plain controls, DEC will do it.

> If within three months of the date by which a local government must qualify
> for participation in the national flood insurance program, the commissioner
> judges that such local government may fail to qualify, the department shall
> develop flood hazard regulations for such local government which meet mini-
> mum federal requirements for participation in such program [14].

Furthermore, if a local government actually fails to qualify, the Commissioner of DEC is authorized to promulgate and enforce flood hazard regulations that meet federal requirements. During the period of DEC administration, the Commissioner assumes the role of appeals board and has the authority to grant variances from the strict letter of the regulations [15]. The state law also requires that stage agencies must minimize flood hazards and losses in connection with state-owned and state-financed buildings, roads and other facilities.

The Town of Islip. All coastal municipalities on Long Island have qualified for the program. The Town of Islip, for example, on November 19, 1974, enacted Article 40 Flood Hazard Districts to be included in the Town Code. It is implemented by the Town Planning Department, which issues building, subdivision and other development permits. Properties located in flood hazard districts are so noted on permit applications and deeds. This information is made available to mortgage lenders, insurance agents, prospective home buyers and other interested citizens. The regulations are enforced by site plan review and field inspections during the permit application review process to ensure that development proposals conform to the regulations. Nevertheless, the national flood insurance program may have the disadvantage of encouraging some development in flood hazard areas. Regulations cannot stop development altogether. Residential and business construction that might never have occurred in these areas may be stimulated in previously unoccupied wetlands, beaches and other high hazard areas. Coastal resources management programs therefore combine flood hazard area management with other means for limiting development, such as designation as geographic areas of particular concern or purchase of property fee ownership or development rights.

The Town of Easthampton. The Zoning Ordinance of the Town of Easthampton is an example of flood area regulations that conform to FIA standards. It was amended June 18, 1976, to include a Special Tidal Flood Hazard Overlay District so that the town could participate in the national flood insurance program. The boundaries of the Overlay District conform to the land elevations at the level that might be reached by a 100-year flood. Its provisions take precedence over any conflicting laws, ordinances or codes and over other provisions of the zoning ordinance. It contains these flood hazard zones:

Special Tidal Hazard areas along the bay shores are designated Zone A5 on the Flood Insurance Rate Maps published by the Federal Insurance Administration. The 100-year flood elevation for this zone is 8 feet above mean sea level.

Special Tidal Flood Hazard areas along the Atlantic Ocean which do not have additional high velocity water hazards (e.g., wave action) are designated Zone A7 on the FIRM. Its 100-year flood elevation is 11 feet above mean sea level.

Special Tidal Flood Hazard areas along the Atlantic Ocean that do have high velocity water hazards are designated Zone V10. Its 100-year flood elevation is also 11 feet above mean sea level [16].

New construction or major improvements to existing structures in any Special Tidal Flood Hazard Zone must have the lowest floor, including the basement, above the elevation of the 100-year flood for that zone; alternatively, together with necessary utility and sanitary facilities, it must be flood proofed up to the 100-year flood level. No land lying at less than 11 feet above mean sea level, which is within Zone V10, may be developed unless the new construction is elevated on adequately anchored piles or columns at or above the 11-ft level, has no basement, and has the space below the lowest floor free from obstructions so that the impact of abnormally high tides or wind-driven water is minimized [17].

The shore erosion and flood protection programs noted here have been paralleled and supplemented by extensive federal, state, county and municipal beach and shore front park systems, nature preserves and reservations. State and local programs for land use regulation, wetlands management and shellfish and other biological resources management, in combination with the other programs mentioned earlier, assure that no part of the marine coast of New York is without some kind of public surveillance and concern. Although controversy surrounds particular projects and programs, management effectiveness may be less than optimal, and intergovernmental and interagency coordination may have room for improvement; nevertheless, a great deal has been accomplished over the years to deal with an extremely complex resources management problem. One of the objectives of the developing New York coastal zone management program is to overcome existing management limitations and deficiencies.

REFERENCES

1. Detailed accounts of coastal geomorphology and shore erosion processes may be found in Joseph M. Heikoff, *Politics of Shore Erosion: Westhampton Beach* (Ann Arbor, Michigan: Ann Arbor Science, 1976); Donald R. Coates (ed.), *Coastal Geomorphology* (Binghamton, N.Y.: Publications in Geomorphology, SUNY at Binghamton, 1973); F. L. Bartholomew and W. V. McGuinness, Jr., *Coast Stabilization and Protection on Long Island.* Regional Marine Resources Council, Nassau-Suffolk Regional Planning Board, February 1972; and D. S. Davies, E. W. Axelrod, J. S. O'Connor, *Erosion of the North Shore of Long Island,* Technical Report No. 18, Marine Science Research Center, SUNY at Stony Brook, 1973.

2. New York Department of Environmental Conservation, *Interim Report on Flood Plain Management, Beach Erosion, and Hurricane Damage Reduction, South Shore Long Island,* April 1976 (Processed) and *Report on Flood Plain Management and Beach Erosion along the New York State Coastal* Zone, May 1977 (Processed).

3. U.S. Army Corps of Engineers, *National Shoreline Study, Regional Inventory Report, North Atlantic Region,* Vols. I, II, 1971.

4. Chief of Engineers, Department of the Army, *Report to Secretary of the Army,* May 27, 1960.

5. Ibid.

6. Letter from Gen. H. G. Woodbury, Jr., to J. Burch McMorran, June 1, 1967.

7. A full account of this case may be found in Heikoff, *The Politics of Shore Erosion: Westhampton Beach,* op. cit.

8. Town of Southampton, *Master Plan,* 1970, p. 93.

9. Town of Southampton, Building Zone Ordinance No. 26, Sec. 2-40-10.03(b), as amended through 1977.

10. Ibid., Sec. 2-40-10.03(1).

11. Town of East Hampton Zoning Ordinance, Sec. 517.1, as amended through 1977.

12. 41 Federal Register 46970, October 26, 1976.

13. New York State, Environmental Conservation Law, Sec. 36-0101, September 1, 1974.

14. Ibid., Sec. 36-0107, 3.

15. Ibid., Sec. 36-0109, 1 and 2.

16. Town of East Hampton Zoning Ordinance, Sec. 518.012.

17. Ibid., Sec. 518.021 and 518.022.

CHAPTER 4

SHELLFISH MANAGEMENT

The Atlantic shore and its estuaries once produced an abundant supply of shellfish. Market supply gradually dwindled, however, as extensive areas of ocean and bay bottom lands were closed to harvesting because the waters were polluted. The entire marine shore of New York State and the tidal waters of the Hudson River provided excellent habitats for shellfish, and its wetlands served as spawning and nursery areas for commercial fisheries species. Gradually New York Harbor, the Hudson River and the waters off western Long Island became inhospitable to marine life or were so polluted that infected shellfish posed serious threats to human health and life. Market demand for shellfish continued high, however, and overfishing posed another threat to the resource.

The marine shellfish resources of New York State include mollusks, crustaceans and conch, a member of the snail family. Blue crabs and lobsters are the familiar crustaceans. They are caught generally in the deeper waters off shore. Squid are also taken off shore by fishing boats. They are shelless mollusks used for both food and bait. The major shellfish harvest, however, comprises the various species of clams, oysters, mussels and scallops.

Shellfish have important ecological value as a link in the food chain that supports fish and wildlife. Only eight species of bivalve mollusks are regularly marketed for food. But 31 species of such mollusks and 37 species of the snail family are native to New York marine waters. These economically unimportant species provide food for crustaceans, fish and wildlife that do have economic value. Lobsters and crabs feed on these species, as do winter flounder, blackfish, cunners and cod. Rails, ibises, ducks and other waterfowl also feed on shellfish. Long Island is a regular winter habitat for about 120,000 waterfowl; some come from as far away as Alaska. In addition, about 150,000 transient birds stop there during migration. Twelve thousand hunters have been licensed to shoot waterfowl, but many more people value them for their beauty and their place in the area ecology [1].

Shellfish are an important economic resource that supports an industry estimated to be worth $100 million or more. Commercial landings in 1974 were valued at almost $20 million. About 740,000 persons were engaged in harvesting shellfish for recreation and their own consumption. The value of this recreational harvest may have been greater than the value of commercial landings [2]. Transportation, wholesaling, retailing and restaurant business, however, account for most of the industry economic product.

Shellfish harvesters have the greatest direct stake in the physical and economic health of the resource. They include the large-scale dredge operators who control privately owned or leased bay bottom lands; independent commercial harvesters, known on Long Island as baymen; and the recreational harvesters. Whereas the large companies use mechanical dredges to bring up their harvest, the baymen operate from small boats using long-handled rakes or tongs. The resource is protected by governmental regulators, who are sometimes regarded as enemies by the harvesters. They include the federal Food and Drug Administration, the New York State Department of Environmental Conservation, and local authorities (Figures 4 and 5).

FIGURE 4 Shellfish harvesting by hand rakes and tongs (Photo by NY State Department of Environmental Conservation).

FIGURE 5 Shellfish harvesting by dredging (Photo by NY State Department of Environmental Conservation).

REGULATION OF SHELLFISH HARVESTING AND DISTRIBUTION

At the federal level, the National Shellfish Sanitation Program (NSSP) was established in 1925 after a serious typhoid epidemic which was attributed to infected shellfish. The program was first administered by the U.S. Public Health Service but it was transferred to the Food and Drug Administration (FDA) in 1968. It is a cooperative effort by federal and state government and the private sector of the industry. NSSP is administered by the FDA Shellfish Sanitation Branch and its regional offices. The states set up their own Shellfish Sanitation Programs. In New York it is housed in the Department of Environmental Conservation. The FDA regional office, the Northeast Technical Field Services Unit, is responsible for reviewing and evaluating the New York program for conformance with the NSSP Manual of Operations. The federal field unit also helps the state by making hydrographic studies and testing water quality in the Long Island bays.

The constitutional foundation for federal involvement is the "commerce clause" (Art. I., Sec. 8(3)), which authorizes regulation of navigation and fisheries. Fisheries are regarded as common property, and all citizens have the right to fish in public waters. Both the federal and state governments have jurisdiction over fisheries within the three-mile coastal zone; federal fisheries regulation now extends to 200 miles off shore.

New York State laws for regulation of harvesting and distribution of shellfish also have a constitutional foundation. Article I, Sec. 6 of the New York State Constitution requires that state laws must promote public health, safety or welfare and not benefit any one special class. Article XIV, Sec. 4 enunciates the state policy to conserve and protect natural resources. The New York State Environmental Conservation Law implements this policy. It grants to the Commissioner of Environmental Conservation the power to protect and manage marine and coastal resources, encourage scientific research, monitor the environment and improve regulatory practices.

The Environmental Conservation Law has antecedents that go back to 1911. Section 11-0105 of the present law gives the state ownership of biological resources:

> The State of New York owns all fish, game, wildlife, shellfish, crustacea . . . in the state, except those legally acquired and held in private ownership. Any person who kills, takes or possesses such fish, game, wildlife, shellfish, crustacea . . . thereby consents that title thereto shall remain in the state for the purpose of regulating and controlling their use and disposition.

Section 11-0305 specifies these powers of the Department of Environmental Conservation to regulate the harvesting and distribution of shellfish:

> To issue the licenses and permits provided for by law, to fix their terms, and the fees therefor, when no statutory provision is made, and to revoke licenses and permits as provided by law;

> To control, manage, propagate and distribute, and to regulate the transportation, importation and exportation of shellfish and crustacea;

> To regulate the examination and inspection of shellfish grounds, boats used in taking and buildings used for storing of shellfish, the handling and shipment of shellfish, the floating of shellfish, the removal of shellfish from unsanitary beds and their deposit on unpolluted grounds;

> To enforce all laws relating to lands under water which have been or shall be designated, surveyed and mapped out pursuant to law as oyster beds or shellfish grounds and to grant leases of such lands, belonging to the state, for shellfish culture, according to law.

New York State and federal laws and programs for managing these resources in coastal waters were in existence long before the federal Coastal Zone Management Act was first passed in 1972. Article 13 of the Environmental Conservation Law was written specifically to deal with marine and coastal resources. Section 13-0103 established the Marine and Coastal District, which was described as including, "the waters of the Atlantic Ocean within three nautical miles from the coast line and all other tidal waters within the state, including the Hudson River up to the Tappan Zee bridge." Under the federal program, the coastal zone is extended up the Hudson to the tidal limit at Troy and it also includes the Great Lakes and St. Lawrence River to the international boundary with Canada. The coastal zone includes coastal lands as well as these waters, the landward boundary to be determined by the state.

Article 13 of the Environmental Conservation Law contains detailed provisions concerning the harvesting, handling and importation of shellfish, water quality and the leasing of state underwater levels for aquaculture. In accordance with this authority, DEC in 1974 issued 8027 permits to individual diggers, 1241 permits to shippers, 18 bed permits, and 6 permits for shellfish hatcheries. DEC also operates the New York Shellfish Sanitation Program (SSP), which assures consumers that shellfish harvested and marketed in the state meet sanitary standards.

According to state law, permits are not required for taking up to two pecks of shellfish per day from certified state waters for home consumption. State residents may take commercial quantities from state waters, buy shellfish from other diggers, process them or ship them in the shell or as fresh or frozen open stock in intrastate or interstate commerce after obtaining the proper class of permit from DEC. Permit holders are subject to the federal and state regulations governing the harvesting, processing and shipping of shellfish and to inspection of their plants and facilities. Town governments issue permits for taking shellfish from certified town waters for home consumption or for sale; but shellfish taken under town permits may be sold only to wholesalers or processors licensed under state permits.

Under the SSP program, all actual and potential shellfish-producing waters within the Marine and Coastal District are classified according to state quality standards. Of the state's 1.2 million acres of underwater lands, 575,000 acres are considered actually or potentially productive for shellfish harvesting; but 139,000 acres, or 24% of these productive waters, were closed because they were polluted. Classification of shellfish-producing waters is based on these technical activities: (1) collection of bacteriological data at water sampling stations, (2) shoreline surveys to identify actual and potential pollution sources, (3) hydrographic studies to determine the impact of major sources of pollution on shellfish-producing waters, and (4) analysis of these data to determine if these waters meet state quality standards and certifying areas for shellfish growing and harvesting.

Oysters and clams are filter feeders; they filter out food and oxygen from the water they take in and circulate out. This traps plant plankton used for food, but bacteria, viruses, metals and pesticides are also trapped and concentrated, for they are not circulated out after the water has been filtered. For example, it has been found that in Moriches Bay soft clams, fecal coliform levels rose from 30 MPN/100 ml of water* to 1600 MPN/100 ml within six hours after a significant rainfall had washed pollutants from the surface of the ground into the bay waters. Increases from 500 MPN/ml to 9200 MPN/ml had been observed in hard clams in Great South Bay even under dry weather conditions when boating and land population densities increased on summer weekends [3], Most water contaminants come from human sanitary and other wastes, even after they have been processed in private septic tanks or sewage treatment plants; from storm water runoff from the land; and from duck farm wastes. The federal Food and Drug Administration has set 70 MPN/100 ml as the standard for water quality acceptable for shellfish harvesting.

DEC maintains surveillance over all wholesale marketing of shellfish in the state. Storage and processing facilities are inspected before a wholesaler is issued a permit to operate. Monthly inspections are made thereafter to assure compliance with the state Rules and Regulations—Sanitary Control over Shellfish. Market samples of oysters and clams are collected for bacteriological analysis, shellfish samples are collected for analysis directly from their underwater beds and vessels used for harvesting are inspected periodically.

Shellfish analysis is performed in DEC's microbiology and chemistry laboratories. Shellfish and seawater samples are analyzed for the presence of organisms, such as fecal coliform and streptococcus bacteria, that indicate pollution. Chemical analysis looks for the presence of pesticides, such as DDT, DDD, DDE, aldrin and dieldrin, and for heavy metals, such as mercury, copper, lead, zinc and cadmium in the air and underwater sediments as well as in the mollusks and water.

DEC and the clammers are often at odds with respect to water quality standards and the prohibition of harvesting in polluted areas. In May 1977, DEC closed 2665 acres, mostly in Great South Bay, because water quality did not meet the standards set by the National Shellfish Sanitation Program and state law. This angered the baymen and other harvesters, who claimed that coliform counts were not a valid basis for establishing these standards. However, the N.Y. Supreme Court in September 1977 denied the request of two baymen for a permanent injunction against closing some of the waters in the Town of Babylon by the Commissioner of DEC. In another decision,

---

*MPN/100 ml means Most Probable Number (of bacteria) per 100 milliliters of water.

the Court upheld coliform counts as the only valid testing standard in a suit by the Towns of Babylon, Islip and Brookhaven against DEC that charged that the coliform count tests were not valid [4].

Meanwhile, DEC agreed to reevaluate the tests and obtained state and U.S. Environmental Protection Agency funds to support the investigation. The state Department of Health, local communities, the industry and officials from neighboring states would be involved in carrying out and evaluating it. Also in June 1977, DEC began a new system of conditional opening of closed areas between April and November, depending on weather conditions and water quality. Under this new ruling, designated areas may be clammed during these months on any day following seven consecutive days when no more than 0.25 inch of rain has fallen on any one of these days. This rule is based on the presumption that the bay waters would be less polluted after a comparatively dry spell, when oils, chemicals, heavy metals and animal feces would not have been washed in by surface runoff from streets, gardens, farms, parking lots and other land areas.

SHELLFISH RESOURCES MANAGEMENT

Department of Environmental Conservation concern for shellfish resources is not limited to regulating the industry. The State is also involved in managing the resource so as to increase the productivity. One of the most important of these programs is the transplanting of shellfish from polluted waters to areas of acceptable water quality, for they can eventually flush out their accumulated disease-producing organisms and toxic materials. Transplantation thus increases the shellfish harvest by making those that are moved safe for human consumption. Between 1965 and 1975, DEC supervised the transplanting of 215,000 bushels of hard clams in almost every town on Long Island. In 1977 alone, 36,000 bushels of clams were transferred from uncertified to certified waters [5].

Removal of shellfish from polluted waters also discourages poaching. Large numbers of shellfish in highly productive polluted waters tempt poachers to harvest them at night, using speedboats that can outrun DEC and local patrol boats. By 1975, however, DEC had increased its complement of enforcement officers to 34. New equipment included fast skiffs with 135 horsepower engines, radar, radio-equipped autos and walkie-talkie radios. Poachers who are caught have their shellfishing permits suspended, and their boats and equipment are seized. To deal with court leniency in sentencing poachers, a special assistant district attorney has been appointed in Suffolk County to prosecute them [6].

Transplantation also helps to increase the shellfish population. In 1976, 3000 clams were transplanted from cool to warmer waters to increase spawning. Oysters and bay scallops are also transplanted, in this case from areas where they are now well established to areas where they were known to be formerly numerous. Initiative for shellfish transplanting must be taken by the Long Island towns whose waters and underwater lands are affected. Costs are shared 50% by the federal government.

It is evident that shellfish must have the proper environment in order to multiply and be marketable. Water depth, temperature, salinity, turbidity and quality must conform to the narrow range of shellfish growth requirements and sanitation. All of these conditions, however, are affected by manmade changes in the environment, particularly pollution, dredging and filling, alteration of wetlands and engineering works that affect tidal flushing and water circulation in the great bays behind the south shore barrier islands. DEC, therefore, carries out shellfish population surveys as part of its management program. Areas to be dredged for navigation channel improvement or other reasons are surveyed to determine if enough shellfish would be affected to make transplanting worthwhile. Where it is advisable, DEC supervises the transplanting, and the costs are borne by the agency or those who would benefit from receiving the transplants. Other surveys are carried out to identify areas for potential transplanting and to lease for shellfish cultivation.

Leasing state-owned underwater lands for shellfish cultivation is the third major element in the DEC management program. This involves the reconciliation of conflicts between the baymen, who are independent harvesters, and the large-scale mechanized shellfish farming operators. Areas leased for cultivation are naturally closed to the baymen. The large-scale operators cultivate the shellfish and then harvest them by mechanical dredging. The baymen, however, use hand rakes or tongs and depend upon nature's bounty for their harvest. In an effort to resolve the conflict, the Environmental Conservation Law (Sec. 13-0301) states that, "lands under water shall not be leased where there is an indicated presence of shellfish in sufficient quantity and quality and so located as to support significant hand raking and/or tonging harvesting." Such state-owned areas are open to baymen without restriction. Other areas that are suitable for cultivation and mechanical harvesting, as determined by DEC, are offered for leasing.

An appreciation of the scale of the various elements of the DEC Shellfish Sanitation Program and other management activities may be gained from this summary of what was done in 1977:

- Completed sanitary surveys on 50 designated shellfish growing areas and determined boundaries of certified waters

- Marked and maintained boundaries of certified waters with buoys and other devices

- Reviewed about 300 applications for shellfish shippers' licenses

- Inspected and evaluated about 300 shellfish shippers' facilities

- Collected shellfish landing statistics on a monthly basis and transmitted the information to the National Marine Fisheries Service

- Analyzed 2,000 shellfish samples to determine quality at the market level [7].

Local Government in Shellfish Management

Town governments on Long Island are deeply involved in shellfish management, for they have an important stake in the resource. The towns own thousands of acres of bay bottom lands where the shellfish grow. They are concerned with regulating the harvesting of shellfish, leasing lands, sanitation, enforcement and increasing productivity. These are the same concerns the State has delegated to the Department of Environmental Conservation. State and local agencies cooperate in these programs, but sometimes there are differences of opinion on how they should be carried out. In any case, DEC is primarily concerned with managing state-owned underwater lands, and the towns have responsibility for their own underwater lands.

Institutions for managing shellfish and other water-related resources vary from town to town. Some have line departments, such as the Department of Environmental Control in the Town of Islip. Some have Boards of Trustees of the Freeholders, which were established by royal charters during colonial times. Both of these forms will be described.

Town of Islip Department of Environmental Control. The Department of Environmental Control was established in 1974 [8]. It replaced the former Departments of Waste Disposal and Marine Affairs. The Commissioner of Environmental Control heads the Department and is appointed by the Town Board. He is given broad responsibility and is:

charged with the protection of the people of the Town of Islip against such activities as would tend to impair, damage, destroy or otherwise infringe upon the natural resources and environment of the Town of Islip or on their enjoyment by the present and future people of the Town of Islip [9].

In order to carry out this charge, the Commissioner is endowed by town law with specific powers. He may:

1. Make rules and regulations, subject to Town Board approval, which may be necessary to ensure the conservation and protection of town natural resources and environment.
2. Intervene in proceedings before the Planning Board and the Board of Appeals in any matter, petition, application or proceeding that affects town resources and environment.
3. Advise and make recommendations to any department, board, committee or other town agency either at their request or on the Commission's own initiative.
4. Hold hearings on matters relating to the conservation and protection of town environment and natural resources [10].

Town law also mandates that the Commissioner of Environmental Control "shall be consulted on all matters affecting the environment and natural resources of the Town of Islip which may come under the jurisdiction of any department, board, committee or other governmental agency of the Town of Islip" [11].

Department operations are carried out by three Divisions: Environmental Facilities, Environmental Management and Environmental Services. The Environmental Management Division supervises and controls waterways and their use in the Town of Islip. It coordinates enforcement of town waterways codes with the Environmental Services Division. Perhaps the most important responsibility of this Division is supervision of the comprehensive shellfish and bay management program, which includes required depuration and transplanting of shellfish from polluted waters. Bay management is also concerned with wetlands restoration or creation.

The Department of Environmental Control has concentrated in its first years of existence on policy and regulating town waterways and developing shellfish production in marine waters. A more ambitious program was visualized for it, however, before it was established in May 1974. During the previous December a report was presented to the Islip Town Board on a "Comprehensive Coastal and Water Management Program."

The proposed comprehensive program would have five components: (1) freshwater resources management, (2) shellfish resource management, (3) wetlands management, (4) inspection and enforcement, and (5) interdepartmental and intergovernmental coordination. Because of its focus on policing and regulating waterways and promoting shellfishing, however, the Department of Environmental Control has not become deeply involved in comprehensive planning. The Department of Planning and Development will assume responsibility for preparing the coastal plan as an element of the Town of Islip comprehensive plan [12]. It will be incorporated in Volume 4, Natural Resources and Environment, of the Town of Islip Comprehensive Plan, which is in preparation.

Demands on the Department of Environmental Control for shellfish resources management has increased because of an important change in Town
policy. The Town of Islip owns most of the land under the waters of the
Great South Bay that are within town boundaries. It amounts to about
4000 acres of prime shellfish-producing bay bottom. In former years, much
of this area had been leased at low rates to commercial firms for exclusive
clamming rights. Now, however, commercial licenses that permit clamming
anywhere in town waters are issued to individual baymen. Residential licenses
are issued to qualified residents to take clams for home consumption.

The Department of Environmental Control operates the shellfish management program under the authority of the Shellfish Ordinance of the Town of
Islip, Chapter 44 of the Islip Code. Personal permits for taking shellfish for
home consumption are issued only to town residents. Commercial permits are
issued to baymen. The Shellfish Ordinance prescribes the harvesting season
for oysters and scallops and specifies the minimum sizes of oysters, scallops
and clams that may be taken. The physical features of tongs or rakes used in
harvesting are also prescribed by the ordinance.

About one-third of all hard clams taken in the Great South Bay were harvested in the Town of Islip. Preserving and enhancing this resource, therefore, has high priority. During 1974, 1000 bushels of sexually mature clams
and more than 60,000 scallops were introduced into town waters in a joint
program with the state DEC to augment the natural shellfish set. Using a
hydraulic dredge, more than 18,000 bushels of hard clams were transplanted
from polluted to certified waters. The Town also had its own enforcement
program to prevent poaching in uncertified areas. It had three patrol vessels,
a seaplane, radar facilities, and seven officers [13].

Town of Southampton Board of Trustees. The eastern towns of Long Island,
including Southampton, East Hampton and Southold have unique colonial
governmental structures. These are the Boards of Trustees that have jurisdiction over town-owned lands and regulate activities in their extensive wetlands and lands under water. The Board of Trustees of the Freeholders and
Commonality of the Town of Southampton, for example, was established in
1686 as the first official government of the town. The charter, or patent, was
granted by Thomas Dongan, Governor of the Province of New York by
authority of King James II. The Board of Trustees remains today as the cus-
todian of about 25,000 acres of town-owned waters, lands and lands under
water.

The Dongan Charter confirmed the ownership by trustees of the original
settlers of all common lands, waters and lands under water, and all their
produce, within the boundaries of the Town of Southampton by right of purchase from the Indians [14]. The New York State Legislature confirmed

these rights in 1818 and 1831. The second act was Chapter 283 of the 54th Session, an act declaring the powers and duties of the Trustees of the Freeholders and Commonality of the Town of Southampton, in the county of Suffolk. It stated that:

> The said Trustees shall have the sole control over all the fisheries, fowling, seaweed, waters, and the production of the waters within the said Town not the properties of individuals, and all the property, commodities, privileges and franchises granted to them by the charter of Governor Dongan in 1686, except so far as they are abrogated, changed and altered by the laws of this state, passed in conformity to the Constitution . . . and they shall have power to make rules, orders, and bylaws for the management thereof and the regulation of their affairs [15].

In 1902, by Chapter 133 of the laws of that year, the state legislature formalized the procedure for choosing trustees. Five trustees were to be elected at the April town meeting every other year to serve for the intervening two-year period.

In spite of these acts of the state legislature, the authority of the Board of Trustees has been challenged by private landowners and state agencies. The Jessup Bridge case was resolved by the New York Court of Appeals in 1903 after 15 years of litigation. The Court of Appeals decision said:

> It is the Court's opinion that although the State has for some time exercised over the Town of Southampton the function of government, the inherent rights of the Trustees as granted by King James still remain until the State acquires that land of the township by condemnation proceedings [16].

In 1932 the Appellate Division of the New York Supreme Court again decided in favor of the Trustees against the State of New York. The issue then was similar to one that has arisen between the Board of Trustees and the New York Department of Environmental Conservation since passage of the Tidal Wetlands Act. DEC claims that its police power right to regulate tidal wetlands under this law supersedes the authority of the Board of Trustees. The same contention was made by the New York Conservation Commission, a predecessor of DEC in the "Southampton Town Clam Case." The State Attorney General, on behalf of the Commission, agreed that the State could not disturb the ownership rights of the Trustees. Nevertheless, the State claimed that:

> In regard to the management of the State and making this property subject to general public law the State retained full power . . . [and] argues that the State may still legislate as to the management of this property in the exercise of the police power [17].

The Court decided against the State and for the Board of Trustees. In the decision, Justice Young said:

> In my judgment, the town in the present case has the absolute right under the ancient charters to control and manage Mecox Bay and its productions, and if there was any right reserved to the State to exercise its police powers over these waters it ceded such right when, by the act of 1831, it gave to the town the sole right to control the fisheries, waters and production of the waters within the Town of Southampton [18].

Now the Department of Environmental Conservation again seeks to assert the State's superior right to exercise police power for the regulation of wetlands under state law. DEC has surveyed Long Island's wetlands and promulgated final regulations for their management by a permit system. They put forward the same argument that was made by the Attorney General in the "Southampton Clam Case;" that the Board of Trustees is the rightful owner of the wetlands, but it must submit in the same way as any other owner to state regulation. Until further court action decides the issue, DEC is implementing its wetlands regulatory system in Southampton and other towns with Board of Trustees [19].

The Southampton Board of Trustees still claims that the State may not preempt its charter rights to regulate its own wetlands. One reason for this, perhaps, is that simple justice demands that Southampton citizens defend their rights. There may be more material values at stake, however. These have to do with dredging and other activities that have economic advantages for the town. The issue was posed squarely by Stephen F. Meschutt who served as Town Supervisor for 15 years before retiring in 1965. He edited a booklet that contained the Dongan charter, the relevant state laws, and the court decisions that have been referred to above. In the conclusion of this booklet, which was intended to present the case against state interference with local self-determination through the Board of Trustees, he made these statements:

> A new fad has appeared upon the horizon. . . . I refer to the sudden upsurge of self-appointed advisors. . . . Let's call them by name, The Shellfish Industry, the pollution and health program, the Commercial Fishing Industry, Sports Fishing groups, Marina operations, Yachtsmen, Boat Yards, and Conservationists.

> The ever increasing demand for more Marinas—both public and private, and careful planning for preservation of our natural resources, all require dredging operations. The dredges under the Town Trustees and Rudolph Kammerer, [Suffolk County] Superintendant of Public Works, has [sic] proven to be seaworthy and well found. Their past record of opening new areas of our shallow creeks which in some instances have never in our life time been cleaned of the decayed vegetation, mud and silt causing them to be condemned areas closed to navigation and polluted. The dredging program has enhanced real estate values by making

existing waterways navigable, keeping our inlets open to commercial fishing boats and yachtsmen which represent a multi-million dollar industry working with the Town Trustees in keeping our channels navigable. They all imply the need for our dredging program to continue [20].

These sentiments were published in 1968 and may not represent the views of the current members of the Board of Trustees. Nevertheless, it may be inferred from these statements that the then newly aroused conservation and environmental movement was regarded as an outside invasion threatening local freedom. The conservationists wanted to preserve the wetlands for their aesthetic values, biological productivity and flood storage function, among others. They also opposed dredging and filling, which not only destroyed wetlands, but also altered the bay bottoms and reduced shellfish production.

The town fathers, however, favored the interests of yachtsmen, commercial and sport fishermen, marine operations and real estate interests. Dredging and filling of wetlands to provide sites for new marinas and high value waterfront lots was given higher priority over environmental conservation. Whether current contention between the Southampton Board of Trustees and the Department of Environmental Conservation is simply a struggle for power or an economic issue between developers and conservationists cannot now be determined. It is one indication, however, of the complexity of the coastal management problem of devising a state management structure to resolve conflicts between interest groups.

REFERENCES

1. J. L. Renkavinsky, "The Noncommercial Value of Shellfish," *Proceedings of a Workshop on the Shellfish Management Program in New York State,* New York Sea Grant Institute, Albany, N.Y., July 1975, pp. 37-8.
2. Anthony S. Taormina, "Overview of New York's Shellfish Resources," *Proceedings of a Workshop,* p. 7.
3. R. B. MacMillan, "Public Health Significance of Shellfish Management," *Proceedings of a Workshop,* p. 18.
4. *NYS Environment,* October 1977, pp. 1 and 12; December 1977, p. 11.
5. *NYS Environment,* December 1977, p. 10.
6. G. W. Thilberg, "The Role of Law Enforcement," *Proceedings of a Workshop,* p. 36.
7. *NYS Environment,* December 1977, p. 10.
8. Town of Islip, Local Law No. 3, 1974, Chapter 10A of the Town Code.
9. Ibid., Sec. 10A-6.
10. Ibid., Sec. 10A-5.
11. Ibid.

12. Interview with Michael LaGrande, Commissioner of Planning, and Stephen Jones, Islip Town Hall, June 22, 1977.
13. *NYS Environment,* February 1, 1975, p. 5.
14. Stephen F. Meschutt (ed.), *The Board of Trustees of the Freeholders and Commonalty of the Town of Southampton,* 1968, pp. 8-17.
15. Ibid., p. 23.
16. *People ex rel. Howell v. Jessup,* 160 N.Y. 249.
17. *People of the State of New York v. Richard Miller and the Trustees of the Freeholders and Commonalty of the Town of Southampton,* 235 AD 226, April 29, 1932.
18. Ibid.
19. NY Department of Environmental Conservation, Division of Environmental Analysis, Albany, N.Y., October 12, 1977.
20. Meschutt, p. 46.

CHAPTER 5

WETLANDS MANAGEMENT

Wetlands management is an important component of the land and water use regulation element in any overall coastal resources management program. In New York State this applies to both marine and freshwater wetlands. There are some freshwater wetlands within the marine coastal zone, but a great segment of New York's coastline includes the freshwater Great Lakes and St. Lawrence River. New York has enacted legislation to manage both marine and freshwater wetlands. The use or alteration of marine wetlands is regulated directly by the State through the Department of Environmental Conservation. The initiative for freshwater wetlands regulation may be taken over by local governments, but if they do not act, the counties may take over. The State must take responsibility if local and county governments fail to do so.

THE NEW YORK TIDAL WETLANDS ACT

The State legislature had attempted to control wetlands destruction before it passed the Tidal Wetlands Act in 1973. The Stream Protection Act of 1966 required that permits had to be obtained for excavating or filling that affected navigable waters as well as contiguous estuaries, marshes and wetlands. Unfortunately, Nassau and Suffolk Counties were excluded from this requirement by reference to the State Navigation Law. Efforts to remove the Navigation Law reference were repeatedly frustrated by various lobbies [1].

Another state law, the New York State Long Island Wetlands Act, had been incorporated in 1959 into the old Conservation Law of 1911 as Sec. 11-2307. It established a program of cost sharing for improving, conserving and managing Long Island wetlands. About 16,350 acres of town-owned wetlands in the Towns of Hempstead, Islip, Oyster Bay and Brookhaven were improved under this program. It was not intended, however, to preserve privately. owned wetlands. Repeated attempts to enact a strong wetlands program were ineffective because of opposition from developers and local governments [2].

81

In 1973, the Tidal Wetlands Act was finally passed and incorporated into the State Environmental Conservation Law as Article 25. It was justified by the legislative finding that, "tidal wetlands constitute one of the most vital and productive areas of our natural world, and that their protection and preservation are essential" [3]. Whereas wetlands had formerly been regarded as mosquito-breeding nuisances that should be filled in and put to some economic use, the legislature recognized that they had both economic and aesthetic value for:

- *Marine food production:* tidal wetlands are a source of nutrients for microscopic organisms, crustaceans and shellfish that are the first links in a food chain that supports fish, wildlife and man; wetlands also are spawning areas, nursery grounds and sanctuaries for fish species that are important for the commercial market and recreation
- *Wildlife habitat:* tidal wetlands provide nesting and feeding grounds as well as cover for wildlife, waterfowl and shore birds
- *Flood and storm protection:* tidal wetlands absorb and store storm waters and serve as a buffer against storm tides and waves, thus minimizing flood damage and erosion
- *Recreation:* tidal wetlands provide opportunities for hunting, fishing, boating, hiking, bird watching, photography and camping
- *Pollution abatement:* tidal marsh vegetation produces great quantities of oxygen from photosynthesis and the wetlands serve as biological and chemical oxidation basins for the conversion of pollutants washed in from upland areas
- *Sediment removal:* tidal wetlands are settling and filtering basins that absorb silt and organic matter that would otherwise obstruct navigation channels
- *Education and research:* tidal wetlands offer opportunities for biological and other scientific research and outdoor classrooms for imparting environmental education and values
- *Open space and aesthetic appreciation:* tidal wetlands comprise a large part of the remaining natural areas along coastal reaches that are under pressure from rapid population growth.

The legislature also found that New York State was in danger of losing these economic and recreational values unless market pressures for altering wetlands could be countered by State regulation:

The legislature further finds that vast acreage in the tidal wetlands in the State of New York has already been irreparably lost or despoiled as a result of unregulated dredging, dumping, filling, excavating, pollution, and like activities; that the remaining tidal wetlands are in imminent jeopardy of being lost or despoiled by these and other activities; that if the current rate of loss continues, most of the State's tidal wetlands will be entirely lost before the end of this century; and that presently many creeks and tidal wetlands are so polluted that shellfish harvesting is banned [4].

About 10,000 acres of tidal wetlands had been lost in Nassau and Suffolk Counties since 1953 [5]. In order to conserve and protect New York's remaining tidal wetlands, the act established a regulatory program. This began with a tidal wetlands inventory and a moratorium on alteration of the wetlands. After completion of the inventory, land use regulations were to be adopted and special permits required for any alteration of the wetlands (Figure 6).

FIGURE 6 Wetland on Long Island (Photo by NY State Department of Environmental Conservation).

Tidal Wetlands Inventory

Aerial photography and ground checks were used to make the wetlands inventory. From this information, maps at the scale of 1 inch equals 200 feet were prepared that show the areal extent of the wetlands as well as variations based on plant types. The different classes of wetland vegetation grow where the duration and extent of regular tidal flow create the proper conditions for their growth. After tentative boundary maps were completed, the Department of Environmental Conservation held public hearings, to which the owners of wetland properties and municipal officials were specially invited.

After considering the information offered at the hearings, the DEC Commissioner established by order the official boundaries of each wetland area.

Six classes of tidal wetlands have been identified and mapped. It is on the basis of information about vegetative types and the degree of tidal inundation that the compatibility of various uses with each wetland class may be determined for writing the regulations. These are the classes defined in the inventory:

- *Coastal fresh marsh (FM):* found primarily in the upper tidal limits of riverine systems where significant freshwater inflow dominates the tidal zone; typical vegetation consists of cattails, brackish water cordgrass, and pickerel weed; this type of wetland is highly productive and valuable for wildlife
- *Intertidal marsh (IM):* lies between the low and high tide lines; dominated by low marsh cordgrass (*Spartina alterniflora*); most productive area for primary nutrients
- *High marsh or salt meadow (HM):* lies above the intertidal marsh; regularly flooded only by spring and storm tides; dominated by salt meadow grass (*Spartina patens*) but also has low vigor *S. alterniflora,* spike grass, and other species; moderately productive, shelter for wildlife, and buffer between uplands and estuarine waters
- *Formerly connected tidal wetland (FC):* normal tide flow restricted by topographic alteration by man; typical tidal wetlands species persist, but common reed (*Phragmites*) may infiltrate; continues as part of marine food web
- *Coastal shoals, bars, and mudflats (SM):* covered by water at high tide and exposed or covered by only a foot of water at low tide; not generally covered with *S. alterniflora* or other rooted vegetation
- *Littoral zone (LZ):* shallow bay bottoms under less than 6 feet of water at low tide; support eel and widgeon grasses; productive for waterfowl, fish, and shellfish [6].

Moratorium on Wetlands Alteration

While the inventory was being prepared, a moratorium was imposed by the Tidal Wetlands Act on any alteration of any tidal wetland or adjacent area. Persons who considered they were suffering hardship because of the moratorium could petition for a permit, which might be granted by DEC after a public hearing. The permitted alteration could continue until the inventory was completed, but the permit could be revoked if its conditions were violated. The moratorium permit would have to be obtained from DEC in addition to any zoning or other permits required by the municipality. DEC regulations were issued for the review and issuance of moratorium permits. They set the general distance of 300 feet from the tidal wetland boundary or the area up to the 10-foot elevation above mean sea level as the limit of the "adjacent area" [7]. The moratorium period regulations were incorporated as Part 660 in the New York Compilation of Rules and Regulations.

Not all applications for moratorium permits had to go through the lengthy review process set forth in the rules and regulations. If a field inspection indicated that the proposed alteration would do little damage to the wetland or would be in an adjacent area and would not adversely affect the wetland itself, the Department of Environmental Conservation issued a "letter of determination of non-applicability," or "D" letter. These letters were usually issued for minor changes to preexisting land uses and activities, for home construction in the "adjacent" area, for repair or replacement of existing bulkheads, for redriving piles that had been displaced and for repairing existing docks.

Applications proposing more serious alteration of wetlands went through the formal moratorium permit review procedures. These included public hearings if there were objections to the project from parties-at-interest or the Department of Environmental Conservation. After detailed consideration, permits were either granted, granted with modifying conditions, or denied. A study by Roy L. Haje, then a permit administrator in DEC, indicated that during most of the moratorium period, only about 20 acres of wetlands were lost as the result of hardship permits granted to property owners. More area was lost by illegal dumping and filling, but the extent of this damage is unknown.

Violators of the moratorium rules and regulations who were caught were punished by administrative DEC action, with fines up to $3000, and were required to restore the area to its former wetland condition. Cases that could not be resolved by DEC were forwarded to the State Attorney General for formal court proceedings. Guilty parties could have civil or criminal penalties imposed on them and be required to restore the wetlands.

Over 50 violation cases were dealt with by DEC and the Attorney General's Office. Accused violators included property owners, developers and even local government agencies. Developers often claimed that the land had been filled before they began work, that the surveyors made bad maps or that the local governments had issued building permits. Sometimes violators were spotted by residents of the area, sometimes by DEC officials. U.S. national wildlife refuges were one of the favorite targets for development encroachment. Hempstead Town workers were charged with illegal filling when they claimed they were trying to clean up a town-owned wetland and convert it into a docking area for boats. Town of Islip officials were also stopped in the middle of a bulkheading project to expand a town marina because they did not have a permit from the Corps of Engineers. Some environmental organizations were not satisfied with DEC efforts to enforce the moratorium regulations. They accused DEC of sabotaging the Tidal Wetlands Act by favoring wetland developers at the expense of the public [8].

Violations continued even after the end of the moratorium period. In New York City there are 10,000 acres of tidal wetlands. The DEC regional office there reported that it was pursuing violators and had collected thousands of dollars in fines. Almost all of those who are caught prefer to pay the fine rather than go through the hearing process. An unknown number of violations are committed by "gypsy dumpers." They own a truck or two and dump anything anywhere they can get away with it. They operate mostly at night and dump earth, garbage, construction refuse and other materials in unguarded corners of the marshes [9].

Tidal Wetlands Land Use Regulation

By mid-1977, about four years after passage of the Tidal Wetlands Act, the wetlands inventory had been completed and hearings held on draft final rules and regulations. The land use regulations were incorporated as Part 661 of the New York Compilation of Codes, Rules, and Regulations effective August 20, 1977.

The heart of the Tidal Wetlands Land Use Regulations is a matrix table that specifies which of 57 categories of use may be permitted in any of six zones. The zones consist of the five types of wetlands mapped by the inventory that have already been described on p. 84 plus the adjacent area (AA). The adjacent area is defined as generally extending 300 feet landward from the boundary of a wetland or to the contour elevation 10 feet above mean sea level, but there are many exceptions and detailed provisions in Section 661.4(b) of the regulations.

The 57 types of land use have been grouped into five classes for determination as to whether or not they may be permitted in any of the six zones:

- Compatible use not requiring a permit or notification letter approval (NPN)

- Generally compatible use, notification letter required (GCn)

- Generally compatible use, permit required (GCp)
  These are uses considered to be compatible with the objective of preserving, protecting, and enhancing the present and potential value of the particular wetland or adjacent area zone

- Presumptively incompatible use (PIp)
  These are uses presumed not to be compatible with the objectives of the wetlands act in the zone in which they are proposed; permits are required for such uses

- Incompatible use (I)
    These uses are not considered compatible with the zone for which
    they are proposed; permits are required

The matrix is reproduced in Table II. It indicates the compatibility or in-compatibility of each type of use with each of the six types of wetlands and adjacent areas.

Property owners or developers who find from the matrix that their pro-posed uses are compatible (NPN) with the areas in which they are proposed may proceed without notifying the Department of Environmental Conser-vation regional permit administrator or applying for a permit. If the proposed uses are classed as generally compatible, but a "notification letter" is required (GCn), project sponsors must notify the regional permit administrator in writ-ing of their intentions so that he may ascertain whether the proposed activity is subject to regulation. The permit administrator returns a written "notifi-cation letter response" informing the sponsor whether he may proceed with the activity or must go through the permit application procedure because it may substantially alter or impair the natural condition or function of the area. For all other intended uses shown in the matrix as (GCp), (PI) or (I), a permit application is required.

The tidal wetlands land use regulations incorporate development standards to protect wetlands and adjacent areas from residential and other kinds of construction for which permits have been granted. These include minimum setbacks from the wetland edge; location and construction of septic tank and other forms of onsite sewage disposal; lot coverage by buildings, parking areas and other impervious surfaces; and minimum lot areas. Substantially increased surface drainage caused by construction must be prevented from running directly into tidal waters classified by DEC as suitable for commer-cial shellfish harvesting or contact recreation, or into other surface waters within 100 feet of such waters. Suitable measures to reduce run off are dry wells, retention basins, filters, and open swales or ponds.

If proposed uses require a permit, application must be made to the DEC regional permit administrator. The application form provides for detailed information about the property, its location, its owners and the proposed development and uses. Copies of the application are sent to officials of the municipality where the wetland is located, and they are made available for public inspection at designated places. The applicant must publish a notice of public hearing, and DEC also follows its own required procedures for pub-lishing a hearing notice. If no formal public objections to the proposals are received by the permit administrator, and if the applicant waives a hearing, then the hearing may be cancelled and DEC may proceed with review of the application.

TABLE II Wetlands Classification for State Regulation

Uses	FM	IM	HM	SM	LZ	AA
1. The continuance of lawfully existing uses (including but not limited to residential, commercial, industrial, agricultural, recreational, and public uses) and the continuance of all activities normally and directly associated with any such use, where such continuance does not involve expansion or significant alteration of the existing use.						
2. Activities of the department of health or of units of local government with respect to public health, when conducted in conformance with section 25-0.01 of the Act.			NPN		NPN	NPN
3. Activities subject to the review jurisdiction of the public service commission or the state board on electric generation siting and the environment under article seven or article eight of the public service law, respectively. The standards and restrictions of this Part will be applied by said bodies in determining whether to issue a certificate of environmental compatibility and public need under such articles.			NPN		NPN	NPN
4. Establishing scenic, historic, wildlife and scientific preserves, without any material alteration of the area involved.			NPN		NPN	NPN
5. Boating, hiking, swimming, camping, picnicking and other similar non-motorized forms of outdoor activity.			NPN		NPN	NPN
6. Depositing or removing the natural products of a tidal wetland (or adjacent area) in the process of recreational or commercial fishing, shellfishing, aquaculture, hunting or trapping, including the erection and maintenance of temporary hides or blinds.			NPN		NPN	NPN
7. Conducting educational and research activities not involving any material alteration of the area involved.			NPN		NPN	NPN
8. Establishing walking trails without material alteration of the area involved.			NPN		NPN	NPN
9. Establishing plantings.			GCn		GCn	NPN
10. Establishing recreational moorings;			NPN		NPN	NPN
11. Operation of motor vehicles, including but not limited to air boats and other all-terrain vehicles, for educational or scientific research purposes (provided this item shall not include operation of aircraft or mechanically propelled vessels other than air boats).			GCn		GCn	NPN

12.	Operation of motor vehicles, including but not limited to air boats and other all-terrain vehicles, for other than educational or scientific purposes (provided this item shall not include the use of aircraft or mechanically propelled vessels other than air boats).	PIp	GCp	NPN
13.	Operation of aircraft or mechanically propelled vessels other than air boats.	NPN	NPN	NPN
14.	Constructing one open pile catwalk and/or dock not greater than four feet in width for any principal building.	GCn	GCn	GCn
15.	Constructing open pile catwalks and docks more than four feet in width; or constructing more than one open pile catwalk and/or dock not greater than four feet in width for any principal building.	PIp	GCp	GCp
16.	Installing a floating dock(s) totalling less than 200 square feet in area.	GCn	NPN	NPN
17.	Installing a floating dock(s) totalling 200 square feet or more in area.	PIp	GCn	GCn
18.	Relocation and/or rearrangement of floating docks, open pile docks, and similar structures within an established marina or boat basin where such activities involve no disturbance of a tidal wetland other than removing and relocating anchors or pilings.	PIp	NPN	NPN
19.	Constructing solid fill docks.	PIp	PIp	GCp
20.	Permanent or seasonal mooring of any vessel or structure to be used as a single family dwelling, multiple family dwelling, commercial use building, industrial use building or public or semi-public building.	PIp	GCp	GCp
21.	Ordinary maintenance and repair (not involving expansion or substantial restoration, reconstruction or modification) of existing functional structures, facilities or improved docks, beaches, piers, wharves, pilings, dolphins, buildings, landscaped or paved areas, lawns, and agricultural and mosquito control ditches. — Including for example, replacing broken boards in docks, repainting structures, redriving pilings, resurfacing paved areas, installing and removing lawful structures on a seasonal basis.	PIp	GCp	GCp
22.	In-kind and in-place replacement of existing functional bulkheads and similar structures.	NPN	NPN	NPN
23.	Routine beach regrading and cleaning, both above and below mean high water mark.	NPN	NPN	NPN
24.	Substantial restoration or reconstruction of existing functional structures or facilities of any kind, except for those covered by items 22 and 26, (provided where the installation of a new structure or facility is listed in this subdivision as GCn or NPN for a particular type of area, the substantial restoration or reconstruction of such a structure or facility on that area shall be treated in the same manner as the installation of such a new structure or facility).	GCp	GCp	GCn

TABLE II (continued)

Uses	Area and Use Categories					
	FM	IM	HM	SM	LZ	AA
25. Expansion or substantial modification of existing functional facilities and structures, except for those actions covered by items 26, 33, 34 or 38 (provided where the installation of a new structure or facility is listed in this subdivision as NPN, GCn or GCp, the expansion or substantial modification of such a structure or facility shall be treated in the same manner in that area).			PIp		GCp	GCn
26. Substantial restoration, reconstruction, modification or expansion of existing functional residential structures which are and will continue to be located 75 feet or more (or 30 feet or more in New York City) from the most landward edge of any tidal wetland.			NA	NA	NA	NPN
27. Dredging.			PIp	PIp	PIp	PIp
28. Maintenance dredging.			GCn	GCn	GCn	GCn
29. Construction or groins, bulkheads, and other shoreline stabilization structures.			PIp	GCp	GCp	GCp
30. Filling.			PIp	PIp	PIp	GCp
31. Disposal of dredged material.			I	PIp	PIp	GCp
32. Construction of berms.			PIp	PIp	PIp	GCp
33. Construction of substantial modification of mosquito control ditches.			GCp	GCp	GCp	GCn
34. Construction or substantial modification of drainage ditches for other than agricultural or mosquito control purposes.			PIp	PIp	PIp	GCp
35. Cultivating and harvesting naturally occurring agricultural and horticultural products, other than activities covered by items 36 and 37 below.			NPN	NPN	NPN	NPN
36. Manual harvesting of salt hay.			NPN	NA	NA	NA
37. Harvesting of salt hay by mechanical equipment.			GCn	NA	NA	NA
38. Substantial modification of agricultural ditches lawfully existing on the effective date of this Part.			GCp	GCp	GCp	GCn
39. New agricultural activities not covered by items 35-38.			PIp	PIp	PIp	GCp
40. Connection of electric, gas, sewer, water, telephone or other utilities from an existing distribution utility facility to an existing structure.			GCn	GCn	GCn	NPN

No.	Activity			
41.	Installation of underground electric, sewer, water or other utilities where such installation will involve restoration of existing ground elevation, other than activities covered by item 40.	GCp	GCp	GCp
42.	Installation of electric, gas, sewer, water or other utilities, other than activities covered by item 40 or 41.	PIp	PIp	GCp
43.	Installation of a dry well, retention basin, filter, open swale or pond.	PIp	PIp	GCp
44.	New discharge of any pollutant requiring a SPDES permit pursuant to the environmental conservation law and complying with the requirements for the issuance of such a permit.	P	P	P
45.	Installation of a sewage disposal septic tank, cesspool, leach field, or seepage pit and discharge of any pollutant into such facilities not requiring a SPDES permit pursuant to article 17 of the environmental conservation laws.	PIp	PIp	GCp
46.	Construction of single family dwellings and multiple family dwellings.	PIp	PIp	GCp
47.	Construction of commercial and industrial use facilities requiring water access and public and semi-public buildings requiring water access; and undertaking commercial and industrial use activities requiring water access.	PIp	PIp	GCp
48.	Construction of commercial and industrial use facilities not requiring water access and public or semi-public buildings not requiring water access; and undertaking commercial and industrial use activities not requiring water access.	PIp	PIp	PIp
49.	Construction of accessory structures or facilities for any use listed in items 46 and 47, other than accessory structures or facilities covered by item 50 or covered specifically in this list.	PIp	PIp	GCp
50.	Construction of accessory structures or facilities for existing residential structures where such accessory structures or facilities are and will continue to be located 75 feet or more (or 30 feet or more in the City of New York) from the most landward edge of any tidal wetland.	NA	NA	NPN
51.	Construction of accessory structures or facilities for any use listed in item 48.	PIp	PIp	PIp
52.	Disposal of any chemical, petrochemical or other toxic material, including any pesticide.	I	I	I
53.	The use or application of any chemical, petrochemical, or other toxic material, including any pesticide, where not authorized by law.	I	I	I
54.	The storage of any chemical, petrochemical, or other toxic material, including any pesticide, for wholesale purposes or for purposes of distribution to persons other than the ultimate user of such materials.	I	I	PIp

TABLE II (continued)

	Uses	FM	IM	HM	SM	LZ	AA
55.	The use of application of any chemical, petrochemical, or other toxic material, including any pesticide, where otherwise authorized by law, or the storage of any such material for purposes other than wholesaling or distribution to persons other than the ultimate users of such materials.			NPN		NPN	NPN
56.	Disposal of solid wastes as defined in section 27-0501 of the environmental conservation law.			I		I	PIp
57.	Any type of regulated activity not specifically listed in this chart and any subdivision of land.			P		P	P

ABBREVIATIONS

Area Categories

FM — Coastal Fresh Marsh
IM — Intertidal Marsh
SM — Coastal Shoals, Bars and Flats
LZ — Littoral Zone
HM — High Marsh or Salt Meadow
AA — Adjacent Area

Use Categories

NPN — Uses Not Requiring a Permit or Notification Letter Approval
GCn — Generally Compatible Use — Notification Letter Required
GCp — Generally Compatible Use — Permit Required
PIp — Presumptively Incompatible Use — Permit Required
I — Incompatible Use
NA — Not Applicable

After a complete official file on the application has been compiled and a hearing held if one is scheduled, DEC staffs review the documents and the permit administrator makes his decision. The permit may be granted, with or without conditions, or denied. The administrator may also order a hearing before making a final decision. The burden of proof "that the proposed activity will be in complete accord with the policy and provisions" of the Tidal Wetlands Act and the Land Use Regulations is on the applicant [10]. The permit process is diagrammed in Figure 7.

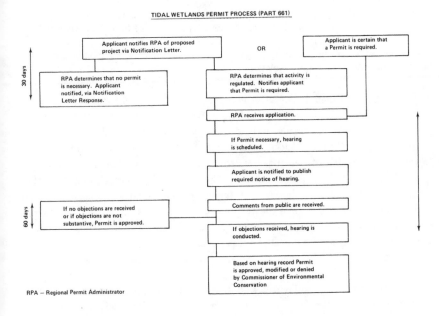

TIDAL WETLANDS PERMIT PROCESS (PART 661)

FIGURE 7 New York State tidal wetlands permit process.

Where there are practical difficulties in the way of complying with all of the regulations, the applicant may request or the permit administrator may on his own motion consider granting a variance. The administrator has the authority:

to vary or modify the application in any provisions [of the regulations] in such a manner that the spirit and intent of the pertinent provisions shall be observed, that public safety and welfare are secured and substantial justice done and that action pursuant to the variance will not have an undue adverse impact on the present or potential value of any tidal wetland [11].

If the applicant or other persons are not satisfied with the DEC decision to issue or deny a permit, they may seek judicial review in the Supreme Court of the county in which the wetlands or adjacent areas are located.

Wetlands Regulation and Tax Assessments

New York State legislators recognized that regulating the development of wetlands would reduce their value as real estate. They therefore included this paragraph in Sec. 23-0302 of the Tidal Wetlands Act:

> The placing of any tidal wetlands under a land-use regulation which restricts its use shall be deemed a limitation on the use of such wetlands for the purposes of property tax valuation, in the same manner as if an easement or right has been acquired under the general municipal law. Assessment shall be based on present use under the restricting regulation.

The law was tested soon after it became effective in September 1973. During the following November, DEC held a two-day hearing on an application to fill 104 acres of wetlands and adjacent area for the development of 607 single-family homes at Lido Beach on Long Island. At the hearing, conservation specialists testified that the project would be environmentally harmful. In March 1974 the Commissioner of DEC denied the application because the land owners had not shown that the project would not damage the tidal marshes, did not challenge the testimony of the conservation specialists and did not show how the development would economically benefit Lido Beach or the State during the moratorium period.

The landowners claimed financial hardship, because they paid $250,000 per year in real estate taxes without realizing any income. One of their attorneys said they could ask that the land be rezoned from its residential classification so that the tax assessment could be lowered, or they might challenge the law's constitutionality in the State Supreme Court [12]. Apparently the provision in the Tidal Wetlands Act that mandated reducing tax assessments on regulated lands could not be invoked until the inventory was completed and regulations were adopted.

Even without following the mandate of the State Law, Nassau County reduced by 50% the assessment on the 70 acres of the Lido Beach property that were actually wetlands. The remainder of the 104 acres was in upland territory. This was the first time that the Board of Assessors had reduced an assessment on ecological grounds. It also started a study of all privately owned wetlands and found that only about 400 acres remained. The Board considered that removing all of these lands from the tax rolls would impose no great financial hardship on the County. In the particular case at Lido Beach, the assessment on the 70 acres of wetlands was reduced from

$800,000 to $400,000. The Environmental Defense Fund, based on Long Island, had supported the assessment reduction in a letter to the Board. It wrote that, "real estate tax policies which impose substantial tax burdens on wetlands and other desirable open space compel the development and destruction of such natural systems without regard to long-term environmental and economic harm to society" [13].

Constitutionality of the Tidal Wetlands Act

Several questions might be raised about the constitutionality of wetlands regulation. First is the reasonableness of a temporary moratorium to keep the status quo until the wetland inventory was completed. An interim permitting system was established to provide relief in cases of hardship, and the act was not challenged during the moratorium period. Nevertheless, state courts have upheld temporary moratoria [14].

Now that final land use regulations have been adopted and the act is in full effect, a more serious constitutional challenge could come on the issue of the legitimacy of the use of the police power, and when regulation becomes so restrictive that it constitutes a taking without compensation. Application of the police power is considered reasonable if its intent and effect is to *prevent harm* to the public. If the objective is to *provide a public benefit,* then the property should be acquired and paid for under the eminent domain power. A Wisconsin court supported the legitimacy of police power regulation of wetlands.

> The changing of wetlands and swamps to the damage of the general public by upsetting the natural environment and the natural relationship is not a reasonable use of that land which is protected from police power regulation. . . .
> Nothing this Court has said or held in prior cases indicates that destroying the natural character of a swamp or a wetland so as to make that location available for human habitation is a reasonable use of that land when the new use, although of a more economical value to the owner, causes a harm to the general public [15].

Wetlands regulation under the police power has been found as legally acceptable as other land use regulations such as zoning. The legal problem is where to draw the line between regulation and taking. Justice Holmes in *Pennsylvania Coal Co. v. Mahon,* one of the leading cases on the issue, found that the line between regulation and taking could be drawn on the basis of how much the economic returns from the land had been diminished [16]. Jeffrey E. Stockholm, who did extensive research on the legal foundation for wetlands regulation in New York, believes that other court decisions are contrary to this point of view:

The distinction between the police power and the power of eminent domain should not be, however, merely a difference of degree as Holmes has suggested. The evolution of the fifth amendment, and the cases decided thereunder, suggest that once a valid police power is exercised curtailing some private objectionable land use, there can be no question of a fifth amendment taking. Once the issue of whether the statute is an exercise of the police power or the power of eminent domain is decided in favor of the former, the amount of value destroyed is irrelevant. . . . The distinction between these two governmental powers should and has been based on a difference in the kind of power that is exercised and not on the extent of the effect of that power [17].

Other contemporary authorities agree with this position. Even the strong concept of private property held by the American Colonists was "a concept . . . which permitted extensive regulation of the use of that property for the public benefit—regulation that could even go so far as to deny all productive use of the property to the owner" [18]. The U.S. Supreme Court itself appeared to disagree with Justice Holmes' position five years before the *Pennsylvania Coal* case: "It is the character of the invasion, not the amount of damage resulting from it . . . that determines the question whether it is a taking" [19].

In New York State, the courts have ruled in zoning cases that to prove a taking, "the land owner must show that the regulations have left him without any beneficial use for which his property is reasonably adapted. . . . Diminution in property values resulting from restrictive regulation is not in itself proof of a taking. Diminutions of over 90 percent have been upheld and 75 percent diminutions often have withstood constitutional attack" [20].

Stockholm has raised another legal argument in favor of the State's right to regulate wetlands that is not usually considered in such cases. Because tidal wetlands lie under the mean high tide line, the State may actually have an ownership interest in them, even if title is held by a private person. Land titles in New York State go back to royal grants. After the Revolution, land titles that had been conveyed to private owners remained with them, and title to royal lands was taken over by the State. Nevertheless, lands under water were a special case, for there were two components to their title, the *jus publicum* and the *jus privatum:*

The king held title to the seas and arms of the seas in his sovereign capacity, for nothing less than a sovereign power could hold them. This title of the king was split into the *jus publicum* and the *jus privatum.* Although grants of either of these would be strictly construed, it was generally held that the *jus privatum* was freely alienable, so long as it did not prejudice any of the public's rights in the *jus publicum.* The *jus publicum,* being a matter of general public concern, was held by the king in trust for the benefit of all the people. It could not be conveyed without the consent of Parliament, or at least the ratification of the colonial legislature. It could only be conveyed to a sovereign entity (not an individual) and was so conveyed in trust. To the extent that title was not conveyed as of the revolution, both the *jus publicum* and the *jus privatum* passed to the state [21].

Stockholm cites cases in New York State where the courts have decided that even where wetlands had been filled to bring the surface permanently above tidal action, the land maintains its original character as land under water. Such filled lands are therefore still vested with the *jus publicum* [22]. As recently as 1971, a New York Court decided that the mean high tide line was the boundary of the *jus publicum*. This line was marked by the boundary between two species of salt marsh grass, *Spartina patens,* which can survive only occasional inundation by salt water, and *Spartina alterniflora,* which thrives on land covered twice-daily by the tides.

Court cases came up during the moratorium period not as challenges to the constitutionality of the Tidal Wetlands Act, but rather to clarify the claims of private ownership and the jurisdiction of various governmental bodies. In October 1973, the Long Island town of North Hempstead filed suit in the New York Supreme Court to recover $10 million from persons and corporations that were alleged to have filled wetlands. The Town asserted that under a Dutch royal patent granted in 1644 and confirmed by the colonial Governor of New York in 1685, it had title to all lands currently and formerly under water. In addition to monetary damages, the Town asked for a Court declaration supporting its ownership of the lands, ordering removal of all fill and debris, and an injunction against further alteration of the property [23].

The North Hempstead Town Supervisor said that the suit was part of an effort to preserve the remaining wetlands. There were only 35 acres left in the town, and the disputed land covered about 50 acres. It had become a dump for earth, demolition rubble, and concrete blocks. The suit alleged that the dumping had been ordered by the "owner" of the property and carried out by an excavating company that had dumped construction refuse for builders. Money recovered by the town would be used to rehabilitate damaged wetlands.

The Town of North Hempstead lost its case in a similar suit against the builder of a home for his own use. The State Supreme Court in July 1974 dismissed the Town's claim on the basis of its finding that the property was inland of the high water mark. The Town attorney had at one time relinquished the Town's claim to the land, but he based the Town's suit to recover ownership on the basis of new information including borings that showed evidence of marine life beneath the soil [24].

A similar case brought in August of 1974 involved the Town of Oyster Bay, Nassau County, and a private property owner. The suit concerned 20 acres of wetlands claimed by the Town under a patent granted in 1667 by Maj. Edmund Andros, then the English Governor of New York. The Town turned over its claim to Nassau County, which wanted the wetland for a wildlife preserve. A building contractor claimed ownership of the wetland on the basis of purchase in 1961 from an Oyster Bay family whose ancestors had held the land since the Andros Patent. The builder filed suit to determine who held title to the land [25].

The question of wetlands ownership was apparently finally settled by a ruling in July 1975 by New York's highest court, the Court of Appeals. It significantly reduced the amount of wetlands to which town trustees could lay claim. The Court of Appeals ruling was unanimous and overturned previously established criteria for defining the line of mean high tide, which separates wetland from upland. Lower court rulings had confirmed the criterion that the high tide line should be set by the boundary between *Spartina patens,* a marsh grass that can tolerate salt water inundation only occasionally, and *Spartina alterniflora* which depends on daily tidal inundation. The Court of Appeals characterized this criterion as "an entirely new technique . . . intellectually fascinating," but they ruled that "the importance of predictability and stability in matters involving title to real property [requires] the application of our traditional and customary method" of establishing the high tide line where all vegetation stops and open water begins [26].

Although this Court of Appeals decision significantly reduces the amount of wetlands that may be claimed by Long Island town boards of trustees, which rely on colonial patents, it should not affect the state regulatory program under the Tidal Wetlands Act. The Act defines wetlands on the basis of types of vegetation. The official wetlands inventory identifies five types of wetlands in the same way, and the land use regulations permit various uses according to their compatibility with these vegetation types. The state land use regulations are based on the police power, and they apply to all wetlands regardless of whether they are publicly or privately owned.

Public Acquisition and Management of Tidal Wetlands

It has already been noted that there was a Long Island Wetlands Act in 1959, before the Tidal Wetlands Act of 1973. More than 16,000 acres of town-owned wetlands had been improved under this state-federal-local cooperative conservation program. Fortunately, the earlier program was incorporated into the 1973 act as Section 25-0301. It provides that the DEC Commissioner may enter into cooperative agreements with any local government or county to preserve, maintain, or improve their publicly owned wetlands. For this purpose, the state may make available personnel and facilities or it may appropriate funds.

An example of this kind of project is the reclamation of a 20-acre wetland near Fire Island Inlet in the Town of Babylon. Construction of houses and roads nearby destroyed the marsh and replaced the birds and fish with mosquitoes. In order to restore the marsh, the soil was stripped off to create five shallow ponds that would fill with freshwater that lay just below the surface of the land. The ponds were stocked with fish that would eat the mosquito larvae, and nature was allowed to take its course. After the marsh grass came up, egrets, hawks and ducks would appear. This had occurred in an earlier project where a freshwater pond was dug on Jones Island in the Town of Oyster Bay. A newspaper account of a visit to this area noted that, "as state ecologists approached it . . . on a path hidden by tall reeds, hundreds of ducks took off in squadrons. Before the pond was fashioned, the ducks went elsewhere in search of freshwater to drink" [27].

The Tidal Wetlands Act maintenance and improvement program is complemented by a public acquisition program. In 1972 New York voters approved the $1.5 billion Environmental Quality Bond Act. Out of this amount, $18 million was earmarked for wetlands purchase. Unfortunately, progress has been slow. Acquisition was delayed by a November 28, 1975, order from the director of the state budget. The poor fiscal situation in the state was the reason for postponing the expansion of the public debt. The Tidal Wetlands Act itself complicated the acquisition program. Regulation of the wetlands, which restricts their development potential and market value, makes appraisal difficult. Purchases were delayed until an appraisal policy could be worked out [28].

By March 1975 wetlands acquisition accelerated. DEC had begun negotiations to buy 20 parcels totaling 2600 acres in Nassau and Suffolk Counties. Prices were also being negotiated with 100 additional property owners. Of the approximately 12,000 acres of wetlands in Suffolk County and 9400 acres in Nassau County, DEC had a long-range goal for acquiring 5000 acres. Rising prices continually jeopardized the achievement of this goal, but the $18 million in state bond funds may potentially be matched by an equal amount from the U.S. Bureau of Outdoor Recreation [29].

MUNICIPAL MANAGEMENT OF WETLANDS

It has been noted in the chapter on shellfish management that local governments on Long Island have natural resources management institutions and programs that parallel those of the state. For example, the Town of Islip has a Department of Environmental Control that is concerned with administering its Wetlands and Water courses law as well as the shellfish program. The Town already owns most of the wetlands within its borders and expects to acquire the remainder still in private hands.

The Town Department of Planning and Development had inventoried all of its wetlands in 1972. Out of about 1700 acres of wetlands in the town only about 600 acres were privately owned. The other 1100 acres were owned by the Town, the Nature Conservancy or the Audubon Society. The Town prepared the inventory in order to take advantage of the State Environmental Quality Bond Issue and use funds from its own capital program to acquire the privately owned wetlands. The Town wetlands inventory report expressed little faith in land use regulations, easements or contracts with private owners to conserve wetlands; "the only guarantee is ownership, and those wishing to preserve the wetlands forever must pay the price" [30].

After the wetlands inventory had been prepared, town officials communicated with owners of private wetlands to seek their cooperation with the conservation and acquisition program. A letter from the Town Supervisor to all owners of wetlands included a property map showing the line between wetland and upland. It suggested several alternatives for property owner cooperation with the Town's preservation effort:

- *Donation:* outright conveyance to the Town of Islip, New York State, the federal government or a public conservation organization

- *Stewardship:* transfer to private conservation agency, such as the Nature Conservancy or the Audubon Society, with tax advantages and life tenancy

- *Clustering:* higher density, less restrictive project design or other modifications of town building and zoning ordinances for development on the upland portion of the property in return for donation of the wetland to the Town

- *Public Acquisition:* negotiation of a sale price for Town acquisition.

The Town of Islip also created an organizational mechanism for managing its wetlands and other properties acquired for conservation objectives. The Town capital budget included $1 million for wetlands purchase where they could not be obtained by any of the other suggested alternatives. The Town also created a Nature Preserve Trust by Local Law No. 5 in 1974. By Town Board resolution, town-owned wetlands and other environmentally valuable lands could be dedicated to the trust. The Department of Planning and Development was given responsibility for recommending which town-owned lands should be dedicated and which private properties should be purchased.

Dedicated Nature Preserve Trust lands were to be kept in their natural state. The Town Department of Environmental Control was charged with management of the preserve. Trust properties were not to be sold, leased or used for any purpose inconsistent with the dedicating resolution. After 10 years, the resolution could be cancelled, amended or extended by the Town

Board after public notice and hearing. Efforts by any town agency to violate the restrictions on trust properties could be restrained by citizen suits. Owners of properties adjacent to nature preserve lands were alerted by letters from the Town Supervisor in these terms: "To complement the Town of Islip Wetland Acquisition Program . . . the Town Board recently passed a law creating the Town Nature Preserve Trust. . . . The regulation of proper conduct by the Town in the management of its properties is dependent on its local citizens . . . We look to your viligance in helping us to preserve these properties" [31].

A wetlands status report issued by the Department of Planning and Development noted that all private owners had been informed of the Town's wetlands preservation program. Building permit applications were carefully reviewed to avoid construction on the wetlands. Cluster plan subdivisions were favored that confined buildings to the upland portion of properties and preserved the wetlands as permanent open space. Since December 1972 development had effectively stopped at the "preservation line" marked on the town wetlands inventory. The State and the Town were both buying wetlands, and some lands had even been donated to DEC and the Nature Conservancy [32] (Figure 8).

REGULATION OF DREDGING AND FILLING

Tidal wetlands are particularly vulnerable to dredging and filling. These operations plus bulkheading are the means by which "useless swamps" are converted to high-value real estate. The technique is simple. A bulkhead is a wall, usually of creosoted wood, sunk into the bottom of the wetland to outline the boundary of the future solid land; its height is determined by the desired future elevation of the land above the water. Then the sediment on the water side of the bulkhead is dredged up and deposited on the other side to create the new land and obliterate the wetland. Deepening the water side by dredging also creates a channel for boats.

It is not always necessary to create the new land by dredging the bottom on the water side of the bulkhead. Fill material may be obtained from building contractors and refuse haulers who need dump sites. Dredge spoil from maintenance of navigation channels or other public projects may be deposited on private lands at little or no cost to the owner. New land created by obliterating wetlands may be used for residential development, which often takes the form of a finger plan with peninsulas of land separated by deadend channels for the boats of the homeowners. Marinas, resorts, ports and industrial plants also are provided with water front sites created by filling wetlands and dredging to facilitate direct water access.

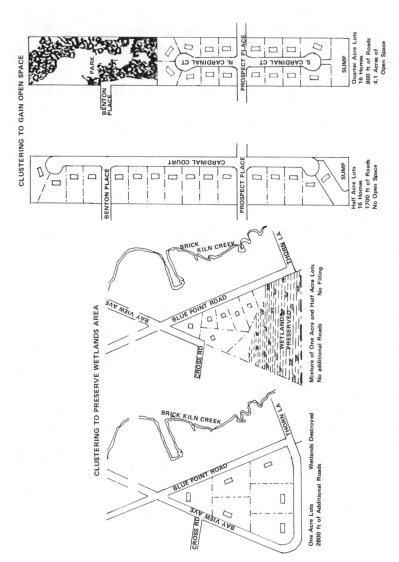

FIGURE 8 Cluster plans for residential development (Courtesy Town of Islip, NY).

Although dredging and filling are often carried out together, one does not always follow from the other. Dredge spoil may be used in other ways than using it for fill, and fill material may be obtained from other sources than dredging. Dredging has its own environmental consequences. It changes the bottom topography, and consequently the shoaling and scouring patterns caused by currents. Potholes are often created in the bottom by sand and gravel mining. The smaller in diameter the pothole and the deeper it is, the more likely it will trap organic material and pollutants. Decay of this material causes oxygen depletion. This, together with increased turbidity, which decreases the penetration of sunlight into the water, and changes in salinity caused by changes in water currents affect the aquatic biota, both plants and animals. Shellfish are particularly affected by dredging, because they dwell on or just below the bottom.

The dredge spoil must be disposed of, and this creates additional problems. Nearby wetlands are the most convenient sites. Filling here obliterates the wetlands, but the spoil may also be used to create artificial islands, which when suitably planted with *Spartina alterniflora* and other tidal marsh plants, create new wetlands. Unfortunately, dredging also stirs up the pollutants that have accumulated on the bottom. Waste from duck farms covers large areas of bay bottom on the Long Island south shore. Clean sandy dredge spoil, however, may serve a useful purpose by replenishing eroded beaches. Fill materials are not obtained solely from dredging. It has already been noted that demolition rubble and building construction and other solid refuse are often dumped into wetlands and waterways.

Local Regulation

Local, state and federal governments are all involved in regulating dredging and filling that affect wetlands. The NY Tidal Wetlands Act has already been described and the permit procedure diagrammed in Figure 7. Local governments on Long Island also have their own regulations and permit procedures. In the Town of Islip, for example, Chapter 67 of the Town Code contains the Wetlands and Watercourses Law, which established major elements of the Town's coastal management program.

The Town wetlands and watercourses were delineated on tax maps showing every privately and publicly owned parcel of land. These areas were consolidated into 42 Wetlands and Watercourses Management Areas on the Islip mainland and on Fire Island. These Management Areas constitute one element of the coastal zone management program requirements under federal law and regulations. This is the identification of geographic areas of particular environmental concern. The wetlands and watercourses maps are incorporated in the Town of Islip Comprehensive Plan as Volume 4A. The boundaries of the Management Areas coincide closely with those on the Flood Hazard Boundary Maps prepared for the federally sponsored flood insurance program. It should also be noted that water areas not included in the Management Area maps, such as navigable waterways and canals that come within the concerns of the U.S. Army Corps of Engineers, are also subject to the Town Wetlands and Watercourses Law.

The Wetlands and Watercourses Law established a permit system to regulate dredging and filling, diversion or obstruction of waterflow, the placement of structures and other uses in town watercourses, coastal wetlands and tidal marshes. The Town Board found that many of these water bodies were being polluted, encroached upon and despoiled. It therefore identified acts that were prohibited in them without Town Board permission.

Sec. 67-5 Permit required for certain acts:

> Except as hereinafter provided, it shall be unlawful for any person, without obtaining a written permit therefor issued upon the order of the Town Board, to:
>
> A. Place, deposit, or permit to be placed or deposited debris, fill or any materials, including structures, into, within or upon any tidal waters or other watercourses, coastal wetlands or tidal marshes of the Town of Islip.
>
> B. Dig, dredge, or in any other way alter or remove any material from submerged lands, coastal wetlands, or tidal marshes of the Town of Islip.

Sec. 67-6 Removal of soil; certain construction:

> The deposition or removal of sand, gravel or any materials and construction of groins, docks, bulkheads, boathouses, dwellings, accessory buildings, roads or other improvements within the coastal wetlands, tidal marshes or watercourses shall be regulated by the provisions of this local law.

Chapter 67 of the Islip Town Code does not include specific standards for evaluating permit applications to dredge, fill or do any of the other things mentioned in Sec. 67-5 and 67-6. Some general guidelines are given in another section, however, which indicate the kinds of activities that may be permitted by the Town Board or Board of Appeals.

Sec. 67-11 Uses subject to permit of Town Board or Board of Appeals:

> The following activities and uses are permissible if done pursuant to terms and conditions of a permit issued upon approval by the Town Board or, when referred by said Town Board to the Board of Appeals, by the Board of Appeals:
>
> A. The building and locating of groins, docks, bulkheads, moorings, boat launching or landing sites and marinas.
>
> B. Temporary storage of materials.
>
> C. Appropriate municipal use such as parks, recreation, wildlife sanctuaries and accessory uses such as concessions.
>
> D. Commercial or private recreation facilities consistent with this local law as determined by the Town Board.
>
> E. Dams and other water control devices, dredging or diversion of water levels or circulation or changes in watercourses to improve hazardous navigation conditions, or for the improvement of fish, shellfish or

wildlife habitat, recreation facilities or drainage improvements deemed
to be consistent with the intent and objectives of this local law by the
Town Board.

F. Driveways and roads where alternative means of access are proven to
be impractical in the considered judgment of the Town Board.

Town of Islip Wetlands and Watercourses Permits. Permits to alter wetlands
and watercourses are not granted routinely. In order that the Town Board,
Planning Board, and Environmental Council may evaluate the environmental
impact of proposed action, the following technical information is required in
the application:

1. Purpose of proposed removal or deposition operations, use or activity
2. Amount of material proposed to be removed or deposited or type of use
3. Description of the area in which removal, deposition or use is proposed
4. Depth to which removal or deposition operations are proposed and angle of
   repose of all slopes, including deposited materials, and sides of channels or
   excavations resulting from removal operations
5. Manner in which material will be removed or deposited, structure installed,
   or use carried out
6. A survey and topographical map, with contours shown at one foot intervals,
   and the area of removal, deposition, use or construction indicated
7. A survey and topographical map with soundings, depth or height of proposed removal or deposition area.

The permit application must also contain evidence that the proposed activity
will be consistent with the purposes of the wetlands and watercourses local
law as stated in the section on legislative intent. Among these purposes are
prevention of damage from erosion, siltation or salt water intrusion; loss of
plant and animal life and habitats; and protection of water supplies and
recreation areas. So that affected property owners may be informed of the
proposal and appear at the Town Board's hearing or take court action against
a Town Board permit decision, the application must also contain the names
and addresses of all owners of lands contiguous to lands and waters where
proposed operations will take place [33].

Wetlands and watercourses permit applications are submitted to the Town
Clerk, who distributes copies to the Town Board, the Planning Board and the
Environmental Council. Within 30 days, comments on the proposal indicating
approval, disapproval or approval with conditions are sent by the other bodies
to the Environmental Council. The Council reviews these comments in light
of its own evaluation of the proposal and sends its final report and recommendations to the Town Board within 14 days. Present town law prescribes
that after reasonable public notice the Town Board is to hold a public hearing
on the application. In practice, the hearing is held by a Watercourses and Wetlands Hearing Board composed of the Commissioner of Planning, the

Commissioner of Environmental Control and the Chairman of the Environmental Council. Although this arrangement is not sanctioned by town law, a bill has been drafted to legitimate this new hearing board. After the hearing, the Town Board renders its decision to approve or deny the application, or approve it with conditions. The applicant or any owner of land within 100 feet of the applicant's property may sue to challenge a Town Board permit decision in the state courts under Article 78 of the Civil Practice Law and Rules [34]. This procedure is summarized in Figure 9.

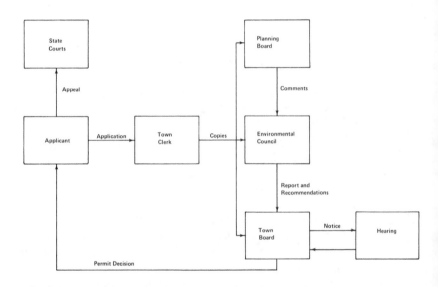

FIGURE 9 Town of Islip wetlands and watercourses permit procedure.

It should be noted that there is no formal requirement in town law that applications must be reviewed by the Department of Environmental Control. Nevertheless, applications are sent to it, the Commissioner of Environmental Control sits on the Hearing Board, and its comments are considered by the Town Board before final decision is made. In the absence of detailed written standards, the Town Board and the Board of Appeals must have the advice of experts in the various agencies of town government in making judgments about whether or not a particular permit should be granted. This advice is obtained from the Department of Planning and Development, the Town Environmental Council and the Town Department of Environmental Control.

The Town Planning Board and the Environmental Council have responsibilities that go beyond reviewing permits for dredging and filling. Permit aplications may be for building construction and land subdivision projects that would be located within watercourses, coastal flood plains, watershed lands, aquifer recharge areas or natural drainage areas. All such application require approval of the Building Inspector in the Department of Planning and Development or the Planning Board. Environmental Council review of these applications is also required [35].

THE FEDERAL GOVERNMENT'S ROLE

New York State and local regulatory procedures for protecting wetlands are paralleled by federal programs. Anyone proposing to alter or use tidal wetlands, marshes or waterways on Long Island must obtain three separate local, state and federal permits. Proposals may therefore be blocked at any of these levels.

The federal agency responsible for wetlands and waterways protection is the Department of the Army, acting through the Corps of Engineers. The two programs most relevant to this concern are authorized by the River and Harbor Act of 1899, as amended, and the Water Pollution Control Act, as amended through 1977. Section 10 of the River and Harbor Act prohibits alteration of or construction in navigable waters without a permit from the Corps of Engineers. (Permits to construct dams or dikes require the consent of Congress, and are issued under Section 9 of this act.) Section 10 permits from the Corps are required for such works as piers, breakwaters, bulkheads, revetments, power transmission lines and aids to navigation. Alterations of navigable waterways that may affect wetlands include dredging, stream channelization, excavation and filling; these also require federal permits.

Until December 1968 the Corps permit program under the River and Harbor Act was limited to waters actually used for interstate or foreign commerce. Subsequently, primary concern for navigation was broadened into a "public interest review" of permit applications. This review includes such considerations as fish and wildlife and resources conservation, pollution, aesthetics and the general public interest.

The second program authorizing federal regulation of waterways and wetlands use and alteration is the Federal Water Pollution Control Act, which was amended in 1972 and 1977. This act is primarily concerned with water quality rather than navigation. The responsibility given to the Corps of Engineers by Section 404 of this act is to regulate any discharge into the "waters of the United States," of dredged and fill materials. Permit application review under this act, as well as under the River and Harbor Act, includes distribution of copies to the State Department of Environmental Conservation and local governments for comment.

The focus of the River and Harbor Act on navigation and of the Water Pollution Control Act on water quality gave rise to the problem of defining the navigable waters of the United States. From the point of view of navigation, these are "waters that are subject to the ebb and flow of the tide shoreward to their mean high water mark and/or waters that are presently used, or were used in the past, or are susceptible to use to transport interstate or foreign commerce" [36]. The Water Pollution Control Act, however, defines navigable waters as "the waters of the United States, including the territorial seas." The Natural Resources Defense Council and the National Wildlife Federation, therefore, brought a court action to force the Corps of Engineers to adopt the broader definition in its regulation of the discharge of dredged or fill materials into the waters of the United States. These organizations advocate regulation of the entire aquatic system, including wetlands and tributary streams that feed into the tidal and commercial navigable streams. The federal District Court of the District of Columbia agreed with this position and on March 27, 1975, ordered the Corps to revise its regulations accordingly [37].

The rules and regulations promulgated by the Army Corps of Engineers to implement the River and Harbor Act, as amended, define the navigable waters of the United States to conform to decision of the U.S. District Court. They are subject to the ebb and flow of the tide; and they are, were, or may be used for interstate or foreign commerce. One of the factors to be used in determining whether a waterbody is a navigable water of the United States is its geographic limits. The shoreward limit of Corps of Engineers jurisdiction in coastal areas "extends to the line on the shore reached by the plane of the mean (average) high water" [38]. In bays and estuaries, where the wetlands are located:

> regulatory jurisdiction extends to the entire surface and bed of all waterbodies subject to tidal action. Jurisdiction thus extends to the edge . . . of all such waterbodies, even though portions of the waterbody may be extremely shallow, or obstructed by shoals, vegetation, or other barriers. Marshlands and similar areas are thus considered "navigable-in-law," but only so far as the area is subject to inundation by the mean high waters [39].

The inclusion of a wide variety of wetlands within the definition of navigable waters or waters of the United States is complemented by a broad definition of "fill material." It is not limited to loose material, such as dredged sand or gravel, but also includes the placement of materials for construction:

The term "fill material" means any material used for the primary purpose of replacing an aquatic area with dry land or of changing the bottom elevation of a water body.

The term "discharge of fill materials" . . . generally includes, without limitation, the following activities: Placement of fill that is necessary to the construction of any structure in a water of the United States; the building of any structure or impoundment requiring rock, sand, dirt, or other material for its construction; site-development fills for recreational, industrial, commercial, residential, and other issues; causeways or road fills; dams and dikes; artificial islands; property protection and or reclaimation devices such as riprap, groins, seawalls, breakwaters, and revetments; beach nourishment; levees; fill for structures such as sewage treatment facilities, intake and outfall pipes associated with power plants and subaqueous utility lines; and artificial reefs [40].

These broad definitions of "navigable waters" and "fill materials" give the Corps of Engineers wide jurisdiction to protect tidal wetlands in terms of what may be taken out of or put into them. Multiple protection is provided by parallel state and local wetlands regulation. In order to avoid including farming and forestry practices in the federal program under Section 404 of the Water Pollution Control Law, the regulations exempt "plowing, cultivating, seeding and harvesting for the production of food, fiber, and forest products " [41]. Materials discharged into the water primarily to dispose of waste are also excluded from the definition of "fill materials" and the permit jurisdiction of the Corps of Engineers. Waste disposal is regulated by the Environmental Protection Agency under Section 402 of the Federal Water Pollution Control Act. This is the national Pollutant Discharge Eliminations System (NPDES), responsibility for which in New York State has been delegated to the Department of Environmental Conservation. The State has a State Pollutant Discharge Elimination System (SPDES).

REFERENCES

1. Roy L. Haje, *The Effects of the New York State Tidal Wetlands Act Moratorium Phase,* Marine Sciences Reserch Center, SUNY at Stony Brook, N.Y., May 1976, p. 3.
2. Ibid., p. 4.
3. New York Environmental Conservation Law, Sec. 25-0101, 1973.
4. Ibid.
5. Haje, p. 2.
6. N.Y. Department of Environmental Conservation, "Tidal Wetlands—Land Use Regulations," Part 661 N.Y. Compilation of Codes, Rules, and Regulations, Sec. 661.4 (hh)(1-6), August 20, 1977. (Processed)
7. Part 600 N.Y. Compilation of Codes, Rules, and Regulations, Sec. 660.1 (c)(1), July 1, 1974.

8. *Newsday,* October 29, 1974.
9. *N.Y.S. Environment,* April 1978, p. 1.
10. NY Environmental Conservation Law, Sec. 25-0402, 1973.
11. Part 661 N.Y. Compilation of Codes, Rules, and Regulations, Sec. 661.13, August 20, 1977.
12. *Newsday,* March 29, 1974, p. 17.
13. *Newsday,* August 14, 1974.
14. *Hasco Electric Corp. v. Dassler,* 143 N.Y.S. 2d 240, 144 N.Y.S. 2d 857 (1955).
15. *Just v. Marinette County,* 201 N.W. 2d 768, as quoted in Haje, p. 35.
16. *Pennsylvania Coal Co. v. Mahon,* 260 U.S. 393 (1922).
17. Jeffrey E. Stockholm, "Can New York's Tidal Wetlands be Saved? A Constitutional and Common Law Solution," *Albany Law Review,* 39 (1975) 460-461.
18. F. Bosselman, D. Callies, J. Banta, *The Taking Issue* (Washington, D.C.: U.S. Government Printing Office, 1973), pp. 91-92, as quoted in Stockholm, p. 462.
19. *U.S. v. Cress,* 243 U.S. 328 (1917), as quoted in Stockholm, p. 465.
20. Haje, p. 35.
21. Stockholm, p. 482.
22. Ibid., p. 484.
23. *N.Y. Times,* October 2, 1973.
24. *Newsday,* July 9, 1974.
25. *Newsday,* August 14, 1974.
26. *Newsday,* July 9, 1975.
27. *Newsday,* November 1, 1974.
28. *Newsday,* June 24, 1974.
29. *Newsday,* March 21, 1975.
30. Town of Islip, Department of Planning and Development, *Marine Wetlands in the Town of Islip,* December 5, 1972, p. 5.
31. Letter signed by Peter F. Cohalan, Town of Islip Supervisor, March 6, 1975.
32. Town of Islip, Department of Planning and Development, *Marine Wetlands in the Town of Islip: A Status Report,* July 18, 1973.
33. Town of Islip Code, Ch. 67, Sec. 67-15, 67-15, June 1, 1973.
34. Ibid., Sec. 67-18, 67-19, 67-20.
35. Ibid., Sec. 67-17.
36. *Federal Register,* Title 33, Sec. 329.4, July 19, 1977.
37. *NRDC v. Callaway,* 392 F. Supp. 685 (DDC 1975).
38. *Federal Register,* Title 33, Sec. 329.12 (a)(2), July 19, 1977.
39. Ibid., Sec. 329.12 (b).
40. Ibid., Sec. 323.2 (m)(n).
41. Ibid.

CHAPTER 6

RECREATION AND ACCESS TO THE SHORE

Demand for recreational use of the shore is no less intense than for other uses, such as ports, heavy industry, power generation and residence. Some of these forms of development that compete for waterfront sites do not necessarily have to locate there. Swimming, boating and fishing, however, which are the most popular forms of shore recreation, must have access to beaches, marinas and launch ramps. Marshes, bluffs and headlands are also uniquely valuable for walking, nature study and just enjoying the beauty of landscapes where land, sea and sky meet.

Federal, state and local governments have assumed responsibility for providing shoreland and water recreation facilities. The national park program of the federal government had paid little attention to the demand and available resources for shore recreation until Congress created the system of national seashores. New York State now has the Fire Island National Seashore and the Gateway National Recreation Area at New York Harbor and Jamaica Bay. These are among the nationally significant natural resource areas that the federal government has acquired for both active recreation and study and conservation of their environmental values.

New York State has developed a great system of parks and conservation areas on Long Island that feature shore recreation facilities, such as the famous Jones Beach State Park. State parks are intended to serve large geographic areas. Visitors must be willing to spend an hour or more to reach them. They serve primarily the relatively affluent class that can travel by private auto and pay the required parkway tolls, parking fees and other charges. Low cost public transportation is not available to most state parks (Figure 10).

Nassau and Suffolk Counties operate park systems to serve countywide recreation demand. Access to these parks is also primarily by private auto. Regional general use parks offer picnic areas and facilities for active use, such as ball fields, tennis and other courts, and sometimes horseback riding and boating. Education-recreational facilities are called interpretive parks, and feature nature trails, natural history orientation and ecosystems conservation. Special facilities in county parks include golf courses, beaches, boat basins

111

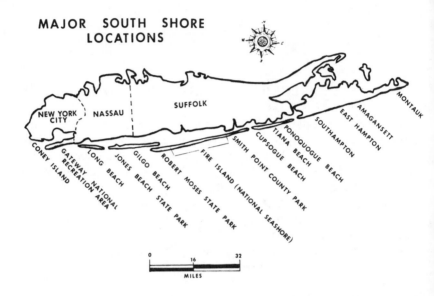

FIGURE 10 Major south shore locations.

and riding stables. Counties also have large reservations for nature and open space preserves. These areas are underdeveloped and have few, if any, visitor facilities.

Towns and villages on Long Island have park and recreation facilities to serve their citizens. Nonresidents are usually excluded on the ground that this is the only way to avoid overcrowding and financial drain on local taxpayers. Nevertheless, local governments on Long Island control significant areas of shoreline for beaches, boating and other recreation facilities.

The recreational resources of Long Island have long been appreciated by the people of the region around it. Federal, state, county and local governments have established hundreds of recreation facilities there, many of which are located on or near the shore. Recreation is therefore a well established element of coastal management by all government levels. This does not mean, however, that there are no management problems or unmet needs still to be served.

Recreation facilities and open space reservations require public agencies to take responsibility for management of a considerable portion of Long Island's coastal resources. The shoreline of Nassau and Suffolk Counties is about 529 miles long. About 140 miles, or 26.4% of the total shoreline, is in public ownership. The south shore has most of the parks and reservations; almost half of its 118 miles are publicly owned (Table III).

TABLE III Ownership of Long Island Shoreline Nassau and Suffolk Counties

Ownership	Approximate Mileage	Percent of Total
Federal	23.5	4.4
N.Y. State	42.0	8.0
County	39.0	7.4
Municipal	35.0	6.6
Private	389.0	73.6
Total	528.5[a]	100.0

[a]This figure does not include the 63 miles of the north side of the narrow barrier inlands of the south shore. Of the south shore's 118 miles, almost half (58 miles) are publicly owned.
Source: N.Y. State Office of Parks and Recreation.

FEDERAL RECREATION AREAS ON LONG ISLAND

The National Park Service, Department of the Interior, operates several historic monuments and national memorials in New York City. Sagamore Hill at Oyster Bay on Long Island was the home of Theodore Roosevelt and is now a national historic site. Large areas of New York's marine coast are under direct National Park Service management. The Gateway National Recreation Area occupies 26,785 acres of some of the last remaining open space around the greater New York harbor. Two of its components are on the Long Island south shore within New York City: Jamaica Bay (15,480 acres) and Breezy Point (2791 acres). The other components are on Staten Island (13,466 acres) and Sandy Hook, NJ (4688 acres). The Fire Island National Seashore has 3400 acres on the Long Island south shore.

The U.S. Fish and Wildlife Service, also in the Department of the Interior, operates extensive wildlife refuges in the Long Island coastal zone. They provide nesting, feeding and resting areas. Waterfowl programs include restoration of wetlands and feed crops. Visitors are welcome for nature study and photography; fishing and hunting are permitted only at certain refuges. Table IV lists the national wildlife refuges on Long Island and indicates their size and permitted activities.

TABLE IV Federal Wildlife Refuges on Long Island

Refuge	Location	Area (acres)	Activity
Target Rock	Lloyd Neck, Huntington, LI	80	Marine and ecological research, environmental interpretation
Amagansett	East Hampton, LI	36	Fishing, hiking, photography
Conscience Point	North Sea, LI	60	Nature
Morton	Nyack Bay, LI	187	Nature study, photography
Oyster Bay	Oyster Bay, LI	3117	Boating, fishing, swimming, hunting, commercial shell fishing
Seatuck	LI	10	Not open for public use
Wertheim	Brookhaven, LI	1937	Natural area

Source: N Y State Office of Parks and Recreation, "Public Access and Recreation Within the Coastal Boundaries of New York State," Albany, N Y , March 1978, p. 58 (Processed).

Fire Island National Seashore

Fire Island is a 32-mile link in the long chain of narrow barrier islands that separate the south shore of Long Island from the Atlantic Ocean. Part of Fire Island is intensively developed with summer homes, but there are still large areas of untouched primitive forest, wetlands, dunes and beaches. The unique character of Fire Island has made it an exceptional recreation resource in the New York metropolitan area. Robert Moses State Park, on the western end of the island, is accessible from the mainland by a causeway, but it is not included in the national seashore. Smith Point County Park is near the eastern end of the island and is also accessible by a causeway. Suffolk County also owns the entire undeveloped eastern end of Fire Island from Smith Point Park to Moriches Inlet. Between these two large parks, which receive thousands of daily visitors during the summer, are several town-owned beaches restricted to town residents, 17 communities of private residences and the extensive undeveloped areas that constitute the federally managed part of the national seashore.

Establishment of the national seashore on Fire Island gives the National Park Service of the Department of the Interior an important role in coastal resources management. Together with the Gateway National Recreation Area, which includes shorelands on Staten Island and Jamaica Bay, Fire Island gives the federal government direct management responsibility for long reaches of the New York State marine coast. This responsibility includes cooperation by the National Park Service with the Army Corps of Engineers, the Coast Guard and other federal agencies. It must also relate to New York State coastal zone planning efforts under the federal Coastal Zone Management Act of 1972 and to local responsibility for land use regulation.

Planning for the Fire Island National Seashore was begun in 1964, but by 1975 three draft plans had failed to receive broad public support. The most recent planning effort, which culminated in the 1977 plan, had to resolve several important issues. These included management of the town and county parks and other lands, the objectives and enforcement of local zoning regulations, access by those who do not own boats and cannot afford the expensive transportation costs to Fire Island, regulation of vehicular traffic on the beaches, and protection from erosion and flooding from hurricanes and northeasters.

The Fire Island national seashore was established by Congress on September 11, 1964 [1]. Its primary objectives were to conserve and preserve the unique natural features of the undeveloped areas and provide recreational facilities in areas where they would be compatible with the natural environment. The national seashore boundaries include the nearby small islands and the waters 1000 feet into the Atlantic Ocean and up to 4000 feet into Great South Bay and Moriches Bay.

The federal law authorizes the Secretary of the Interior to acquire lands, by condemnation if necessary, and to supervise the regulation by local authorities of land use on privately owned lands. The Secretary is authorized by Section 3(b) to "issue regulations, which may be amended from time to time, specifying standards that are consistent with the purposes of the act creating the national seashore" [2].

By February 1977 the National Park Service had acquired 2792 acres. In 1965 Congress added to the national seashore the 612-acre William Floyd Estate, which was once owned by a signer of the Declaration of Independence. The estate is on the mainland, separated from Fire Island by Moriches Bay. Congress originally authorized $16 million for land acquisition. Additional land will be acquired as funds are appropriated. The federal government does not own the beach, the primary dune line, the marshlands or other unimproved lands on Fire Island that are outside the boundaries of its land holdings. The dunes and marshlands are important natural features of the barrier island. As there has been little success in preventing development on them by local land use regulation, eventual purchase by the National Park Service is the only way to maintain them in their natural state (Figure 11).

It has been noted that the Robert Moses State Park and the Smith Point County Park are accessible by auto. They receive several million visitors each year, and they resemble other highly used parks in the New York metropolitan region. They do not offer the unique Fire Island recreational experience, however, which has been described this way:

Constantly reworked by wind and wave, the sand that makes up the island is molded into an orderly mosaic of dunes and flats, which are continually built, then destroyed. Fire Island's vegetative communities are widely differentiated due to great changes in environmental conditions from place to place.

In some areas, visitors can take a walk through wind-swept grasslands, moist maritime forests, and saltwater tidal marshes—each community being associated with its own particular environment. It is obvious that visitors will not feel the same on the beach as they do at the edge of a vast tidal marsh or in a secluded holly forest, and the visitor's opportunity to relate with the sounds, sights, smells, and sensations of each of these outstanding natural environments, without interference from development, is an integral part of the Fire Island recreational experience [3].

FIGURE 11 Beach houses on Fire Island dunes. Continuous private ownership restricts public access to the beach, and house construction may accelerate destruction of dunes.

Access to the Fire Island National Seashore

Relatively few people will be able to enjoy this unique national seashore experience. The problem is transportation. Fire Island is on the edge of the most densely populated region in the United States, but there is no land access to the national seashore. The Suffolk County south shore is difficult to reach from the heart from the Metropolitan area because the Long Island

Expressway and the state parkways are congested during the recreation season. Public transportation is inconvenient, undependable and expensive. Inexpensive lodging on Fire Island and in the nearby Long Island communities is scarce. Use of this national recreation facility is therefore limited to "relatively affluent New York suburbanites, and primarily those residing in Suffolk and Nassau Counties. The provision of an inexpensive, convenient means of public transportation is the only way by which the national seashore is likely to become more accessible for a variety of socioeconomic groups. The possibility of such a system appears relatively remote" [4].

Consider the plight of even those relatively affluent city dwellers who want to take advantage of the unique Fire Island experience, which their tax dollars help to make available.

Visitors who do not have access to private boats may have to endure many frustrations before reaching Fire Island National Seashore. Those who arrive by car may have to battle several hours of traffic on Long Island highways, only to become lost enroute to the ferry slip because routes are poorly marked. At the ferry slip, public parking costs $2 to $3 per day, and the insufficient parking area is often full. Visitors must then leave their cars some distance away, occasionally at the risk of an illegal parking fine. Their frustration may be magnified when they see the parking lot contains many empty stalls, which are reserved for the exclusive use of local residents. If visitors miss a ferry connection, they may have to wait an hour or more for the next one. Once on the ferry, visitors have about a 30-minute ride to the island; round trip ferry rides cost $3.00 to $3.75 per person [5].

Efforts to improve access to the national seashore, however, will confront the National Park Service with a management dilemma. Better and cheaper access will help release some of the pent-up demand for seashore recreation, especially by city dwellers who must seek relief from summer's heat in competition with hundreds of thousands of their fellows. Intensive use is not compatible, however, with the objective of conserving and preserving the environmental and ecological features that make Fire Island unique in the United States.

Among the planning premises included in the 1977 Fire Island general management plan are these:

The primary management concern is preservation and enhancement of the serenity and natural beauty of the island, which includes protection of the beaches, dunes, and other natural features fundamental to the concept of Fire Island National Seashore.

Increased use of federal recreational areas will be minimal, with emphasis placed on the quality of facilities and visitor experiences and not on quantitative increases. This general management plan recognizes that Fire Island National Seashore serves a definable population of known and potential visitors. Basically,

Fire Island provides for, and will continue to serve, the recreational needs of
Suffolk and Nassau Counties and to a lesser degree the needs of New York City
[6].

National Park Service recreation facilities within the national seashore
will be limited to those that are environmentally compatible with conservation and preservation objectives. Aside from the heavily used state and
county parks accessible by auto, which do not provide the unique Fire Island
experience, recreation facilities will be provided on federal lands at only four
sites: Old Inlet, Sunken Forest, Talisman and Watch Hill. Access to Old Inlet
will be limited to owners of small boats and hikers willing to walk miles from
other access points. Sunken Forest, Talisman and Watch Hill will be accessible
only by ferry and private boats. The General Management Plan proposed that
combined daily peak visitation to all three areas be limited to 3292 arriving
by ferry and 1908 by small boat. Even this number of visitors would not be
reached until 1987, when ferry service would have to be improved [7].
    The Final Environmental Statement of the Fire Island General Manage-
ment Plan acknowledges the social consequences of the limited accessibility
of the National Seashore.

Emphasis in the general management plan on recreational development that is
in keeping with existing environmental values precludes the possibility that the
areas of Fire Island under federal jurisdiction may be used for mass public
recreation. . . . Nothing in the proposed plan promises to significantly reduce
the high cost of obtaining access to the seashore, which precludes use by many
people. The isolation of the island's federal developments makes provision of
public access expensive. . . . With the exception of increased use by visitors
with small boats, the difficulty of access will continue to limit use of park areas
by lower income families, by a disproportionate number of lower income residents of Nassau and Suffolk Counties and of New York City, by minorities
(particularly blacks and Latins), and by elderly persons living on fixed incomes.
Access to the seashore will continue to be difficult for these people, except when
they participate in organized parties and school or scout groups, for whom free
or inexpensive access could be provided by local government or sponsoring
organizations, or unless a subsidy system to defray the high cost of transportation
can be arranged [8].

It has already been noted that there are mass recreation facilities available
on Fire Island at Robert Moses State Park and Smith Point County Park.
Both have excess capacity, and the Smith Point Park may be easily expanded.
Both these parks are accessible by auto. Nevertheless, low-income people,
especially from New York City, would not be able to go to these Fire Island
Parks unless low-cost rail and bus transportation could be made available. The
Fire Island recreational experience is unique, but after future development
the Gateway National Recreation Area, which has components in New

Jersey, Staten Island and Jamaica Bay, will provide extensive new seashore recreational opportunities available to residents in the metropolitan area.

NEW YORK STATE PARKS
ON LONG ISLAND

Since 1924, 21 state parks have been established within the coastal boundaries of Long Island. Swimming and beach facilities are world famous at Jones Beach and Robert Moses State Parks on the south shore barrier islands, but they are also available on Long Island Sound, Great South Bay, Zachs Bay and Gardiner's Bay. Horticulture is the main feature at Bayard Cutting and Planting Fields Arboretums, former private estates. Caumsett, Connetquot and Nissequogue State parks are underdeveloped as ecological preserves for a variety of Long Island natural nabitats and their plant and animal life. Sunken Meadow, Orient Beach and Wildwood State Parks have representative examples of the north shore ecology. All of the developed parks have facilities for picnicking, active sports and passive recreation. Table V lists state parks within the Long Island coastal zone, their size and attendance in 1976. In addition to these state parks and arboretums, there are boat launch areas at Freeport and South Jamesport and 146.3 miles of parkways that provide access to the parks and offer opportunities for pleasure driving.

A Wild, Scenic, and Recreational Rivers System was established by the State Legislature in 1972 [9]. After study by the NY Department of Environmental Conservation, selected river segments are designated into the system by the Governor and Legislature. The intent of the state law was not to restore the rivers to their primitive conditions, but rather to preserve them from the effects of further development. Segments of designated rivers fall into three classes:

1. *Wild River:* free from diversions or impoundments, inaccessible except by water, or foot or horse trail through primitive and undeveloped area;

2. *Scenic River:* free from diversions and impoundments except for log dams, limited road access through largely primitive and underdeveloped areas or used predominantly for agriculture, forest management, or other dispersed activities;

3. *Recreational River:* may have had some diversion or impoundment, readily accessible by road or railroad through areas that have some development.

Most of the rivers in the system are in the Adirondack Mountains, but two are coastal rivers in Suffolk County. In 1973, 10.25 miles of the Carmans

TABLE V New York State Parks in the Long Island Coastal Zone

Park Name	Acres	Attendance in 1976 (thousands)
Nassau County		
Hempstead Lake	792	664
Jones Beach	2413	11311
Massapequa	596	Underdeveloped
Planting Fields	409	115
Valley Stream	97	129
Suffolk County		
Bayard Cutting	690	50
Belmont Lake	459	463
Camp Hero	165	Underdeveloped
Captree	298	Included with Jones Beach
Caumsett	1500	28
Connetquot River	3473	
Gilgo	1223	30
Heckscher	1657	922
Hither Hills	1755	Included with Mohawk Pt.
Montauk Point	724	645
Napeague	1278	Underdeveloped
Nissequogue River	543	19
Orient Beach	363	82
Robert Moses	1000	2049
Sunken Meadow	1266	1282
Wildwood	769	487
Total	21470	18276

Source: N Y State Office of Parks and Recreation, "Public Access and Recreation Within the Coastal Boundaries of New York State," Albany, N Y , March 1978, Table 8, p. 24. (Processed)

River was designated as "scenic," and an additional 3 miles classified as "recreational." In 1974, 5 miles of the Connetquot River were classified as "recreational." An adjoining 0.75 mile headwaters section has been proposed for designation in this class. Detailed boundaries have been established for these river segments, and a special moratorium on development is in effect within these areas until state regulations are adopted to control land use. The Nissequogue River in Suffolk County is also under study for inclusion in the system.

Access to State Recreation Facilities on Long Island

Access to state parks on Long Island is subject to the same limitations as those already noted for the Fire Island National Seashore. There are no legal restrictions on access to state parks, but physical problems of transportation, cost and socio-economic factors limit access and the preferences of users.

Regional recreation demand comes primarily from residents of New York City and Nassau and Suffolk Counties. The transportation problem, which affects commuting to work and access for other activities as well as recreation, is the result of low-density and sprawling development on Long Island and the consequent reliance on autos and trucks for transportation services. An extensive network of expressways, parkways and arterial highways has been developed, but congestion persists.

> In Nassau County, about 60% of the state highway mileage was operating at or beyond its design capacity in 1972. The Long Island Expressway was operating at approximately 180% of design capacity, while both the Northern and Southern State Parkways operated at an average level of about 125% of design capacity. In Suffolk County, approximately 43% of the state highway mileage was operating at or beyond design capacity with another 25% operating near maximum capacity [10].

On summer weekends, congestion of the entire system prevents free flow of traffic.

With the decline of public transportation, the elderly, young, poor and handicapped residents of the region are unable to reach recreation facilities on Long Island. One approach to improving access by these people, as well as to reducing congestion, is by expanding bus and train service. Walkways and bikeways could improve short range access.

The NY State Department of Transportation favors expansion of bus use of expressways and recommends that buses be permitted on parkways that are capable of accommodating them [11]. Buses are banned from state parkways, and quotas have been set for the number of buses that may enter state parks. On Sundays, buses are excluded from *all* state parks except Heckscher. Jones Beach, for example, is the most heavily used Long Island state park. It is served by two six-lane expressways and has parking for 23,000 cars. Parking and other fees are $2.00. Franchise and charter bus service is available from New York City and Nassau County, except on Sundays; but in 1976 only 3.9% (357,013) of all visitors to Jones Beach (10.5 million) came by bus.

The Long Island Railroad provides transportation service along the south shore out to Montauk. But the stations are several miles from the state parks, and local connecting buses do not run on weekends and holidays. Taxis provide the only service at these times. Families that cannot afford cars are not likely to be able to afford the cumulative costs of public transportation, especially from New York City, even if they would be willing to spend several hours in travel for a day's outing.

Access limitations are inequitable, and they also prevent efficient utilization of park facilities. Very often parking lot capacity determines the capacity of the park, although some of its facilities may be underutilized. Jones Beach State Park in Nassau County, for example, usually closes early on summer weekend mornings because the parking lots are full, although there is still plenty of room on the beaches. Other state and county parks are similarly underutilized. This situation could be avoided if bus transportation were available from parking lots at shopping centers and other locations within reasonable travel times from the parks.

Robert Moses and State Policy on Access. The great system of state parks on Long Island was created by Robert Moses. Yet he is reported to have deliberately limited access to these parks by blacks and poor people. Robert A. Caro, in his detailed study of Moses in *The Power Broker,* claims that he had a deep distaste for the people who were using the parks. Franklin D. Roosevelt was Governor of New York during part of Moses' reign, and would not interfere with his policies. Frances Perkins, who later became Roosevelt's Secretary of Labor, is quoted by Caro as saying this about Moses:

> He doesn't love the people. It used to shock me because he was doing all these things for the welfare of the people. . . . He'd denounce the common people terribly. To him they were lousy, dirty people, throwing bottles all over Jones Beach. 'I'll get them! I'll teach them!'. . . . He loves the public, but not as people. The public is just *the* public. It's a great amorphous mass to him [12].

This reputed distaste for the public was apparently incorporated into a deliberate Moses policy to limit access to the Long Island parks to only the prosperous, white middle class. We must trust Caro for the veracity of these assertions:

> Now he began taking measures to limit the use of his parks. He had restricted the use of state parks by poor and lower-middle-class families in the first place, by limiting access to the parks by rapid transit; he had vetoed the Long Island Rail Road's proposed construction of a branch spur to Jones Beach for this reason. Now he began to limit access by buses; he instructed Shapiro to build the bridges across his new parkways low—too low for buses to pass. Bus trips therefore had to be made on local roads, making the trips discouragingly long and arduous. For Negroes, whom he considered inherently 'dirty,' there were further measures. Buses needed permits to enter state parks; buses chartered by Negro groups found it very difficult to obtain permits, particularly to Moses' beloved Jones Beach; most were shunted to parks many miles further out on Long Island. And even in these parks, buses carrying Negro groups were shunted to the furthest reaches of the parking areas. And Negroes were discouraged from using 'white' beach areas—the best beaches—by a system Shapiro calls 'flagging'; the handful of Negro lifeguards (there were only a handful of Negro employees

among the thousands employed by the Long Island State Park Commission) were all stationed at distant, least developed beaches. Moses was convinced that Negroes did not like cold water; the temperature at the pool at Jones Beach was deliberately icy to keep Negroes out. When Negro civic groups from the hot New York slums began to complain about this treatment, Roosevelt ordered an investigation and an aide confirmed that 'Bob Moses is seeking to discourage large Negro parties from picknicking at Jones Beach, attempting to divert them to some other of the state parks.' Roosevelt gingerly raised the matter with Moses, who denied the charge violently–and the Governor never raised the matter again [13].

Robert Moses went beyond limiting physical access to Jones Beach and other state parks by imposing financial barriers. Practically all users of these parks had to be affluent enough to own cars and pay for the gasoline, parkway tolls and parking fees. During the Depression, these were effective economic constraints on park attendance by the New York City and Long Island poor. Roosevelt had asked Moses to reduce parking fees at Jones Beach, but Moses refused on the ground that maintenance standards would have to be lowered. In the face of one of Moses' frequent resignation threats, Roosevelt not only dropped this request, he vetoed a bill passed by the state Legislature prohibiting fees in state parks [14].

State Recreation Planning

The NY State Office of Parks and Recreation (OPR) prepared in 1978 a Statewide Comprehensive Recreation Plan. This is the third such plan prepared to meet the requirements of the Federal Land and Water Conservation Fund Act of 1965. OPR manages the federal grants made available by the Fund, which cover up to 50% of the cost of land acquisition for parks and recreation and for certain types of facilities. Grants may be made from the state fund for local recreation projects as well as for state facilities.

OPR has provided the NY Coastal Management Program with planning information on coastal recreation facilities. Existing facilities and their capacities for various kinds of recreation activity are listed on the computerized Outdoor Recreation Facilities Inventory. Forecasts of recreation participation up to the year 2000 have been made from a mathematical model that incorporates these factors: population, age, leisure time, income, mobility and access. A demand model has been developed based on the three variables of age, income and population density, which are considered to be the most important explanatory factors. The model can account for demand from residents of all parts of the state and forecasts peak as well as average demands.

New York City is the largest source of recreation demands in New York State, followed by Nassau and Suffolk Counties. Recreation resources in New York City are considered inadequate and will continue so, even though a 12% population decrease is projected for the year 2000. As the result of overcrowding and pressure on existing facilities, New York City residents who can afford it travel to other areas for recreation. Long Island is a favorite destination.

Population in the Nassau-Suffolk County Region is expected to grow rapidly, adding to the demand for recreation from the City. As a major source of recreational services for the entire New York metropolitan area, deficiencies are already evident in Nassau County. This area adjoins Brooklyn and Queens, and it is itself heavily urbanized. Population movement eastward, however, will also produce recreation deficiencies in Suffolk County by the end of the century. Table VI indicates the scale of future requirements.

TABLE VI Projected Public Design Day Deficiency, by Region, 2000   (Deficiency in number of people served)

	Population	Deficiency	Percent Share of Statewide Deficiency
New York City	7,891,563	788,848	49.7
Long Island	2,555,868	212,415	13.4

Source: N Y State Office of Parks and Recreation, "People, Resources, Recreation in 1978: New York Statewide Comprehensive Recreation Plan" (Draft) March 1978.

The state comprehensive recreation plan pays particular attention to the problem of access:

> The most important problems facing outdoor recreation systems in the next 25 years, superseding increases in demand, will be meeting the needs of those segments of the population currently being underserved. . . . The inner city resident, the elderly, the handicapped, the economically underprivileged, and the young are among the groups significantly underserved. . . . OPR can do little to resolve socio-economic disparities among various population groups, such as automobile ownership, personal income, physical and mental health, etc., which have such a great influence on ability to access state parks and other natural resources areas. But efforts can be advanced to maximize all practicable options for those persons currently excluded from full participation in recreation experiences [15].

It has been noted that nonresidents are excluded from municipal beaches and parks on Long Island. Nevertheless, some of these facilities receive federal and state grants and should be open to all. Municipalities may charge fees to offset costs of their use to local taxpayers, but the state has found difficulty in insuring implementation of its policy to discourage discriminatory restrictions against nonresidents in facilities receiving matching grants-in-aid. Part of this problem results from the already overcrowded conditions at local facilities, particularly on weekends. There are also less manageable problems of race and socio-economic class relations. White middle-class residents on Long Island fear that New York City people, with "strange" appearance and behavior, may discourage attendance by local people.

Improving access to recreational facilities is socially desirable, but it may have negative environmental consequences. Use may increase beyond their physical carrying capacity:

> Resource areas, intended for preservation, have been destroyed by the over-crowding brought about by improved accessibility. Lowering personal costs by easing access raised social and environmental costs beyond the bearable limits of the resources involved. The fragile ecological balance has been lost complete-ly and irreparably for some natural areas [16].

COUNTY PARKS ON LONG ISLAND

Nassau and Suffolk Counties operate their own park system. Nassau County is half the size of Suffolk, but its population is greater. It adjoins New York City and was developed earlier and more densely. Development fever, especially after World War II, allowed little public concern for reserving parks, nature preserves or other kinds of open space. The Nassau County Planning Commission has acknowledged that Nassau County and its municipalities will never reach the standards suggested by professional recreation specialists. What little open land that remains is insufficient and too costly [17]. Suffolk County, by comparison, is still largely undeveloped. It also has the advantage of a county government that recognized coming development pressure and acquired large tracts of land while they were still available and reasonably priced.

Table VII indicates the total amount of park and open space land available in Nassau and Suffolk Counties. The table includes land owned by federal, state and municipal governments. Although this table shows that compara-tively large areas of land are in public ownership for recreation and open space uses, not all of it is available to all comers. Nassau County parks are re-stricted to residents and their guests. Entrance to these parks is strictly con-trolled, and residents must show their "leisure pass" to get in. Suffolk County has a similar policy, but it is not strictly enforced. Admission to Suffolk County Parks is essentially open to any visitor.

Suffolk County Department of Parks, Conservation, and Recreation

The Suffolk County Department of Parks, Recreation, and Conservation plays an important role in coastal resources management. Extensive areas of

TABLE VII Acreage of Park and Open Space Lands in Nassau and Suffolk Counties

| Ownership | Nassau County | | | Suffolk County |
	1963	1974	1977	1977
Federal	117	117	3234	3391
N.Y. State	4877	5201	5261	18545
County	2557	5111	5111	14787
Nature Conservancy	NA	NA	203	1079
Municipalities	3626	4283	4283	10106
Schools[a]	NA	NA	4452	7160
Private	NA	NA	5164	11348
Total			27708	66416

[a]Available recreation area estimated at 50% of local school acreage.

Source: Nassau County Planning Commission, "Parks and Recreation Study," December 1974, Table 1; Nassau-Suffolk Regional Planning Board, "A Recreation and Shoreline Access Subplan for Nassau and Suffolk Counties," August 31, 1977, Table 3.

the Suffolk County shoreline are occupied by facilities and reservations operated by it. These include county public parks, beaches, wetlands, playgrounds, athletic fields, recreation centers, marinas, golf courses, open spaces and areas publicly owned and acquired for the conservation of natural resources.

Ownership and operation of parks, recreation facilities and natural area preserves and reservations by Suffolk County removes these coastal areas from the threat of private development and puts their management responsibility directly into the hands of the county agency. Coastal zone management objectives for development control and protection of ecological and environmental quality are achieved by direct county action.

The Department of Parks, Recreation and Conservation is jointly managed by a Commissioner and a Board of Trustees. The Commissioner is the administrative head of the Department and is responsible for the operation and maintenance of all its facilities and properties. Department policy, however, is made with the participation of the Board of Trustees.

Acquisition and development of new parks and recreation facilities is managed jointly by several county agencies. The Commissioner and Board recommend such actions to the county legislature. Preparation of maps, engineering design, letting of contracts and supervision of park construction is done by the Department of Public Works. However, architectural and engineering services for park buildings and the letting of contracts and supervision of construction are responsibilities of the Department of Buildings and Grounds.

Access to Westhampton Beach. One of the obstacles to public access to beaches on Long Island is the barrier of privately or municipally owned land between the access road and the shore. On Westhampton Beach, for example, a public road parallels the beach, but practically continuous private owner-ship of the land between the road and the beach prevents access. Where access ways or even public recreation areas are located, they are restricted to town residents and even parking is restricted. Nevertheless, the beach itself below the high water line is state property. It would be open to anyone were access not barred.

The question of access to Westhampton Beach was debated by the Suffolk County Legislature in connection with a federal government project to con-struct groins to control shore erosion. The groins were to be long narrow ridges of great rocks piled at right angles to the shore to capture sand from the shore current. As part of its contribution to the project, Suffolk County was supposed to provide easements over private property fronting on the beach to provide access for groin construction and later on for inspection and maintenance. The property owners agreed to donate rather than sell the ease-ments if Suffolk County agreed not to allow them to be used for public access to the beach or groins for swimming or fishing.

This condition was approved by the Army Corps of Engineers in spite of its own policies. The Corps required certain written assurances of cooperation before the project could go ahead. The Suffolk County Legislature approved an "Assurance of Local Cooperation" that contained these statements:

the state will provide without cost to the United States all lands, easements, and rights-of-way . . . necessary for construction of the project. . . . the state will maintain during the economic life of the project continued public ownership of the non-Federal publicly owned shores and continued avail-ability for public use of privately owned shore equivalent to that upon which the recommended Federal participation is based [18].

The County Board of Supervisors approved these commitments on behalf of the State in August 1963 by Resolution No. 365-1963. Nevertheless, in the following year by Resolution No. 364-1964 it declared that the 25-foot wide easements from Dune Road to Westhampton Beach

be limited to use solely and only by governmental agencies and their duly authorized representatives, employees and contractors for the sole purpose of inspecting, maintaining and repairing said stone groins, with control over said parcels to remain in the owners thereof.

This contradictory resolution closing the county easements to public use were not objected to by the Corps of Engineers in spite of its own conditions for County participation in the project. At a meeting of the Board of Super-visors, one member noted that a federally aided erosion control project in New Jersey included the requirement that access to the groins and shore be

open to the public. He wondered why this requirement was waived for
Westhampton Beach. The minutes of the meeting contain no answer to this
question [19].

MUNICIPAL PARKS IN COASTAL
MANAGEMENT

Long Island municipalities also contribute park and open space lands as a
public ownership component to coastal management. Accurate data about
municipal public lands in the Long Island coastal zone are not available.
Tables included in this chapter show only approximate totals for lands in
municipal ownership, but they are a fair indication of their place in coastal
management because about three-quarters of all of Long Island is included in
the defined coastal zone. It would be impractical to survey all of the municipalities for this study, but the Towns of East Hampton and Islip provide examples of municipal programs.

The Town of East Hampton

For the Town of East Hampton, surveys, plans and implementation programs were already available for two elements of coastal zone management
programs: geographic areas of particular concern and recreational access. The
Town Plan for Open Spaces was published as a newspaper supplement on
April 11, 1974, by the East Hampton Star. This document contained a survey
of such areas already in public ownership or in privately owned preserves
open to the public. It also listed lands to be acquired for additional parks or
park expansions.

Open space holdings within the unincorporated area of East Hampton
comprised about 10% of the total land area, or 4508 acres. Federal, state and
Suffolk county properties accounted for 3467 acres. Negotiations were also
underway to transfer 117 acres from Camp Hero to Montauk Point State Park
and to acquire 900 acres for a proposed Indian Field County Park. The Town
itself owned 719 acres. Privately owned open spaces totalled 322 acres: 187
acres reserved for the exclusive use of residents of certain subdivisions; 16
acres only for the use of members of private associations; 119 acres held by
the Nature Conservancy and generally accessible to the public. The Open
Spaces Plan called for the Town of East Hampton to acquire 482 acres for
additional parks and a joint program with Nature Conservancy to acquire 200
acres; all these are sites identified for their environmental and recreational
value.

The Nature Conservancy plays a unique role in environmental conservation.
As a private organization, it can engage in direct action to preserve areas of

concern without the long political, administrative and fiscal hassles to which local governments are subject. All Nature Conservancy needs is the money to buy at market prices unique properties threatened by development. Fortunately, East Hampton has many wealthy residents. The local chapter of Nature Conservancy recently collected $300,000 by a fundraising campaign to buy 17 acres of dune land [20]. The land value of $17,647 per acre indicates the price it would bring in the open market. Nine thousand dollars for a 0.5-acre lot or even $18,000 for a 1-acre lot could be easily obtained for unique dune sites. The area consists of two parallel lines of sand dunes separated by a low-lying shrub forest and fresh water ponds. The beauty of the landscape is matched by its ecological interest, for it houses a diverse community of unusual plant and animal species. It will be called the Atlantic Double Dunes Preserve.

The Town of East Hampton Planning Board has developed procedures to conserve even small areas of open space of significant environmental value in land subdivisions. The Town Board enacted in 1968 an Open Space Zoning Ordinance to supplement both its regular zoning ordinance and subdivision regulations. This ordinance grants the developer some flexibility in determining lot sizes and subdivision design in exchange for the preservation of particular open spaces. The Planning Board staff works closely with the developer as it reviews subdivision proposals and points out the advantages of conserving significant open areas.

Recreation Planning in the Town of Islip

The Town of Islip Comprehensive Plan contains a volume devoted to recreation and open space. The Department of Planning and Development conceived a threefold role for the Town within the context of federal, state and county recreation programs. These aspects of the Town's role are:

1. To protect the natural resources which constitute the most important component of Islip's leisure environment by guarding against encroaching development near watercourses, the Great South Bay, on the ocean beaches, and around Lake Ronkonkoma;
2. To utilize the natural components of the leisure environment, making natural areas and regional facilities accessible to all the Town's people for their collective enjoyment through improved transportation, public information and instructional programs;
3. To provide as many of its people as possible with opportunities to meet their everyday needs for basic public recreation necessary to maintain a healthy and balanced existence [21].

This element of the Islip Comprehensive Plan contains population and economic profiles of each of the Town's planning areas and detailed analyses of their leisure environment and facilities and opportunities for recreation and enjoyment of open space. On the basis of this information, policy recommendations were drawn up for consideration of the Town Board, and operational target programs were proposed for each of the areas. As the Town of Islip borders on the Great South Bay and includes a portion of Fire Island, much of the Town's recreation land and open space reservations are on the shore.

Recreational Land Use in the Town of Islip

A considerable amount of land on and near the shoreline is devoted to recreation in the Town of Islip. Boating, fishing and swimming are the most popular recreation activities, but nature study, enjoyment of the landscape and passive recreation are also provided for. Thousands of acres of recreation areas and open space reservations are also owned by federal, state and county governments as well as by private organizations, such as the Nature Conservancy and Audubon Society.

The 1973 land use inventory of the Town of Islip, which was prepared by the Department of Planning and Development, indicates that extensive areas of coastal land were publicly owned for recreational use. They included state, county and town facilities. Management of these coastal lands is a direct public responsibility. As they include undeveloped areas of environmental concern as well as developed beaches and parks, management of these lands becomes an element in the coastal program for the Town of Islip. This one town contained these publicly managed lands:

Federal lands	792 acres
State Parks and conservation areas	5578
County parks	1202
Town of Islip parks	908
Nature Conservancy	207
Audubon Society	73
Total	8760 acres

The approach that the Town of Islip has taken toward combining recreation with areas of particular environmental concern is illustrated by its management plan for the South Shore Nature Center. The Nature Center is adjacent to Heckscher State Park and close to the Great South Bay. It is based on the former Hollins estate, but parts of its 206-acre area were contributed by Suffolk County and the Nature Conservancy in a cooperative arrangement with the Town of Islip

Only the Town-owned Nature Center has the original Hollins buildings, and it will be developed as the reception and educational area. The remaining property will be maintained in its natural state. This area has been very little affected by the works of man since the first white settlers arrived on Long Island. Its flora and fauna have been painstakingly inventoried, and the Nature Center program is designed to conserve these resources. Nature trails will be the only facilities provided and attendance will be limited in order to accomplish this objective.

Suburbanites have a vague, oftentimes unsatisfied feeling, of living in the country. Their very numbers, have, of course, defeated what they sought, but regardless of lifestyle, most people have lost the traditional ties with nature. . . . People are becoming discerning in their choices for leisure time. There is a demand for more than parking lots, picnic tables, fireplaces, and beaches. People are increasingly interested in learning something about the natural world in which they live. They find that through appreciation and the development of sharper sensibilities, they can realize a higher sense of personal values and thereby gain richer, fuller lives [22].

REFERENCES

1. Public Law 88-587, 78 Stat. 928, September 11, 1964.
2. Ibid., Sec. 8 (a).
3. U.S. Department of the Interior, National Park Service, *Fire Island National Seashore: General Management Plan*, Patchogue, N.Y., 1977, pp. 15-16.
4. Ibid., p. 13.
5. Ibid.
6. Ibid., p. 23.
7. Ibid., p. 91.
8. U.S. National Park Service, *Final Environmental Statement, General Management Plan, Fire Island National Seashore*, New York, 1977, pp. 201-202.
9. N.Y. State Environmental Conservation Law, Article 15, Title 27.
10. Evan R. Liblet, "Long Island State Park Mass Transit Access Improvement Study," N.Y. State Office of Parks and Recreation. Revised May 1977 (processed), p. 3.
11. Ibid., p. 5.
12. Robert A. Caro, *The Power Broker: Robert Moses and the Fall of New York* (New York: Vintage Books, 1975), p. 318.
13. Ibid., pp. 318-319.
14. Ibid., p. 319.
15. N.Y. State Office of Parks and Recreation, "People, Resources, and Recreation in 1978: New York Statewide Comprehensive Recreation Plan" (Draft), March 1978, p. 365.

16. Ibid., p. 98.
17. Nassau County Planning Commission, *Parks and Recreation Study,* Mineola, N.Y., December 1974 (mimeographed).
18. Assurance of local cooperation for the beach erosion control and hurricane protection project for Fire Island Inlet to Montauk Point, N.Y. furnished in pursuance of the River and Harbor Act of 1960 (Public Law 86-645, 86th Congress), August 14, 1963.
19. Joseph M. Heikoff, *The Politics of Shore Erosion: Westhampton Beach* (Ann Arbor, Michigan: Ann Arbor Science, 1976), pp. 88-91.
20. *NYS Environment,* March 1978, p. 3.
21. Town of Islip, *Comprehensive Plan: Recreation/Open Space,* Vol. 5, January 1977, p. 2.
22. Town of Islip, *South Shore Nature Center: Management Plan,* October, 1976, p. 31.

CHAPTER 7

WATER QUALITY MANAGEMENT

There is no need to emphasize the obvious point that water is one of the major resources of the coastal zone and that water quality is one of the major concerns of coastal zone management. The federal Coastal Zone Management Act requires that state coastal programs must include a water quality element as well as one for air quality. Coastal programs under this Act, therefore, must be coordinated with water and air quality programs under the current versions of the Clean Water Act and the Clear Air Act. Each of these federal laws acknowledges the need for coordination with the other.

Section 307 (f) of the Coastal Zone Management Act states that the programs developed to implement the Clean Water Act and the Clean Air Act are to be incorporated into the state coastal management programs to meet their water and air pollution control requirements. At the same time, Section 510 of the Clear Water Act of 1977 provides that this Act does not preclude the right of any state to adopt its own water quality standards, as long as they are no less stringent than those required by federal law, nor does it impair the jurisdiction of the states with respect to their waters, including their coastal waters.

State coastal resources management, therefore, is aided by ongoing state water quality management programs to the extent that they operate in the coastal zone. On the other hand, coastal zone management programs have the opportunity to participate in and influence the determination of water quality standards, effluent limitations and performance standards for public and private wastewater treatment facilities in the coastal zone. Land use planning in the coastal program should also help in the achievement of water quality objectives in this zone.

Management of environmental quality is a responsibility assigned to the NY State Department of Environmental Conservation (DEC). This is one of its three basic responsibilities mandated by the Environmental Conservation Law of 1970:

1. Management of air and water *quality*—the abatement of pollution,
2. Management of water *resources*—assuring adequate supplies of freshwater,
3. Management of *natural resources*—including plants and forests, fish and wildlife, and their habitats.

In order to carry out these responsibilities, DEC has been organized into these program divisions:

1. Air Resources Division — air quality management,
2. Pure Waters Division — water quality and resources management,
3. Solid Waste Management Division,
4. Marine Resources Division — management of shellfish, crustaceans and marine fish species,
5. Fish and Wildlife Division,
6. Land Resources and Forest Management Division,
7. Environmental Analysis and Permits, a branch of DEC that parallels the program divisions.

The Division of Pure waters has lead responsibility in DEC for water quality management. It is concerned with implementing water quality programs mandated by federal and state laws. Planning support for preparation of the state Water Quality Management Plan, a requirement of Section 208 of the Clean Water Act, was provided by the Resources Program Development Subdivision of the Division of Land Resources and Forest Management. Water quality management in DEC incorporates a variety of coordinated strategies and programs, some of which will be described below. They are:

1. Development of an annual state strategy,
2. Water quality assessment,
3. Construction grants for new wastewater treatment works,
4. Monitoring and surveillance of water bodies and wastewater sources,
5. A continuing planning process,
6. Wastewater discharge permit program.

DEC is not the only state agency responsible for water quality management. The NY State Department of Health plays a major role by analyzing and certifying drinking water supplies. The Environmental Conservation and Health Departments cooperate in carrying out their water quality and water resources management programs. An interstate agency, the Interstate Sanitation Commission, helps to coordinate the New York and New Jersey water quality programs in the New York Metropolitan Area.

Municipal and regional agencies also participate. The Nassau-Suffolk Regional Planning Board is the designated agency to prepare the regional Water Quality Management Plan under Section 208 of the federal Clean Water Act. Long Island County governments and municipalities have responsibility for the supply and quality of drinking water. Their future land use, water supply and wastewater treatment plans will have to conform to the final regional Water Quality Management Program and the provisions of the Clean Water Act.

Intergovernmental coordination and cooperation are further complicated by the responsibilities of federal agencies involved in implementing the federal Clean Water Act. The Environmental Protection Agency has overall responsibility for establishing the national water quality standards and approving state programs. The U.S. Army Corps of Engineers has an operational role in reviewing proposals for dredging and filling and issuing permits, which is especially significant for wetlands conservation. The Coast Guard is responsible for regulating tankers and other vessels and the cleanup of oil spills.

KINDS AND CAUSES OF WATER POLLUTION

Contaminating substances and organisms that pollute water bodies and even underground water resources have been classified as follows [1]:

1. *Oxygen demanding materials.* An important indicator of good water quality is the presence of adequate amounts of dissolved oxygen. Excessive growth rates of algae and the decomposition of the mass of dead cells, for example, are organic causes of oxygen depletion. Chemical pollutants also combine with oxygen, removing it from the water. Water quality measures include biochemical oxygen demand (BOD) and chemical oxygen demand (COD).

2. *Infectious agents.* These are bacteria and viruses that cause disease. Fecal coliform and streptococcus bacteria are indicators of the presence of such organisms.

3. *Nutrients.* Nitrogen and phosphorus are essential to the growth of algae. Overabundance of these elements in the water causes algal blooms that make water unfit for swimming. The nutrient content of water may also be indicated by its acidity (pH) and taste or odor.

4. *Toxic substances.* These are chemicals that are poisonous to humans and aquatic animals. Mercury and other heavy metals, chlorine compounds such as polychlorinated biphenols (PCB), some nitrogen compounds, and organophosphates are such substances. Although they may be present in minute quantities in the water or sediments, they are taken up by microorganisms and higher forms that feed on them. Eventually they may concentrate in fish to levels that make them unfit for human consumption.

5. *Thermal pollution.* Fish and other aquatic organisms thrive within a rather narrow range of water temperature. Temperature may be raised above optimum levels by the discharge of industrial or power plant cooling waters.

6. *Sedimentation and minerals.* Excessive erosion washes soil and minerals into water bodies. Disturbance of the bottom by dredging also increases the amount of dissolved and suspended solids. The consequent turbidity reduces the penetration of sunlight and affects the growth of microorganisms. Currents may also carry the sediment and cause unwanted deposition or changes in bottom configuration. Wastes from mining operations also change water acidity and other characteristics.

7. *Oil and hazardous substances.* These are petroleum products and other fuels and chemicals usually transported in bulk by ship, railroad or truck. They may be leaked or spilled during storage, transfer or transport, sometimes in very large quantities. They are poisonous to aquatic organisms; cover the feathers of wildfowl and cause their death; and foul beaches, boats, shorelines and property.

8. *Radioactive materials.* Wastes from nuclear military activities and civilian power plants may be stored in liquid form and leak from their containers or leak into the soil. They may also be spilled during handling and transportation to disposal sites. Because no solution has yet been found for the permanent safe disposal of nuclear wastes, the proliferation of military facilities and electricity generating plants is producing increasing volumes of waste material in temporary storage.

Although it is known that these materials are hazardous, poisonous or otherwise undesirable contaminants of water bodies, the exact concentration at which they threaten human health and damage to the environment is not always known. Effective water quality management, however, requires the establishment of numerical standards that mark the boundary between "safe" and "unsafe" levels of contamination. So far EPA/DEC standards have been determined for dissolved oxygen, coliform organisms, turbidity, phenolic compounds and radioactivity. Standards are under consideration for toxic materials, hazardous substances, and nutrients (Tables VIII and IX).

Water quality management requires the identification and control of the sources of these contaminants. There are two general classes of sources, "point" and "nonpoint." Point sources are those that have a specific place or point of discharge, such as a pipe, conduit, channel or even a ditch. Municipal sewage treatment plants and industrial plants are the most obvious point sources, but even single houses that discharge sanitary wastes directly to a stream or lake are point sources. Some communities have sewer systems, but no treatment plants. They discharge raw sewage directly into nearby water bodies, but even treated sewage effluents may contain pollutants.

Point sources can be relatively easily identified. Where effective technologies are available, the discharge of pollutants can be measured and controlled. It is much more difficult to deal with nonpoint sources, such as surface runoff from farm lands, parking lots and urban areas, for there are no reasonably economical control technologies. Fertilizers, pesticides and herbicides, animal wastes, heavy metals, petroleum and rubber compounds, and asbestos particles are washed freely into water bodies from nonpoint sources by rain.

Various point and nonpoint sources produce contaminants in a great variety of combinations. The technology of water quality management is complex because each source may produce many kinds of pollutants. These are some examples [2]:

1. *Municipal discharges.* These come from publicly owned sewage treatment works, package treatment plants for residential subdivisions and private plants that pretreat industrial wastes before they are discharged into publicly owned systems.

2. *Industrial discharges.* Industrial plants may discharge wastewaters directly to nearby waters or indirectly through municipal treatment works, with or without pretreatment to remove particular contaminants.

3. *Residual waste sources.* After wastewaters are subjected to various degrees of treatment and contaminant removal, the liquid effluent is discharged to water bodies. But then the residual materials removed from the wastewaters must also be disposed of. They may be solids, such as trash and sediment, or practically liquid, such as treatment plant sludge. Residual wastes are also produced by air pollution control devices, such as scrubbers and precipitators that remove contaminants from stack gases. Residual wastes, therefore, include all solid and liquid wastes that remain in municipal treatment plants, package plants, septic tanks and air pollution control systems, and also nuclear wastes and solid wastes. Ocean dumping and burial in landfills have been the final disposal methods. Nevertheless, these residuals pollute the ocean dump sites and nearby waters directly, or they may leak into groundwaters from land fills.

4. *Combined sewers.* These are municipal systems that collect both storm water surface runoff and sanitary sewage. During dry periods, all of the waste waters are conveyed to the municipal treatment plant. These plants do not have the capacity, however, to handle the large volumes of combined wastewaters collected during and after heavy rains, so they are bypassed around the treatment plants and discharged directly into surface waters.

5. *Urban storm water runoff.* Rain water in urban areas flows over roofs, paved areas, lawns, gardens and other surfaces where it may pick up many kinds of contaminants. Even where it is collected into separate stormwater sewers, it runs directly without treatment into water bodies. This constitutes a point source of pollution; but much of the surface water drains directly into water bodies without being collected in sewer lines first. Urban areas, therefore, are both point and nonpoint sources of water pollution.

6. *Hydraulic/hydrologic modifications.* Water quality problems may result from activities that regulate or alter water flow, including channel

TABLE VIII Classifications and Standards for Marine Waters

Class	Best Usage	Dissolved Oxygen (min.)	Coliform Level				Toxic and Deleterious Substances
			MPN Any Time	Monthly Median	20% of Sample	Monthly Geometric Mean	
SA	Shellfishing for market; primary and secondary contact recreation; all other uses	5.0 mg/l	Less than 70/100 ml	—	—	—	None in amounts that will interfere with primary contact recreation or be injurious to propagation or marketing of edible fish or shellfish or impair best usage of waters
SB	Primary and secondary contact recreation; any other use except shellfishing for market	5.0 mg/l	—	Less than 2,400/100 ml coliform	Less than 5,000/100 ml coliform	Less than 200/100 ml fecal coliform	None in amounts that will interfere with primary contact recreation or be injurious to propagation or marketing of edible fish or shellfish or impair best usage of waters
SC	Fishing and other uses except primary contact recreation and shellfishing for market	5.0 mg/l	—	—	—	Less than 10,000/100 ml coliform & 2,000/100 ml fecal coliform	None in amounts that will interfere with secondary contact recreation or be injurious to propagation or marketing of edible fish or shellfish or impair best usage of waters
SD	All uses except shellfishing for market, primary and secondary contact recreation, and fishing	3.0 mg/l	—	—	—	—	None alone or in combination with other substances in amounts to impair survival of fish life or best usage of waters

I	Secondary contact recreation and any other use except primary contact recreation and shellfishing for market	4.0 mg/l	—	—	Less than 10,000/100 ml coliform and 2,000/100 ml fecal coliform	None in amounts that will interfere with secondary contact recreation or be injurious to propagation or marketing of edible fish or impair best usage of waters
II	Not primarily for recreation, shellfish culture, or development of fish life	Average of not less than 30% saturation during any week, but adequate for fish & shellfish	—	—	—	None alone or in combination with other substances in amounts injurious to or affect saleability of fish or shellfish

Other Standards

Refuse	No garbage, cinders, ashes, oils, sludge or other refuse
Acidity (pH)	Normal range not to be exceeded by more than 0.l pH unit
Turbidity	No increase except from natural sources
Color	No change from manmade sources that will affect best usage assigned to waters
Solids	No suspended, colloidal or settleable solids from sewage, industrial or other wastes that will cause deposition or affect best usage assigned to waters
Oil and floating substances	No residue attributable to sewage, industrial or other wastes; no visible oil film or grease globules
Thermal discharge	None that will be injurious to fish life or affect best usage assigned to waters

Source: adapted from N.Y.S. Department of Environmental Conservation, *Water Quality in the New York Coastal Zone*, Table 1, Classification and Standards for Marine Waters, p. I-12.

TABLE IX Classification and Standards for Fresh Surface Waters*

	AA	A	B
Class			
Best Usage	water supply for drinking or food processing	water supply for drinking or food processing	contact recreation & other uses except water supply & food processing
Conditions	waters will meet Health Dept. standards	waters will meet Health Dept. drinking water standards with approved treatment	—
Dissolved Oxygen — Trout Waters — Spawning	7 mg/l	7 mg/l	7 mg/l
Dissolved Oxygen — Trout Waters — Min. Daily Avg.	6 mg/l	6 mg/l	6 mg/l
Dissolved Oxygen — Trout Waters — Min.	5 mg/l	5 mg/l	5 mg/l
Dissolved Oxygen — Nontrout Waters — Min. Daily Avg.	5 mg/l	5 mg/l	5 mg/l
Dissolved Oxygen — Nontrout Waters — Min.	4 mg/l	4 mg/l	4 mg/l
Coliform — Monthly Median Value	less than 50/100 ml coliforms	less than 5000/100 ml coliforms	less than 2400/100 ml coliforms
Coliform — 20% of Sample	less than 240/100 ml coliforms	less than 20,000/100 ml coliforms	less than 5000/100 ml coliforms
Coliform — Monthly Geometric Mean	—	less than 200/ml fecal coliforms	less than 200/ml fecal coliforms
pH	6.5-8.5	6.5-8.5	6.5-8.5
Total Dissolved Solids	as low as practicable; less than 500 mg/l	as low as practicable; less than 500 mg/l	none detrimental to aquatic life; waters with less than 500 mg/l shall remain so
Phenolic Compounds	less than 0.005 mg/l (phenol)	less than 0.005 mg/l (phenol)	—
Radioactivity — Gross Beta	less than 1000 pc/l (in absence of Sr^{90} and alpha emitters)	less than 1000 pc/l (in absence of Sr^{90} and alpha emitters)	—
Radioactivity — Radium 326	less than 3 pc/l	less than 3 pc/l	—
Radioactivity — Strontium 90	less than 10 pc/l	less than 10 pc/l	—

—	—	Natural
—	—	Natural
—	—	Natural
—	—	—
none detrimental to aquatic life. water with less than 500 mg/l	—	Natural
6.5-8.5	6.0-9.5	Natural
less than 10,000/100 ml coliforms and 2000/100 ml fecal coliforms	—	Natural
—	—	Natural
—	—	Natural
4 mg/l	3 mg/l	Natural
5 mg/l	—	Natural
5 mg/l	—	Natural
6 mg/l	—	Natural
7 mg/l	—	Natural
—	waters must be suitable for fish survival	no waste discharges without approval, filtration through 200 of unconsolidated earth
fishing and other uses except water supply, food processing, and contact recreation	secondary contact recreation; waters not suitable for propagation of fish	enjoyment of water in its natural condition for whatever compatible purposes.
C	D	N

*Source: Adapted from N.Y.S. Department of Environmental Conservation, Water Quality in the New York Coastal Zone, Table 2, p. I-13.

modifications, impoundments, construction, resource recovery from solid waste conversion, groundwater withdrawal and recharge and also from natural erosion.

7. *In-place pollutants.* These are called benthic materials, because they are in bottom sediments. They are the accumulation of past discharges. Duck farm wastes are major in-place pollutants in the Great South Bay of Long Island. PCBs in sediments in the Hudson River have closed it to commercial fishing.

8. *Nonpoint sources.* Urban runoff is only one form of nonpoint sources of pollution. Rural areas also produce serious pollution problems because surface waters become contaminated from agriculture. Pesticides and herbicides may be toxic, fertilizers contribute excessive nutrients, feedlots and barnyards produce animal wastes, and plowing and cultivation produce sediment.

WATER QUALITY IN THE NEW YORK MARINE COAST

Atlantic Ocean and Long Island Sound coastal waters have been designated by DEC as Water Basin No. 17 for purposes of water quality management. About 85% of New York State residents live in this basin—8 million in New York City and 3 million on Long Island. In this densely urbanized region, it is natural that municipal and industrial discharges produce most of the water pollution load. New York harbor must be periodically dredged to maintain adequate depth in navigation channels and adjacent to piers and docks. Dredge spoil must be disposed of, but it contains in-place (benthic) pollutants. Residual wastes were formerly dumped at sea miles from land, but EPA has decreed that this must be stopped. Port activities also contribute pollution by sanitary and wastewater discharges from vessels, by accidental spills, and by refuse from cargo handling. Parts of the West Side of Manhattan and the Red Hook section of Brooklyn still discharge raw sewage into New York harbor.

Atlantic Ocean waters and the Long Island south shore bays as well as Long Island Sound also suffer from pollution, although it may not be as obvious as in the waters of New York harbor.

Shellfishing Areas

Shellfish are a major economic resource in Long Island coastal waters. Unfortunately, about 139,000 acres, or 24% of productive shellfishing waters are closed because they do not meet federal and state water quality standards. Pollution is caused by combined storm and sanitary sewage system overflows, inadequate treatment of collected municipal sewage and disinfection of the effluents, and stormwater runoff from urban and agricultural land. Remedial measures have been taken that increase the shellfish harvest, but continuing pollution forces the closing of increasing acreage.

Groundwater and Water Supplies

The quality of surface water is especially important on Long Island because it affects the quality of groundwater, which is the only freshwater supply. For this reason, activities that affect groundwater quality and supplies have been regulated. Well drillers on Long Island must be registered and must file reports on all wells drilled, including information about pump capacity and the drilling log. DEC must also approve any wells that would supply more than 45 gallons per minute on any single property, except for agriculture and fire protection [3].

The State Commissioner of Health has delegated to county and municipal health departments authority to certify that a water supply is of substandard quality and to order reasonable improvements. Land subdivisions and lots offered for sale must have approved water supply and sewage disposal. The federal Safe Drinking Water Act (PL 93-523) and its federal and state implementing regulations further regulate water quality.

These regulations concerning water supply quality are supplemented by regulation of the discharge of wastewater. Point sources must obtain permits for such discharges from DEC under the State Pollutant Discharge Elimination System. Treated municipal wastewater is being recharged to the ground on a small scale. Recharge basins are also excavated as part of large-scale private and public developments to receive surface runoff and return it underground. Surface waters recharged into these basins may, however, pick up contaminants from agricultural and urban nonpoint sources.

Long Island groundwater levels and quality have been survey and monitored by county, state and federal agencies, including the U.S. Geological Survey, county health departments, the North Atlantic Regional Water Resources Study, the North Eastern United States Water Supply Study and the Temporary State Commission on the Water Supply Needs of Southeastern New York Study.

Nevertheless, Long Island ground-waters have become polluted in some areas. Some wells have had to be closed or abandoned and replaced by deeper wells, beaches have been closed because of seepage from polluted groundwaters, nutrients have been leached to surface water bodies, and salt water has intruded into aquifers near the shore [4].

Water Quality and Recreation

The annual contribution of the recreation industry to the Long Island economy has been estimated at between $600 and $800 million. Access to the ocean beaches is the prime attraction Long Island has to offer. Between June 15 and July 1, 1976, about 30 miles of ocean beaches along the south shore between Rockaway and East Hampton had to be closed to public bathing. Even after the beaches were reopened, attendance was slow in reaching normal volume. The cost of this pollution episode was estimated to be about $30 million to the local economy plus $100,000 in public clean-up costs [5].

Beaches were first closed after two great sludge holding tanks in Island Park, Nassau County, exploded. A million gallons of sludge were spilled. Two weeks later, raw sewage, sludge, oil, tar balls, produce and plastic and wooden containers began washing ashore on Fire Island between Robert Moses State Park and Moriches Inlet. Soon afterward, these materials began to appear to the east and west until almost the entire south shore was affected. The sources of this unusual volume and variety of refuse and contaminants have not been fully determined.

The economic impact and loss of recreation benefits from the stranding of sludge and wastes along the south shore of Long Island appear to justify the fears of business firms and residents that exploration for and the extraction of oil from the Outer Continental Shelf could cause similar losses in the event of a major spill. During the spring and summer, prevailing winds and currents are from the south and east. Oil spills resulting from tanker traffic between drilling platforms on Georges Bank and refineries in New Jersey could wash ashore during the tourist seasons. The NY Office of Parks and Recreation has determined that:

> A major oil spill would have the same effect as the sludge and waste pollution problem of the summer of 1976. If a spill occurs in the spring or summer it is possible that, in addition to severe ecological damage to marine life and water fowl, beaches will be fouled and forced to close down for periods much longer than two weeks [6].

ELEMENTS OF WATER QUALITY MANAGEMENT

New York State established its own water resources and water quality management programs before federal legislation created the Environmental Protection Agency and gave it responsibility for administering the Clean Air and Clean Water Acts. Federal programs, however, have improved environmental quality programs in New York and other states by providing financial assistance, and they have established uniform environmental standards and management procedures. The federal Clean Water Act provided for two basic approaches to water quality management: (1) achievement of water quality standards for water bodies, and (2) application of good practices to the control of pollution from point and nonpoint sources.

Achievement of Water Quality Standards

Streams, lakes and marine waters have been classified according to their "best usage," in descending order, for drinking, swimming, shellfishing, fishing and boating. Standards for dissolved oxygen, coliform count, toxic substances, pH, dissolved solids, phenolic compounds and radioactivity have been specified for each class of usage. The management goal is to maintain the water quality of each water body so that it will meet the standards for its assigned best usage classification. Violation of these standards is an administratively determinable condition of pollution. Best usage classifications and the corresponding water quality standards for marine and freshwaters are presented in Tables VIII and IX.

Application of Good Practices to Pollution Control

Standards for water bodies are concerned with maintaining *ambient* water quality. But the quality of water bodies depends on what is discharged into them from point and nonpoint sources. Ambient water quality standards must therefore be supplemented by effluent limitations from point sources and control of nonpoint sources. Federal regulatory jargon has produced two terms to describe controls for these two sources. "Best practicable treatment" (BPT) refers to national effluent standards for *point* souce discharges, such as those from municipal sewage treatment works and industrial plants. "Best management practices" (BMP) apply to *nonpoint* sources, such as agricultural, forest and urban surface runoff. Uniformly applicable control technology and standards have not yet been established for nonpoint sources. Attempts have been made, therefore, to identify best management practices for field crop and livestock production and forestry that will minimize pollution from these sources and for controlling the quality of runoff from urban areas. Pollution control enforcement, however, is now limited for practical reasons to point sources, and it is carried out by the State Pollutant Discharge Elimination System, which will be described later.

Water Quality Assessment

In order to implement water quality improvement programs, it is necessary to continually inventory surface and groundwaters and to monitor their quality. Specific objectives for pollution control enforcement may then be established.

> Assessment of water quality is an essential step in achieving the state and national water quality goals. Assessment provides the basis for determining the need for revised program strategies for deployment and management of scarce resources, evaluates the reasonableness of existing and proposed water quality standards, and serves as a means for evaluating the effectiveness, cost-benefits, and environmental impacts of point and nonpoint source control strategies [7].

Federal grants have been made to states that have developed monitoring programs in accordance with Section 106 of the Clean Water Act. Monitoring and analysis results of the physical, chemical, biological and groundwater aspects of water quality, together with classification of lakes by trophic condition (nutrient concentration) are incorporated into the DEC Water Quality Inventory and Assessment Report, which is required by Section 305(b) of the Clean Water Act. The report contains these components:

1. description of existing quality of New York waters in relation to EPA "Quality Criteria for Water," state water quality standards and best usage classifications in comparison with 1983 water quality goals,
2. analysis of: (a) extent to which elimination of discharge of pollutants has been or will be achieved, (b) extent to which water quality adequate for a balanced community of aquatic life and recreation in and on the water has been or will be achieved, and (c) recommendations for action necessary to achieve these objectives and identification of waters where this action is necessary,
3. estimation of environmental impact and economic and social costs and benefits of achieving the objectives of the Clean Water Act and projected dates for such achievement.
4. assessment of nonpoint source pollution, recommendations for abatement programs, and estimates for implementation costs.

Major Water Quality Programs

Responsibilities of DEC for managing environmental resources and achieving state conservation objectives have been noted, and the nature of the water quality management problem has been briefly described. Two organizations in DEC had major responsibility for water quality management. The Division of Pure Waters was the operating unit. The Resources Program Development Subdivision in the Division of Land Resources and Forest Management was the planning unit. This was a rather inefficient administrative arrangement, and it may be expected that these water quality management planning and operating functions will be brought together.

The operating strategy of the Division of Pure Waters has been developed around a set of specific operating programs. These programs conform to the structure of the federal Clean Water Act of 1977 and its predecessors as well as to pertinent articles in the state Environmental Conservation Law. The major water quality programs are:

1. Construction Grants
2. State Pollutant Discharge Elimination System (SPDES)
3. Nonpoint Source Management
4. Water Quality Standards
5. Monitoring
6. Enforcement
7. Toxic Substances Control
8. Public Water Supply
9. Residual Waste Management

Space in this report cannot accommodate a full description of each of these programs. Only the first two listed above, the construction grants program and the State Pollutant Discharge Elimination System, will be surveyed briefly. The planning aspect of water quality management, which is the responsibility of the Resources Program Development Subdivision, is concerned with implementing Section 208 of the federal Clean Water Act. The "208" planning program will also be discussed in a later section.

Treatment Works Construction Grants

In the national effort to improve water quality, priority has been given to reducing municipal sewage discharges into rivers, lakes and marine waters. Municipalities have often discharged raw or inadequately treated sewage, becoming major point sources of pollution. Municipal sewage systems also sometimes collect industrial wastes, which may or may not have been pretreated to remove heavy metals, toxic substances or other dangerous substances.

The national objective and state implementation programs aim at universal secondary treatment of municipal wastes and meeting operating standards for efficiency and effectiveness of the treatment works. Some economists claim that this is an economically inefficient method of dealing with the problem. They say that some plants should be required to have more intensive, and costly, forms of treatment, while others may provide simpler treatment, depending on the quality of the receiving waters and objectives for "best usage" for them. In other words, instead of spreading the available capital around uniformly, it should be distributed more heavily where the water quality problems are more severe. Such a system might indeed make more efficient use of the limited capital resources available, but it has been found politically difficult to design and implement a system that has differential effluent standards and financial support. In any case, under existing regulations DEC may require that more stringent effluent standards should be imposed for discharges into "water quality limited segments" of surface bodies where the uniform requirements will not improve ambient water quality to meet national standards.

Federal grants are authorized by Section 201 of the Clean Water Act to pay for 75 percent of the construction cost of municipal wastewater treatment works. Financial aid is available in three steps: preliminary design (Step 1 grants), final design (Step 2 grants), and construction (Step 3 grants). The U.S. Environmental Protection Agency makes the grants and monitors local efforts, but it has delegated review authority to DEC for these program aspects: analysis of infiltration of groundwater into sewer lines, plans and specifications, bid materials, change orders, construction inspections and plans of operation.

The Construction Grant Program started in New York State in 1956 under the original Water Pollution Control Act. It was expanded under the amendments of 1966 and 1972 and the Clean Water Act of 1977. By October 1, 1977, 497 grants had been authorized for total eligible costs of $2.861 billion. Of this amount, $2.146 billion had actually been awarded for design and construction grants.

Most of the early development of Long Island, especially residential subdivisions relied on septic tanks. Population growth and high densities of recent development require conversion to sewage systems because septic tank effluents threaten to pollute the groundwater, Long Island's only source of drinking water. Nassau and Suffolk Counties and their municipalities are therefore actively participating in the "201" construction program.

Many wastewater treatment works have been designed as multipurpose projects. Pumping stations may have rooftop overlooks where they are adjacent to water bodies or scenic areas. Piers where sludge is loaded into carriers for ocean or other disposal may also serve as fishing piers. Treatment plants may have rooftop parks, and their sites may also accommodate baseball fields, picnic areas, ice skating rinks and recycling centers.

Sewage treatment facilities planning is generally initiated voluntarily by municipalities. Nevertheless, DEC monitoring of water quality may identify municipalities that cause a heavy pollution load, but have not taken any action to begin facilities planning. In such cases, pollution abatement procedures may have to be used by DEC, which include Commissioner's Orders to stop the discharge of pollutants; and under the State Pollutant Discharge Elimination Program, operating permits may be denied or revoked.

Facilities construction is an important and costly phase of water quality improvement efforts, but it must be supplemented by effective operation of the treatment works after they are built. If the operators are not technically qualified or plant management is inefficient, effluent and ambient water quality standards may not be achieved. New York State grants are available to municipalities, therefore, to pay up to one-fourth of the annual cost of sewage treatment plant operation and maintenance.

Narrow concern with the design and construction of individual treatment works may also fail to produce a system of facilities that will actually meet regional or statewide water quality objectives. Federal law, therefore, requires that facilities planning and construction must take place within the framework of broader planning for water resources and water quality management. In the Clean Water Act, Section 208 provides for assistance to states to prepare areawide water quality management plans; and Section 303 provides for water resources planning for every water basin in the state. The Water Management Bureau in the Division of Pure Water reviews facilities plans to see that they conform to these broader planning activities (Figure 12).

FIGURE 12 Sewage treatment plant (Photo by NY State Department of Environmental Conservation).

Policy Issues on the Construction Program. Sewage treatment plant construction affects Long Island differently from most other regions. Long Island's water supply comes entirely from underground. Because of the permeable soil, pollutants from surface runoff and septic tanks may readily degrade the water supply. Sewerage and wastewater treatment systems reduce groundwater pollution, but they may aggravate another problem—salt water intrusion into the underground freshwater supply. When freshwater is drawn from the ground, used for various purposes, and then sent through sewerage systems out into the Atlantic Ocean, salt water tends to be drawn into the aquifers—especially near the shore. Evidence of salt water intrusion in water supply wells suggests that wastewater should receive tertiary treatment to prepare the effluent for recharge into the ground-water supply. There are advocates on both sides of this controversial proposal, which is being tested on a small scale.

A more general criticism that has been levelled at the federal construction grants program is that it has been regarded locally as just another public works program. Thomas A. Jorling, Assistant EPA Administrator for Water and Hazardous Materials, has said that, "pressure to 'spend the money' has often prevailed over legitimate concerns about the cost effectiveness of a proposed facility and its associated environmental impacts." [8]

Treatment plant construction may have some undesirable side effects. It may encourage poor land use patterns by opening areas to development that should remain in agriculture or other open uses and may therefore increase pollution from nonpoint sources. Small communities have incurred severe burdens of debt and operating costs that threaten their fiscal integrity. Some of these problems might have been avoided if Section 208 Water Quality Management Plans, which will be described in a later section of this chapter, had been available to guide the construction program. Unfortunately, 208 planning has lagged behind construction, so that some treatment plants have been built without consideration of data on population, land use or nonpoint source pollution. Sanitary engineering professionals and the governments involved have not given enough consideration to innovative alternatives to large-scale sewerage systems, which may actually encourage wasteful use of water resources. Informed public participation should be fostered to avoid some of these problems in the future [9].

State Pollutant Discharge Elimination System

The State Pollutant Discharge Elimination System (SPDES) is concerned with regulating wastewater discharges from point sources. Discharges from municipal sewer lines, sewage treatment plants and industrial plants are major point sources, but they include any discharges that come from pipes, conduits or ditches. SPDES was established by the New York Environmental Conservation Law, Article 17, Section 3-0301. It assumed the permitting authority delegated by the federal government. The National Pollutant Discharge Elimination System (NPDES) was established by Section 402 (b) of the Federal Water Pollution Control Act Amendments (PL 92-500) and continues under the Clean Water Act of 1977. The State Department of Environmental Conservation now operates the System to implement both federal and state laws.

DEC issues permits under SPDES for the discharge of pollutants from industrial, municipal, commercial and institutional point sources. Other point sources, such as vessels, uncontaminated stormwater discharges and major steam electricity generating facilities, are not included in SPDES, but are regulated under other laws. Dischargers who are covered by the System must obtain a permit from DEC and comply with its conditions. Failure to comply may result in revocation of the permit or assessment of damage payments.

Granting of a permit is not a license to pollute; rather it is a means of reducing the discharge of contaminants so that the wastewater itself and the receiving water body will meet water quality standards. The time limit on permits is five years, but they may be issued for shorter periods. The permits specify the limits on contaminants that may be contained in the wastewater, requirements for self-monitoring and schedules of compliance. Public notice and hearing are included in the permit application review process, and applications are also reviewed by the U.S. Environmental Protection Agency, the Coast Guard, the Corps of Engineers, and any other state whose waters may be affected by the discharge.

Effluent contamination limits include chemical, physical and biological parameters, and discharges are monitored to see that they comply with permit conditions. The limits established for each discharge source are based on the volume and content of the wastewater, the existing quality of the receiving waters, and other environmental and economic factors.

Section 301 of the Clean Water Act contains guidelines for determining effluent limits:

1. *Publicly owned sewage treatment plants* were to have secondary treatment by July 1, 1977.
2. *Publicly owned treatment plants* must achieve effluent quality standards based on 'best practicable waste treatment technology' by July 1, 1983.
3. *All other point sources* were to have effluent limitations based on 'best practicable control technology currently available' by July 1, 1977.
4. These private sources discharging 'conventional' (non-toxic) pollutants, which are identified in Section 304 (b)(4), must reach effluent limitations based on 'best conventional pollutant control technology' by July 1, 1984.
5. Private sources discharging *nonconventional, non-toxic* pollutants must reach effluent standards based on 'best available technology economically achievable' not later than three years after such limitations are established or not later than July 1, 1984, whichever is later (but in no case later than July 1, 1987).

6. Private point sources discharging *toxic* pollutants, which are identified in House Committee Print 95-30, must reach effluent limitations based on 'best available technology economically achievable' by July 1, 1984.
7. Private point sources discharging *toxic* pollutants *other than those listed* in House Committee Print 95-30, must reach standards based on 'best available technology economically achievable' not later than three years after such effluent limitations have been established.

Guidelines for establishing effluent standards for *new* point sources in the above categories are contained in Section 306 of the Clean Water Act. The general criteria stated in the federal legislation, such as "secondary treatment," "best practicable waste treatment technology," "best conventional pollutant control technology" and "best available technology economically achievable" are being converted to operational standards by the Environmental Protection Agency and published in its regulations and technical reports.

The NPDES/SPDES system is based on the expectation that prescribing effluent limits on point sources will in fact reduce and eventually eliminate pollution in the nation's streams, lakes and marine waters. This may indeed occur in some segments of these various waters, but other segments may be subject to heavy pollution from nonpoint sources, which are not regulated. These waters may already be so overburdened by pollution from complex causes that regulating point source discharges into them cannot significantly improve their quality.

Federal regulatory jargon includes separate designations for these two situations. When waters that receive regulated point source discharges do indeed reach acceptable water quality standards, these parts of water bodies or stream segments are called "effluent limiting segments." Waters where normal point source regulation cannot improve water quality to meet national and state standards are called "water quality limited segments." In this situation, wastewater dischargers may be required to provide extraordinary measures of abatement. These requirements are determined on a case-by-case basis, taking into consideration technical feasibility and economic, political and environmental factors.

Although the SPDES program has succeeded in improving the quality of some state water segments, point source discharges still pollute the marine coastal zone. Municipal sewage discharges are the main problem in Long Island Sound and the Atlantic Ocean. For many years, New York City discharged untreated or inadequately treated sewage. Although most New York City sewage now receives secondary treatment, the west side of Manhattan and the Red Hook area of Brooklyn still discharge raw sewage into the Hudson River and New York Harbor. New treatment plants under construction are designed to stop this problem. Treatment plant effluents may require measures beyond secondary treatment to abate pollution of marine waters and to permit recharge of effluents into groundwaters. These are being considered in current areawide water quality management studies. It has already been noted that there are intermittent problems caused by municipal discharges in addition to those caused by regular treatment plant effluents. The intermittent pollution is caused by the bypassing around treatment plants of raw sanitary sewage and stormwater runoff collected by combined sewer systems during rainstorms, when the treatment facilities cannot handle the large volume of wastewater.

Implementation Problems. The State Pollutant Discharge Elimination System to control point sources of pollution and protect drinking water supplies from toxic chemicals will succeed or fail depending on the effectiveness of its enforcement. Past experience with permit programs has not always been good.

The New York Public Interest Group and the Environmental Defense Fund detailed severe permit program problems in their 1977 study of toxic pollution in the Hudson River entitled, *Troubled Waters.* None of the hundreds of permits that study investigated required thorough control of toxic discharges. Even worse, the regulatory authorities didn't know exactly what pollutants dischargers were dumping. Little or no analysis had been performed in the past of industrial effluents. Yet most heavy industries are known to empty vast amounts of dangerous oils, solvents, dyes and other hazardous wastes into the state's waters [10].

Uncontrolled dumping along the Hudson River, even with a permit system, resulted in severe degradation of its waters. The Nassau-Suffolk Regional Planning Board discovered that the ground-water supply around certain industrial areas was contaminated with industrial wastes. This was learned during the preparation of a "208" Water Quality Management Program for Long Island. The Regional Planning Board asked for an additional grant from the Environmental Protection Agency to investigate the problem of industrial pollution in detail, but no funds were available. Areawide wastewater management planning and the pollutant discharge permit system are vital elements in the national and state effort to reach the goal of waters clean enough for swimming and fishing by 1983. But without sufficient funds and manpower for research, monitoring and enforcement, even well-conceived programs may not be able to do the job.

SLUDGE AND SPILLS

Sewage Sludge Disposal

The problem of improving water quality by regulating point sources of pollution is not finally solved by municipal and industrial treatment of wastewater. The treatment process itself produces residues, or sludge, that must be disposed of. Private septic tanks and cesspools also accumulate sludge, which must be periodically removed and disposed of. Sewage sludge is mostly water containing suspended and settleable solids, and possibly pathogenic organisms, toxic metals and chemicals. Sludge may therefore be a hazardous waste that must be conditioned in some way before being disposed of by incineration, pyrolysis, ocean dumping, land fill or land dispersal.

Unrestricted dumping of sludge in the Atlantic Ocean has been replaced by a permit system controlled by the U.S. Environmental Protection Agency, The dump site is a designated area 12 miles offshore in the New York Bight. EPA has mandated, however, that ocean dumping must stop in 1981. In a search for alternatives, it supported a study by the Interstate Sanitation Commission [11]. The Commission's report suggested a phased development of composting and land dispersal of sludges accumulated in rural areas; for urban-generated sludges, it recommended pyrolysis and land disposal of residual ashes. Thus the treatment of wastewater to reduce pollution is a complex process in which treatment produces sludge residuals, which must in turn be treated and its own residuals disposed of. In the composting process, sludge is dewatered to contain between 20% and 40% solids. This is mixed with wood chips or other organic material and allowed to weather. The resulting material is free of pathogens; if it does not contain heavy metals or toxic substances, it may be used as a soil conditioner. Pyrolysis is a retorting process in which the sludge solids are decomposed by heat in the absence of oxygen. It produces less air pollution than incineration, and the ash residue may be disposed of in land fills or in the ocean, if this is permitted. Sludge treatment final residues that contain metals, DDT, PCP and other toxic chemicals must be disposed of on land so that these materials do not leach out into surface or groundwaters.

Spills of Oil and Hazardous Substances

Marine water quality is particularly vulnerable to large-scale spills of petroleum products and hazardous substances because much of its production and transportation take place along the coast. Oil spills result in unsightly waters, damage to boat hulls and dock facilities, closing of beaches, death of fish and waterfowl, tainted sea food and long-term inhibition of fish migration and reproduction patterns. Hazardous substances other than oil, particularly chemicals in bulk quantities, cause similar damage to shorelines and living resources as well as threats to human health. The national policy as stated in laws and regulations is that there shall be *no* discharges of oil or hazardous substances into coastal waters. Management objectives, therefore, are the prevention of illegal or accidental spills and effective action to minimize damage.

A National Oil and Hazardous Substances Pollution Contingency Plan has been prepared to implement Section 311 of the Clean Water Act. It includes these elements:

1. Assignment of duties and responsibility among federal departments and agencies in coordination with state and local agencies,
2. Identification, procurement, maintenance, and storage of equipment and supplies,
3. Establishment or designation of strike forces to carry out the Plan,
4. A system of surveillance and reporting designed to insure the earliest possible notice of discharges,
5. Establishment of a national center for coordination and direction,
6. Procedures and techniques for identifying, containing, dispersing and removing oil and hazardous substances,
7. A schedule, prepared in cooperation with the states, to identify dispersants and other chemicals to carry out the Plan,
8. A procedure for reimbursing states for reasonable costs incurred in cleaning up the spills [12].

The discharger has primary responsibility for cleaning up spills of oil and hazardous substances. If he does not act promptly or effectively, the federal government may take charge and assess the responsible parties for damages. The Coast Guard coordinates cleanup activities in navigable coastal waters and contiguous waters subject to tidal action. The EPA coordinates activities for inland waters, and state agencies coordinate remedial action for ground waters.

The plan described above is for action to deal with a spill after it occurs. Different plans have been prepared to prevent spills. These are the Spill Prevention, Control and Countermeasure Plans for action to be taken by owners or operators of onshore or offshore facilities that may cause spills. These plans include estimates of the amount and characteristics of spills that may occur, the placement of diversionary or containment structures and written commitment for manpower, equipment and materials to control and remove spills.

Spills often occur from vessels during transfer or transportation. The Coast Guard must approve the transfer of more than 250 barrels (10,500 gallons) of cargo oil, and the operator must submit an operations manual as part of the permit review procedure. The Coast Guard also regulates the design and operation of tankers and vessels that handle oil and hazardous substances.

WATER QUALITY MANAGEMENT PLANNING

This is a very complex program involving DEC in its own network of institutions that function under a variety of state and federal laws. At the federal level, the regulatory and funding umbrella is provided by the Federal Water Pollution Control Act Amendments of 1972, PL 92-500 and the Clean Water Act of 1977. State Eligibility for grants, authority to administer the National Pollutant Discharge Elimination System (NPDES), and setting water quality standards depends on its carrying out a Continuing Planning Process for water pollution control. The Continuing Planning Process must be approved by the Environmental Protection Agency, which administers the federal laws. As it covers regional and statewide water pollution control planning and will even influence land use planning, the Continuing Planning Process has become a significant element of state planning.

The Continuing Planning Process is expected to produce a state Water Quality Management Plan. In New York, the planning process incorporates county, drainage basin and statewide planning, which were established originally under separate programs. DEC must now integrate them into the Water Quality Management Plan for the state.

County-level studies were initiated in the early 1960s, a decade before PL 92-500 was enacted. This program was wholly financed by the State under Article 17 of the Environmental Conservation Law. It consisted of basic engineering studies for sewage collection and treatment projects from one or more municipalities. These studies are the basis for implementation planning and provide data for basinwide plans, by which they contribute to the Continuing Planning Process.

Basinwide plans were called for by Sec. 303(3) of PL 92-500. They were initially intended by EPA to lead to statewide water quality plans. Seventeen major basins in New York are covered by these plans. They identify water quality problems; classify streams; identify significant industrial, municipal and nonpoint pollution sources; and propose effluent limitations, abatement schedules and remedial solutions and priorities. These basin plans constitute Phase I of the process for preparing the State Water Quality Management Plan. They were scheduled for completion early in 1977.

Statewide water quality management planning, Phase II of the planning process, was initiated under Sec. 208 of PL 92-500. Under this program, six areas have been "designated" for planning by regional or local agencies. These are: (1) Erie and Niagara Counties, (2) part of Chemung and Steuben Counties, (3) a five-county Central New York Region, (4) Westchester County, (5) New York City, and (6) Nassau and Suffolk Counties. The rest of the state will be covered by DEC itself. It should be noted that these designated "208" planning areas cover much of New York's marine and fresh water coastal zone.

Consolidation of state-funded, Sec. 303(e), and Sec. 208 programs for the production of a state Water Quality Management Plan has great significance for coastal zone management program development. DEC is the agency designated by Governor Carey to take responsibility for coordinating and accomplishing the Continuing Planning Process for water quality management. EPA has extended the deadline for approval of the initial Water Quality Management Plan to May 28, 1979. This plan will influence governmental decisions that go beyond improving water quality by planning for sewage collection and treatment. Because of high urban densities, ground-water problems on Long Island and the problem of pollution from nonpoint sources, improving water quality will also require land use regulation and even restriction of development. State water quality planning will therefore have to be integrated with state planning for water and associated resources, air quality maintenance, coastal zone management and land use and housing studies by municipal and regional agencies. Water quality cannot be improved without control of the whole development process that converts raw land into an urban environment. On the other hand, much development may not take place unless sewage collection and treatment facilities are available to make urbanization possible. Water quality, water supply, natural resources and land use planning are coming to be seen as interrelated aspects of a single environmental management process. Recognition and implementation of these interdependencies will have great significance for coastal zone management.

For Long Island, the Nassau-Suffolk Regional Planning Board was designated by the Governor to prepare the "208" Water Quality Management Plan. It received a $5.2 million grant from the U.S. Environmental Protection Agency, which was used to finance its own staff work, to support cooperative work by local agencies and to engage consultants. Plan making was preceded by intensive data collection and analysis. Early in the program the Nassau County Health Department, the Suffolk County Department of Environmental Control and the Town of Islip carried out water sampling surveys of the main embayments of the Long Island coast. Laboratory analysis was provided by the Nassau County Health Department, the Suffolk County Departments of Health and Environmental Control, the Suffolk County Water Authority and the Region I Office of the state Department of Environmental Conservation. The water survey data were used by a consulting firm to develop water quality models for each of these bays.

An engineering consultant completed an inventory of point sources of water pollution in the two counties and identified alternatives for point source management. The Soil Conservation Service cooperated by collecting samples of surface water runoff, which were used to analyze the nature and magnitude of nonpoint source pollution. The Cooperative Extension Service collected data on pesticide and fertilizer use on farms and residential properties to evaluate alternative control measures. The Nassau-Suffolk Regional Planning Board used these and other data to prepare reports on:

1. population projections,
2. existing economic base,
3. economic base projections,
4. industrial activity projections,
5. land use projections,
6. projected wastewater service areas, and
7. projected wastewater flows and loads.

A Technical Advisory Committee of professional people and a Policy Advisory Committee of public officials and citizens were also organized [13].

As survey and planning work proceeded, unexpected amounts of organic chemicals from industrial sources were found in the groundwater from community and industrial supply wells. Additional funds and time were requested from EPA to study this problem [14].

As the December 1978 completion deadline for the Nassau-Suffolk "208" plan approached, the following technical reports were issued:

1. Demographic projections,
2. Point and nonpoint source treatment alternatives,
3. Ground and surface water quality,
4. The use of models in water quality management planning,
5. Sampling data,
6. Environmental and economic assessments, and
7. Animal waste: nonpoint source pollution [15].

The last of these reports presented the results of studies by the Suffolk County Soil and Water Conservation District. The report concluded that dogs and semiwild Pekin ducks were the major unregulated sources of nonpoint animal waste pollution. It found that dog and other animal wastes were responsible for most of the closing of shellfish growing areas during a severe pollution episode. In order to identify the scale of this problem and make recommendations for animal waste control, data had to be collected on animal populations, animal waste characteristics, animal waste impact on surface water quality and animal waste controls. The report recommended that dog cleanup ordinances be adopted by municipalities that have an average density of more than 100 residences per square mile and that neutering programs be funded to reduce dog populations in critical watershed areas. Control measures for duck and horse wastes were also recommended [16].

The draft Summary Plan was issued by the Nassau-Suffolk Regional Planning Board on March 17, 1978. It showed how the bicounty region was divided into eight hydrologic zones according to varying ground- and surface water concerns. For each zone, the plan listed pollution control options that integrated structural measures, such as treatment works, and nonstructural measures, such as regulation of waste sources and water conservation. Water supply was found to be adequate for the next twenty years, provided that management techniques were implemented to maintain water quality standards. These were the major recommendations of the plan:

Sewer construction: Sewering should be continued in areas where studies have shown the need for it. In developed areas, sewers should replace septic tanks and other on-site systems where the density is three dwelling units or more per gross acre. In undeveloped areas, sewers should be installed when new housing projects are at densities of two or more units per acre. Environmentally sensitive areas require sewers when densities are as low as one dwelling unit per acre.

Hazardous wastes: a regional treatment plant is needed for hazardous wastes collected from the whole area.

Industrial wastes: pretreatment should be required before discharge to municipal sewers.

Water conservation: should be promoted to reduce the volume of wastewater discharge.

Stormwater runoff: control is required where pollution loads are heavy or water supplies are threatened. Street sweeping to remove contaminants before they are picked up by rainwater and improved land grading practices are recommended. Nearly 3,000 recharge basins collect rainwater runoff. Many of them may have to be modified so that the quality of the runoff water may be acceptable for percolation into the groundwater supply.

Septic tanks: must be properly operated, and sales of certain hamful chemical cleaners should be banned.

Solid wastes: landfill operation should be improved and should be replaced by resource systems in environmentally sensitive areas.

Animal wastes: dog control and cleanup ordinances are required and the sale of Pekin ducks as pets should be banned.

Fertilizers: use on farms and gardens is a major source of water pollution; a public education campaign should be initiated to reduce fertilizer use, and certain kinds of fast release inorganic fertilizers should be banned [17].

The final Water Quality Management Plan for Nassau and Suffolk Counties will be reviewed by the state DEC and then considered by the Governor. If he finds it acceptable, the plan will go to the Environmental Protection Agency for final action. Once the plan is approved there, all wastewater treatment projects will have to conform to it and implementation measures will have to be developed to regulate point and nonpoint source pollution to achieve federal and state water quality goals.

NEW YORK STATE/ENVIRONMENTAL PROTECTION AGENCY AGREEMENT

It is evident from this necessarily brief survey that water quality management is a large and complex undertaking. It requires the coordination of many programs established under a multiplicity of federal and state laws and the cooperation of many federal, state and local agencies. Citizen review and participation in the management process is an important component of the whole program. In an effort to streamline water quality planning and implementation in New York State, the Commissioner of DEC and the Regional Administrator of EPA prepared a written agreement, "to ensure the orderly integration of water quality management planning and implementation activities which are being pursued by the various entities representing Federal, State, and local government, and to ensure that these activities are consciously geared to achieve the attainment and maintenance of the objectives of the Clean Water Act" [18]. The agreement has been summarized this way in a State DEC release:

Purpose

The State of New York represented by the Commissioner of Environmental Conservation and the Federal Environmental Protection Agency represented by the Regional Administrator of Region II are in the process of concluding an Agreement for the State's water quality program intended to accomplish three basic purposes:
* determine the timing and level of detail for future water quality planning required by Federal Law;
* provide a comprehensive five year strategy document to guide State and Federal programs for water quality management in New York; and
* organize and simplify program reporting requirements (will substitute for separate documents for annual strategy, water quality assessment, and planning work document).

Scope

The scope of the Agreement is wide, encompassing all of EPA's water-related programs and their counterpart programs at the State level. Key federal legislation covered in the Agreement includes:
* Clean Water Act
* Safe Drinking Water Act
* Toxic Substances Control Act
* Resource Conservation and Recovery Act

The Department of Environmental Conservation is EPA's counterpart for administering these laws with the exception of the Safe Drinking Water Act for which the State Health Department is responsible. Implementation of the Agreement will require cooperation of many other agencies:
* federal (Corps of Engineers, U.S. Geologic Survey);
* interstate (Tri-State, Delaware River Basin Commission, Susquehanna River Basin Commission);
* State (Health, Parks & Recreation, Economic Development Board, State Soil and Water Conservation Committee, Interagency Planning Advisory Committee);
* regional (six designated areawide planning agencies, regional planning boards);
* local (municipal sewage treatment agencies, health departments, soil and water districts);

Status

Work on the Agreement, which actually amends an existing much more limited agreement, was started in Fall 1977 by a joint State-EPA task force. EPA representatives included their Washington Headquarters because it will serve as a national model. Because of the priority placed on it by EPA they also supplied the services of a consulting firm to assist, particularly with writing and production of the document and accompanying public information materials.

DEC and EPA will take the draft Agreement to an extensive series of meetings around the State during May and June in cooperation with areawide agencies and DEC policy advisory committees to obtain public comment and recommendations on priorities. The final document will then be signed by the DEC Commissioner and the EPA Regional Administrator. Subsequently, the document will be periodically updated [19].

INTEGRATION OF WATER QUALITY AND COASTAL MANAGEMENT

The New York coastal management program in the Department of State has tentatively identified the Long Island landward boundary of the official coastal zone. It will follow roads, power lines, railroads, jurisdictional boundaries and other such features by which it may be readily identified on the ground. It may have to be adjusted, however, to take account of "geographic areas of particular concern," which require special attention under the federal Coastal Zone Management Act.

The coastal zone boundary defines a relatively narrow strip along the shore, but water quality planning and regulation follow hydrologic basins. The quality of Long Island marine coastal waters and their freshwater tributaries may be affected by land and water uses anywhere in the Long Island Sound and Atlantic Ocean basins that are separated by the Island's glacial moraine ridges.

Because there are differences between the "legal" coastal zone boundary and the "natural" hydrologic basin boundaries, institutional mechanisms will be required to coordinate the Coastal Zone Management Program prepared in the New York Department of State and the Water Quality Management Program produced by the Department of Environmental Conservation. This will be of special significance for establishing and revising "best usage" classifications for the various coastal waters. Department of State designation of "permissible land and water uses" for particular segments of the coastal zone will have to be compatible with DEC classification of "best usage" for the same water bodies.

Water quality and coastal management goals may require mutual adjustment of land use and water quality classifications. For example, coastal management has objectives for both environmental protection and economic development. Water quality classifications may possibly have to be lowered for areas designated by the coastal program for port, waterfront industrial or other economic development. On the other hand, such land use designations may be constrained by DEC "best usage" classification of the affected waters.

Nevertheless, land use and water quality designations may help each other. Land use controls may help to achieve water quality standards in particular areas by limiting or prohibiting uses that might cause waste discharges that would degrade water bodies below water quality standards. But water quality performance standards, such as effluent limitations and required "best management practices" to reduce nonpoint source pollution, may help to achieve land use objectives.

REFERENCES

1. N.Y. State, Department of Environmental Conservation, *New York State/ EPA Agreement* (Draft), Albany, N.Y., March 28, 1978, p. I-2 (Mimeo).
2. Ibid., pp. 1-8 and I-9.
3. N.Y. State, *Environmental Conservation Law,* Article 15.
4. N.Y. State, Department of Environmental Conservation, *Water Quality in the New York Coastal Zone,* Albany, N.Y., July 1977 (Mimeo).
5. N.Y. State, Office of Parks and Recreation, *Long Island Waste Pollution Study: An Economic Analysis,* Albany, N.Y., November 1976 (Mimeo).
6. Ibid., p. 21.
7. N.Y. State, Department of Environmental Conservation, *New York State/ EPA Agreement,* p. I-56.
8. Thomas A. Jorling, "EPA's New Direction on Construction Grants," *Sierra Atlantic,* New York, N.Y., June 1978, p. 13.
9. Ibid.
10. Walter Hang, "The National/State Pollution Discharge Elimination System Under the State/EPA Agreement: Will it Be Implemented?" *Sierra Atlantic,* June 1978, p. 5.
11. Interstate Sanitation Commission, *New York-New Jersey Metropolitan Area Sewage Sludge Disposal Management Program,* October 1976.
12. N.Y. State, Department of Environmental Conservation, *Water Quality in the New York Coastal Zone,* p. A-IV-2.
13. N.Y. State, Department of Environmental Conservation, *208 Bulletin,* No. 3, December 1976, p. 16.
14. Ibid., No. 4, April 1977, p. 7.
15. Ibid., No. 5, July 1977.
16. Ibid., No. 6, October 1977, p. 23.
17. Ibid., No. 8, Spring/Summer 1978, pp. 4-5.
18. New York State/EPA Agreement, p. iii.
19. Memorandum by Thomas P. Eichler, March 17, 1978 (Mimeo).

CHAPTER 8

ENERGY PRODUCTION

Energy production makes important demands on the coastal zone. Electric generating stations are located on the coast because they require large amounts of cooling water. They must also receive bulk fuel shipments, either oil or coal, and water transportation in the cheapest mode. The visual and environmental effects of power stations on their surroundings, however, make such facilities undesirable neighbors for other uses. Steam generation produces air pollution, thermal pollution and the threat of oil spills. Nuclear generation may increase levels of ambient radiation, but the major objection to it is the unsolved problem of how to dispose of spent fuel and contaminated wastes.

Generation of electricity is only one component of energy production. Another is the transportation, storage and refining of petroleum products. Fuel production and handling facilities are unsightly, but air pollution and the threat of oil spills make them even less desirable. Nevertheless, they are essential for the health of the economy and the comfort of our homes. Fuel production is of special concern for the New York marine coast because it lies between the Outer Continental Shelf potential oil sources at the Georges Bank to the north and the Baltimore Canyon to the south. There is little immediate prospect that Long Island coastal sites will be sought for support facilities for exploratory drilling or production platforms, or for receiving and refining crude oil. Nevertheless, if oil is found at Georges Bank and transported to refineries in New Jersey by tanker, then spilled oil may very well wash up on Long Island beaches.

EXISTING ENERGY PRODUCTION FACILITIES

There are 27 electric power generating stations in New York City and on Long Island. They are all located on waterfront sites and make a significant impact on the New York marine coast. The geographic location of these facilities is shown on Figure 13; their generating capacity, type of facility and utility company, are shown in Table X.

163

VIII-2a

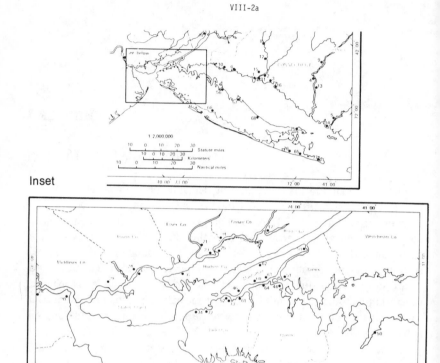

FIGURE 13 Electric generating facilities location.

These electricity generating stations have measurable effects on the environment. Electric utilities that used fossil fuels were responsible nationwide for 62% of the sulfur oxide, 25% of the nitrogen oxide, 14% of the particulate, 0.4% of the hydrocarbon, and 0.2% of the carbon monoxide air pollution. Electric power production also uses more than four-fifths of the total cooling water drawn in the nation. Nuclear plant effluents are relatively small in quantity and routine radioactive releases are lower than permitted by national standards. Nevertheless, major accidental radioactive releases that pose considerable hazard have occurred. Thermal pollution from nuclear plants is about one-third higher than from fossil fuel plants where direct cooling is used [1].

Four types of cooling systems are in use, and they all have significant environmental effects. Once through cooling takes water from the water body source, uses it directly to condense the boiler steam and then discharges the heated cooling water back into the source. This is the least expensive and most efficient system, but it has the greatest environmental impacts: entrapment and entrainment of fish and larvae, dissolved oxygen depletion, discharge of chemical additives (used to reduce corrosion and fouling of the system), and raising the temperature and creating currents in the receiving waters. Pond cooling uses an artificially created pond, not a natural water body with its established ecosystem, as the source of cooling water. Cooling occurs by evaporation of the pond water. It does little damage to natural water bodies; but large land areas are required, from 1-3 acres/megawatt [2].

Wet cooling towers dissipate the heat of the spent steam by letting water fall over the condenser tubes and then passing air, by natural or mechanical draft, over the water as it falls from the top of the tower. The towers are large structures that require land areas of 2-4 acres/1000 megawatts. The wet towers tend to produce ground fog and icing conditions and consume considerable amounts of water. Large quantities of chemicals must also be used to retard corrosion and algal growth. Dry cooling towers release heat directly to the atmosphere by convection and radiation. Mechanical draft wet or dry towers use huge fans to move large quantities of air. The fans are noisy and generally cause thermal updrafts. Dry towers require more land than wet towers, 3-8 acres/1000 megawatts. Dry towers are also higher in cost and less efficient than wet towers, but they do not affect the water source directly [3].

The environmental impacts of some electric power generating plants in the New York marine coastal area are shown in Table XI. These impacts are determined by the kind of fuel used, generation efficiency (the amount of fuel required per kilowatt hour of output), the installed air pollution control equipment and the method of using cooling water. Plants of similar size may have different environmental impacts, depending on these variables. All of these plants use ocean water for condenser cooling, but none have cooling towers (Figure 14).

SITING OF NEW ELECTRIC POWER GENERATING PLANTS

The New York Public Service Commission is a state agency that has been given authority under the Public Service Law to regulate the siting of new generating facilities. It also regulates other kinds of public utilities and common carriers that are privately owned, but its specific supervision over energy production extends to:

TABLE X Electric Power Facilities, New York City and Long Island

Plant Name	Map Key	Utility Company	Capacity (MW)	Type
Manhattan				
59th Street	62	Consolidated Edison	185	Conventional steam
			35	Gas turbine
Sherman Creek	59	Consolidated Edison	217	Conventional steam
74th Street	63	Consolidated Edison	65	Conventional steam
			144	Conventional steam
			37	Gas turbine
Waterside	60	Consolidated Edison	140	Conventional steam
			572	Conventional steam
			14	Gas turbine
East River	46	Consolidated Edison	734	Conventional steam
			60	Conventional steam
Brooklyn				
Narrows	74	Consolidated Edison	348	Gas turbine[a]
Gowanus	72	Consolidated Edison	344	Gas turbine
			344	Gas turbine[a]
Hudson Ave.	52	Consolidated Edison	715	Conventional steam
			90	Conventional steam
Hudson Ave.	73	Consolidated Edison	28	Conventional steam
			8	Hydroelectric
Kent Ave.	61	Consolidated Edison	108	Conventional steam
			28	Gas turbine
Staten Island				
Arthur Kill	43	Consolidated Edison	912	Conventional steam
			18	Gas turbine
Bronx				
Hell Gate	51	Consolidated Edison	70	Conventional steam
			401	Conventional steam
Queens				
Astoria	44	Consolidated Edison	1551	Conventional steam
			700	Gas turbine
Ravenswood	64	Consolidated Edison	1828	Conventional steam
Far Rockaway	48	Consolidated Edison	471	Gas turbine
			114	Conventional steam
Nassau County				
Glenwood Landing	50	L.I. Lighting Co.	377	Conventional steam
			16	Gas turbine
			100	Gas turbine[a]
Barrett	47	L.I. Lighting Co.	375	Conventional steam
			330	Gas turbine
Rockville Center	58	Municipal	27	Internal combustion
			6	Internal combustion[a]
Freeport	49	Municipal	34	Internal combustion
Suffolk County				
Northport	56	L.I. Lighting Co.	774	Conventional steam
			387	Conventional steam[a]
			16	Gas turbine

TABLE X (continued)

Plant Name	Map Key	Utility Company	Capacity (MW)	Type
Port Jefferson	57	L.I. Lighting Co.	467	Conventional steam
			16	Gas turbine
Shoreham	68	L.I. Lighting Co.	850	Nuclear[a]
			53	Gas turbine
			3	Internal combustion[a]
Southhold	75	L.I. Lighting Co.	14	Gas turbine
West Babylon	66	L.I. Lighting Co.	109	Gas turbine
South Hampton	76	L.I. Lighting Co.	11	Gas turbine
East Hampton	65	L.I. Lighting Co.	6	Internal combustion
			22	Gas turbine[a]
Montauk	77	L.I. Lighting Co.	6	Gas turbine

[a]In construction
*Source: H. G. M. Jones, H. Bronheim, and P. F. Palmedo, Electricity Generation and
Oil Refining, MESA New York Bight Areas Monograph 25, New York Sea
Grant Institute, Albany, N.Y., July 1975, p. 10.

FIGURE 14 Nuclear power plant on the shore (Photo by NY State Department of Environmental Conservation).

TABLE XI Environmental Impacts of Steam-electric Generating Plants, 1970

Plant Name	Capacity (MW)	Annual Fuel Use			Annual Plant Emissions[a] (Thousand tons)			Cooling Water (ft^3/sec)	
		Coal (thousand tons)	Oil (thousand barrels)	Gas (thousand cubic feet)	Particulates	SO$_2$	NO	Rate of withdrawal and discharge	Rate of consumption
Consolidated Edison Co.									
59th Street	185		1,464	2.20	0.25	4.22	3.23	870	7.48
74th Street	269		1,426		0.24	4.02	3.14	175	1.51
Arthur Kill	911	1,001	3,069		0.44	26.92	15.78	929	7.99
Astoria	1,551	1,223	3,321	22,655	1.28	27.62	22.75	1,743	15.00
East River	833		2,437	23,399	0.34	6.54	9.94	1,230	10.58
Hell Gate	611		4,419	4,695	0.74	11.70	10.64	744	6.40
Hudson Avenue	765		6,162	17	1.04	16.54	13.59	798	6.86
Ravenswood	1,828	360	8,386	8,217	1.33	29.61	23.32	1,464	12.59
Sherman Creek	216		1,450	153	0.24	3.60	3.23	261	2.24
Waterside	712		3,712	13,642	0.62	9.71	10.84	787	6.77
Long Island Lighting Co.									
Barrett	375		2,314	4,559	0.34	7.92	6.00	412	3.54
Far Rockaway	114		713	729	0.09	2.15	1.71	127	1.09
Glenwood	380		1,807	3,378	0.24	5.40	4.64	368	3.16
Northport	774		7,574		0.19	63.02	16.70	660	5.68
Port Jefferson	467		4,021		0.36	32.38	8.87	600	5.16

[a]Steam electric plants only, excluding gas turbine and hydro-electric.

Source: H.G.M. Jones, Bronheim, and P.F. Palmedo, Electricity Generating and Oil Refining, MESA New York Bight Atlas Monograph 25, New York Sea Grant Institute, Albany, N.Y., July 1975, pp. 14-15.

The manufacture, conveying, transportation, sale or distribution of gas (natural or manufactured or mixture of both) and electricity for light, heat or power, to gas plants and to electric plants and to the persons or corporations owning, leasing or operating the same [4].

Specific concern for power plant siting is delegated to the New York State Board of Electric Generation Siting and the Environment, which is in the Department of Public Service, the operating arm of the Public Service Commission. The chairman of the Board of Electric Generation Siting and Environment is the Chairman of the Public Service Commission. Other members are the state Commissioners (department heads) of Environmental Conservation, Health and Commerce. The fifth member of the Board is an ad hoc member appointed by the Governor. This member is to be a resident of the judicial district in which a proposed facility is to be located and serves only until the Board has made its determination on the application for the new facility. If the Board approves the application, it issues a Certificate of Environmental Compatibility and Public Need [5].

The legislative findings that justified establishment of the Board on Electric Generation Siting and the Environment and its review procedures included these statements:

It is recognized that such facilities cannot be built without in some way affecting the physical environment where such facilities are located, and in some cases the adverse effects may be serious. The legislature further finds that it is essential to the public interest that meeting power demands and protecting the environment be regarded as equally important and that neither be subordinated to the other in any evaluation of the proposed construction of major steam electric generating facilities. . . .

The legislature further finds that the present practices, proceedings and laws relating to the location of major steam electric generating facilities are inadequate to protect the environmental values and to take into account the total cost [to] society of such facilities and result in delays in new construction and increases in cost which are eventually passed on to the people of the state in the form of higher utility rates. Furthermore, the legislature finds that existing provisions of law do not provide adequate opportunity for individuals, groups interested in conservation and protection of the environment, municipalities and other public bodies to participate in a timely and meaningful fashion in the decision whether or not to locate a specific major steam electric generating facility at a specific site. The legislature therefore hereby declares that it shall be the purpose of this Act . . . to provide for the expeditious resolution of all matters concerning the location of major steam electric generating facilities presently under the jurisdiction of multiple state and local agencies, including all matters of state and local law, in a single proceeding in which the policies heretofore described shall apply and to which access will be open to citizens, groups, municipalities and other public agencies to enable them to participate in these decisions [6].

An application for a Certificate of Environmental Compatibility and Public Need is filed with the Chairman of the Board on Electric Generation Siting and the Environment and contains detailed information about the proposal. This includes a description of the physical and ecological features of the site, the source and volume of cooling water, and an environmental impact statement. The gaseous, liquid and solid wastes to be produced by the facility are to be described, and also plans for treating, concentrating and disposing of the wastes. Construction and operation of the facility would have to comply with environmental, health and safety standards and regulations under state and municipal laws. The application must also justify the need for the facility and show how it will meet load demands and contribute to system reliability. Alternate locations must be described and reasons given why the proposed location is best.

Copies of the application or notice that the applications has been filed must be sent to the municipalities affected, the state attorney general and secretary of state, members of the legislature from affected districts, and individual persons and organizations that have expressed an interest in receiving such notice. The utility company must pay with the application a fee of $150,000, which is to be used to defray the expenses of affected municipalities and other local parties to the proceeding that may have to engage expert witnesses and consultants [7].

A hearing is to be held on the application between 180 and 210 days after receipt of the application. The hearing is conducted by a presiding examiner appointed by the Department of Public Service. An associate hearing examiner, who may file a dissenting report on his conclusions and recommendations, is appointed by the Department of Environmental Conservation. The Board is to make its final decision on the basis of the record of the hearing, briefs and exceptions to recommendations of the presiding examiner and the report of the associate examiner, and oral arguments permitted by the Board. In connection with its written decision, the Board is to issue an opinion stating its reasons for approving or disapproving the application. No other state agency nor any municipal agency may require separate permits or conditions for the construction or operation of a power plant approved by the Board unless so authorized by the Board or by state law. Only the Appellate Division of the State Supreme Court of Appeals, the state's highest court, has jurisdiction to hear or determine matters arising out of a decision by the Board.

Applications for two new electric power generation stations with proposed locations on the New York marine coast are before the Siting and Environmental Board. One is a fossil fuel plant proposed by the Power Authority of the State of New York to be located on the western shore of Staten Island near the existing Arthur Kill station. It would generate 700 MW of electric power. The other is a nuclear plant proposed by the Long Island Lighting Company for the north shore of Long Island. It would be a large facility to generate 1150 MW of power. Two sites have been proposed, one at Jamesport in eastern Suffolk County and the other at Shoreham near a nuclear plant already under construction to the west of Jamesport. The utility company prefers the Jamesport site, while the Public Service Commission staff recommends the Shoreham site. A final determination by the siting board is being held up pending a review of need for the additional generating capacity [8] .

A complicating factor is the declaration by Governor Hugh Carey that new nuclear power plants would be discouraged until the problem of the disposition of radioactive wastes has been solved. This is a rather uncertain proscription, however, for a new nuclear plant would not be ready for operation in any case for nearly a decade, even if approval were granted now. By that time the problem of nuclear waste disposal might be under control. Another factor in determining the fate of the proposed north shore plant is that the Governor does not have authority to veto decisions of the Board on Electric Generation Siting and the Environment. The Board is supposed to make its decisions on the basis of the record produced at the hearings presided over by the hearing examiner and his associate. Nevertheless, the Governor appoints the Chairman of the Public Service Commission, the cabinet members and the ad hoc member who make up the siting board. It might be possible for the Governor to persuade the individual board members to disapprove the proposed nuclear plant in spite of official findings that the facility is needed and environmental safeguards would be assured.

State Energy Planning

A technical framework for determining the need for future electric power generating facilities is also provided by the state Public Service Law. It requires the members of the New York Power Pool to prepare annually a single comprehensive long range plan, which is to include a forecast of demand for the next ten years, the additional generating capacity needed and an inventory of the major facilities and the lands owned as future sites by the utility companies that are members of the New York Power Pool.

The state energy planning process has been expanded by the establishment of the State Energy Office. The NY Power Pool plans will be integrated by the State Energy Office into a state energy master plan. The energy industry's contribution will be complemented by a strong state effort to assure public participation in preparing the state master plan. A fund of $200,000 has been established to help public interest organizations and interested citizens pay the expenses of technical preparation and participation.

The state energy master plan and related long-range electricity and gas studies will analyze state energy policy options and try to forecast demand for energy by households and business firms. As of January 1, 1980, these forecasts will be binding on the Board on Electric Generation Siting and the Environment and the Public Service Commission in their determinations about need and location for electric generation and transmission facilities. By April 1, 1979, electric, gas, coal and oil companies in the state are to provide the State Energy Office with their projections of energy supplies and demands. A two-stage public hearing process will be scheduled before the master plan is expected to be adopted around the end of November 1979. The plan will be evaluated and adopted by an energy planning board made up of the State Energy Commissioner, who heads the State Energy Office, the Commissioner of Environmental Conservation, and representatives of the Public Service Commission and the legislative Senate and Assembly.

The New York Power Pool is in the process of investigating potential sites for future power generation stations. Over 200 sites were identified in the initial screening. Further analysis will lead to the selection of 30 sites around the state where future facilities proposed by the energy master plan might be located.

POWER INDUSTRY PROBLEMS
WITH REGULATION

The electric power industry recognizes that electricity generating plants have a great impact on their air and water environments, the land resources they use and the visual aspects of the landscape around them. Regulation of the industry may be necessary, but it involves costs to the power companies that are inevitably passed on to the consumers. We have become so used to electric power that we expect our demands to be met whenever we turn on the switch. Our dependence on electricity is immediately demonstrated when there is a power failure. The problem for the power companies, therefore, is that they must make instantly available in quantities demanded whenever the consumer wants it of a product, electricity, that cannot readily be stored to meet variable needs [9].

Power companies, both public and private, find their attempts at planning to be plagued by uncertainties, but at the same time they form one of the most highly regulated industries in the economy. Because electricity production requires a monopoly on supply, regulation is a necessary substitute for competition. Regulation to assure adequate and economical service to retail consumers is mostly the responsibility of the states. The federal government regulates wholesale rates and interstate power sales.

Supplying electric power is a complex process. The system operated by a single power company may be composed of several separate power plants, each one containing several generating units that may use different fuels. The output of the generators is stepped-up by transformers to high-voltage buses that connect to the high-voltage transmission lines that link the units in the system. Power from the main transmission lines is stepped down to lower voltages for distribution to retail customers at transformer substations. Power systems are made more complex, but more dependable, because the separate utility systems are synchronized into large regional networks. New York state companies are tied into a network that covers the eastern part of the nation and extends into Canada. Planning and operating these technically complex systems must be carried out in an atmosphere of uncertainty as to the future demand for electricity, the time and cost of constructing additional generation and transmission facilities, and the availability and cost of fuel.

Power Needs

Future demand for electricity is the key variable for planning electric power production. Load forecasting is inherently difficult, but it is complicated by controversy about whether or not electricity demand and supply should be allowed to grow as determined by market conditions or be limited by a national "no-growth" policy to conserve fuel and protect the environment. The utility industry has been accused of exaggerated extrapolation of past trends into a forecast of exponential growth that would continue the doubling of load every ten years. In fact, instead of straight line projection, many utilities use econometric models in forecasting that include such variables as the rising cost of electricity, its price elasticity, the effects of conservation, and the availability and substitutability of oil and gas as fuels.

At present, the power industry has estimated an increase in the demand for electricity of about 5.2 percent per year, compounded annually over the next 10-year period. This compares to a projection of 4.4 percent, compounded cumulatively, in President Carter's National Energy Plan of April 1977. Regardless of the precise growth rate, both figures clearly indicated the need for additional power production and power supply facilities if the nation's demand for electric power is to be met [10].

In New York State there are wide differences in power demand forecasts by the utility companies and state agencies. It has already been noted that the state Board on Electric Generation Siting and the Environment has been delaying a decision on a new 1150-MW nuclear generating station proposed for Jamesport or Shoreham on the Long Island Sound shore pending review of the need for new generating capacity. State utility differences are also illustrated by the proposal for a nuclear plant, also of 1150-MW capacity, in the

Town of Sterling on Lake Ontario east of Rochester. Four utility companies, Rochester Gas and Electric, Orange and Rockland, Central Hudson Gas and Electric, and Niagara Mohawk are partners in the proposal. The Board had suspended its certification of the project in May 1978 because projections of growth of future demand by the power companies themselves were significantly lower than estimates they had made only four months earlier.

The Sterling station proposal was the first of six new applications for facilities in the state to reach the Board, and this was the basis for the claim by utilities that the one for Sterling should be approved. The state Department of Environmental Conservation, however, appeared before the Board in September 1978 to emphasize the significance of the new demand forecasts. DEC attorneys claimed that there was no proven urgent need for the Sterling plant, and the Board should therefore take the time to review and compare the probable impacts of all current applications in view of declining forecasts of statewide energy needs [11].

The DEC position is that if too much generating capacity is built, consumers will pay higher electric bills, and the environment will be unnecessarily jeopardized. It believes that the need for additional generating power is so far in the future that building new plants now would certainly cause environmental damage, and they could be obsolete or inefficient by the time they are really needed. The alternatives of smaller, more dispersed facilities and new technologies for burning solid waste and coal would be precluded if the Sterling plant were built now.

Facility Siting

Finding locations for new generating plants and routes for transmission lines poses another problem of uncertainty in planning. Power plants have certain basic requirements that limit location choices. They require large land areas for the plants themselves and for fuel handling and storage; but a buffer zone to separate them from other activities is desirable. They need an adequate supply of cooling water to condense the spent steam that has passed through the turbine generators. Rail or water transportation facilities are required for receiving bulk shipments of fuel and heavy equipment. Plant location should also permit reasonable integration into the system of transmission lines.

Transportation and cooling water requirements are the main reasons for the desirability of waterfront sites, especially in coastal areas such as New York City and Long Island. Major generating plants have closed steam cycles. Boiler feedwater, which may be heated as high as $1000°F$, is highly purified and treated to remove contaminating minerals that would corrode the boiler tubes. In order not to waste this water, the high-temperature, high-pressure steam is injected into a condenser where it is cooled back into water. Large amounts of outside water must be circulated through the condenser to cool the steam, but this water becomes hot also and causes thermal pollution of the water body into which it is discharged.

The physical constraints on power plant siting are augmented by public opposition, mostly on environmental grounds, to new plant construction. Nuclear power plants have more exacting siting requirements than fossil-fueled plants, and there is strong organized opposition to nuclear generation. Utility companies must also contend with the elaborate requirements of the federal Nuclear Regulatory Commission. These have grown in complexity, and "the crucial problem . . . is not so much the need to meet a given set of requirements as the uncertainty regarding changing criteria and future standards for plant location and design" [12].

There is also public opposition to the location of transmission lines, mostly on aesthetic grounds. Opposition to extra-high-voltage lines, of 750 kV ac, is also based on their possible health hazard. Scientific evidence one way or the other is not conclusive. In any case such lines would not be required to serve the heavily populated marine coastal areas of New York state.

Regulatory Delays and Construction Lead Time

Planning uncertainties are compounded by uncertainty about the length of time it will take for new facility approval to get through the maze of the regulatory process. Some applications never do get through, perhaps rightly so, but then the utility company cannot be sure that it will be able to meet all consumer demands, especially during emergencies. Power system planners must try to meet an anticipated load level and a set of contingencies that past experience has shown to be possible. Service to customers may be feasible without additional power production or transmission capacity up to the point at which load level reaches available capacity or the potential crises materialize. When blackouts occur, the fault may lie with the system operators, if they fail to take proper action. But the problem may also be the result of the years of delay in bringing new facilities on line because of regulatory hurdles. The power industry sees the problem this way:

> The regulatory process, with its many opportunities for intervention and public hearings, has now made it necessary to commit fossil generating plants as long as 8 to 10 years in advance of need, with a minimum lead time of 6 years. Nuclear plant lead times for regulatory approvals and construction are now a minimum of 10 years and in several instances have reached as long as 14 years. Major transmission lines now require lead times of 6 to 8 years; in the past, such construction required only 2 to 4 years [13].

Air quality management poses another regulatory obstacle. The power industry claims that emission standards are not based on scientific evidence of threats to health and social welfare; nor are they based on cost-benefit analyses, especially the enormous costs involved in securing the last bit of incremental gain in air quality improvement. To compound the problem, the regulators continually change emission standards. Electric power production is the most capital-intensive industry in the economy. Air quality requirements have demanded huge capital investments for emission control devices in a period of cost inflation.

The environmental impact assessment process and the preparation of draft and final environmental impact statements add another couple of years to the regulatory process. This does not include the time required for public intervention and hearings. As we have seen, New York state law now requires power companies to obtain not only certificates of public need but also of environmental compatibility. This is the conclusion of an industry spokesman:

> Public concern and involvement in the siting process is essential in a free society. In a complex, industrialized (but orderly) society, however, complex issues require the application of specialized knowledge by those trained and experienced. In other words, a specialized technical activity such as power system planning cannot be carried out in an open forum or in the atmosphere of a town hall. This means that the entire intervention process needs to be circumscribed by certain rules, so that its duration and scope are limited and the issues raised are relevant to the matter at hand. The alternative can be nothing less than confusion and chaos [14].

OIL AND GAS EXPLORATION ON THE OUTER CONTINENTAL SHELF

When geologic studies indicated the probable presence of oil and gas reserves under the Atlantic Outer Continental Shelf (OCS), the U.S. Department of the Interior and the petroleum industry began preparations for exploratory drilling. The first step was the auction by Interior of leases to OCS underwater tracts. The Georges Bank lease area is southeast of Cape Cod. The Baltimore Canyon Area is east of Cape May, New Jersey. The second step is to prepare onshore support bases for assembling drilling rigs and supplies and for transporting men and materials to the offshore drilling rigs. The third step, if oil and gas are actually found in commercial quantities, is the erection of permanent drilling platforms and transportation of the product by tanker or pipeline to storage and refining facilities on shore.

The major onshore impacts of OCS petroleum resources exploitation are caused by the waterfront construction of support bases for drilling and eventual production, and construction of transportation, storage and processing facilities. This construction has secondary impacts on coastal communities, for large numbers of construction workers and drilling crew members and their families must be provided with temporary housing and community services. The permanent work force to handle oil and gas production, if it materializes, would be much smaller, but they would have a long-term impact on the economies and physical and social structures of the affected coastal communities. It has been noted in the chapter on water quality management that oil spills during transportation between the production platforms and refineries could foul Long Island beaches and affect the tourist industry.

Section 308 of the Coastal Zone Management Act, as amended in 1978, provides loans and grants to coastal states and communities to prepare for and deal with the onshore impacts. The NY State Department of Environmental Conservation was assigned responsibility for using federal funds to study the positive and negative impacts, both onshore and offshore, of oil and gas exploration and extraction on the Outer Continental Shelf. This new form of resources development along the East Coast could be expected to have impacts on the state economy, its environment, its legal and institutional structure, and on the availability of energy supplies. Contributions to the impact analysis were made by the State Geological Survey, the State Office of Parks and Recreation, the Nassau-Suffolk Regional Planning Board, the New York City Department of City Planning and the Port Authority of New York and New Jersey.

In October 1977 the Department of Environmental Conservation published its summary report of impact analyses made by the various contributors [15]. The report noted that until exploration of the Atlantic Continental Shelf has been completed, it is not possible to estimate realistically the amount of available petroleum reserves or the impacts on the shores of New York State. Its conclusions were therefore based on hypothetical resource finds estimated by the U.S. Geological Survey, and impacts were analyzed on the basis of high- and low-find scenarios. Environmental and economic impacts most relevant to coastal management concerns were identified as follows:

Environmental Implications. OCS development may adversely affect both the offshore and nearshore ocean environments and may cause conflicts with the established commercial fishing and tourism and recreation industries. The possibility of both major and minor oil spills is perhaps the most detrimental aspect of OCS development. According to information to date, pipelines will probably be utilized to transport oil from the Baltimore Canyon (Mid-Atlantic) leasing areas to the shore. Pipelines, if properly designed, constructed and maintained, are a relatively safe method of transporting hydrocarbons. In the case of the Georges Bank (North Atlantic) leasing areas, however, tankers will most likely be used to transport oil to refineries in the Mid-Atlantic. Because oil spills from tankers are more likely than from pipelines, there has been great concern that additional tanker traffic may subject Long Island to a high degree of risk. It should be noted that the possibility of tanker spills in the present traffic lanes exist regardless of OCS development [16].

Economic Benefits. It is not possible to predict exactly what facilities may be located in the State, as companies make individual siting decisions on where to locate after specific sites that meet technical criteria have been identified. The actual kinds and numbers of facilities that may locate in New York State will be dependent upon the successful marketing of various sites in competition with other sites on the East Coast [17].

OCS Exploration and Production Facilities

The onshore impacts of OCS energy resources development and the need for onshore facilities will vary with the kinds of activities involved in each of the five phases of the development process: (1) leasing, (2) exploration, (3) development, (4) production, and (5) shutdown. After the lease sale, the oil companies look for temporary support bases to service the offshore drilling rigs. If commercially exploitable reserves are found, permanent support bases are needed for the development and production phases. The exploratory phase is expected to last about five years. Depending on the size of oil and gas discoveries, production may continue for 15-30 years. Small finds of oil would be transported from production platforms to refineries by tanker. Large finds are more economically transported by pipelines, which are also more desirable because they pose lower chances of oil spills. Commercial finds of gas would also be transported by pipeline. Once the recoverable supplies are exhausted, probably before the end of this century, the wells are shut down and sealed, the production platforms are removed, and the pipelines are abandoned.

Temporary and permanent service bases provide supplies and personnel transfer facilities from shore to the drilling rigs and platforms. Permanent service bases also provide repair and maintenance facilities. Other onshore installations include yards to fabricate production platforms, pipe coating yards and pipeline installation facilities, landfalls and shore terminals for pipelines and tankers, and gas processing plants. Information about these facilities and their characteristics is summarized in Table XII.

Not all of the facilities listed in this table are likely to be located in New York State. Steel platform fabrication yards and refineries require larger land areas than would be available, and air and water quality problems in the New York Metropolitan area would preclude the additional pollution load imposed by a refinery. In any case, existing refineries in New Jersey and around

TABLE XII Characteristics and Physical Requirements for Various OCS Related Activities

	Land (acres)	Waterfront		Employment		Average Wages		Capital Investment (Millions)
		Wharf (ft)	Depth (ft)	Onshore	Offshore	Onshore	Offshore	
Temporary Service Base	5-10	200[a]	15-20	45	150[a]	$17,000	$17,000	$0.15-25
Permanent Service Base	25-50	200[b]	15-20	50-60	200[b]	$17,000	$17,000	$ 10-3.0
Steel Platform Fabrication Yard	200-1000	200[b]	15-30	250-550[a]	–	$19,000	–	$ 30-60
Steel Platform Installation Service Base	5	200[b]	15-20	25[b]	100[b]	$17,000	$18,000	NA
Pipelines and Landfalls	See Footnote c	NR	NR	20[d]	250-350[d]	$16,000	$15,000-25,000	See Footnote e
Pipeline Installation Service Bases	5	200[f]	15-20	25	–	$17,000	–	NA
Pipe Coating Yards	100-150	750	20-30	100-200	–	$11,500	–	$ 8-10
Partial Processing Facilities	15	NR	NR	10	–	$14,000	–	$ 13
Gas Processing and Treatment Plants[h]	50-75	NR	NR	45-55	–	$15,500	–	$ 85
Marine Terminals	15-60	–	30-60	25-65	–	$16,000	–	$ 10-93
Refineries[i]	1000	–	–	440	–	$15,300	–	$815

Source: Adapted from NERBC Factbook.

NA is not available; NR is not required.

[a] per exploration rig

[b] per platform

[c] 50-100 foot right-of-way for landfall; 40 acres if pumping station required at landfall; 60 acres if tanker and barge terminal required.

[d] Onshore at figure assumes terminal or pumping station; offshore figure is construction jobs per lay barge spread.

[e] Capital investment is $700,000 per mile for 8" pipe; $2.0 million per mile for 42" pipe; shore terminal $2.5 million

[f] per installation spread

[g] assumes 100,000 barrel/day capacity

[h] assumes 1 billion cubic feet/day capacity

[i] assumes 250,000 barrel/day capacity

Philadelphia could be expanded more economically than building a new one. The distance of the leasing areas from New York also probably precludes the landing there of oil or gas pipelines from the platforms. Massachusetts or Rhode Island would offer more likely sites for pipelines from the Georges Bank area, and New Jersey and Delaware are more accessible from the Baltimore Canyon area. Associated facilities, such as gas treatment plants, would therefore also not be located in New York State. The kinds of facilities that could possibly be located in the state are temporary and permanent service bases, pipecoating yards, pipeline installation service bases and steel platform installation or module construction bases.

In order to identify possible sites for these facilities, the NY State Department of Environmental Conservation contracted with the Port of New York and New Jersey Authority, the New York City Planning Commission and the Nassau-Suffolk Regional Planning Board to explore possibilities within their jurisdictions. Twelve potential sites were identified in New York City and on Long Island. They are listed in Table XIII, and their locations are shown on the map in Figure 15.

The Port of New York offers some advantages. It is the closest major port to the Baltimore Canyon area, and it contains a wide variety of ancilliary services and industries. Vacant and underutilized waterfront facilities are available that would require less capital investment than starting from undeveloped land. The Port has excellent rail, highway, and air transportation facilities and housing and community services to meet the needs of temporary and permanent employees. Nevertheless, the DEC report notes that:

> The ultimate decisions on siting will be made between the oil companies and the local governments. Exploration support bases have already been established in Davisville, Rhode Island and Atlantic City. Whether additional or replacement support base sites will be used and where they would be located will depend on factors in addition to economic and social considerations. Among the most important of these are oil company perceptions of the desirability of different areas, taking into account such matters as labor relations and community attitudes [18].

TABLE XIII Possible New York State OCS Support Sites

Location	Acres		Zoning[a]	Water		Transportation		Utilities	Environmental Restrictions
	Upland	Under-water		Front (ft)	Depth (MLW)	Road	Rail	Adequacy	
• Brooklyn Navy Yard; Brooklyn	58	—	m3	4,600	20	I-278	Float	Partial	Historical Landmarks
• Erie Basin & Columbia St. Marine Terminal; Brooklyn	47	99	m3	9,287	30	I-278	Float	no	none
• Northeast Container Terminal; Brooklyn	83	45	m3	15,200	35	I-278	yes	yes	none
• Shapleton Piers; Staten Island	52	139	m3	4,000	45	I-278	yes	no	none
• St. George Area									
a. Alcoa	33	—	m2	1,900	18-35	NY rts	yes	Partial	none
b. Coast Guard	9	—	Fed. land	600	18-35	NY rts	no	yes	none
• Brooklyn Army Terminal; Brooklyn	70	26	m3	8,000	40	I-278	yes	yes	none
• Fort Pond Bay; L.I.	50	—	ind	3,000	40^2	NY 27	yes	no	none
• Greenport, L.I.	NA	—	Resident	500	40^2	NY 25	yes	no	none
• Port Jefferson, L.I.	5	—	ind	500	35	yes	yes	yes	none
• Freeport, L.I.	NA	—	ind	200	10-17	yes	yes	NA	none
• Oceanside, L.I.	5	—	ind	200	11-12	yes	yes	NA	none
• Yaphank-Shirley	333	—	ind	none	none	46-A-66	yes	NA	none

[a]m3 and i3: Allows maximum flexibility and essentially heavy industrial use, even those with low performance standards.

m2 and i2: Prohibits natural synthetic gas production processing storage as distribution.

ind: Industrial zoning.

N/A: Not available.

240 feet 200 yards offshore.

Source: Port Authority; New York City Department of Planning; Nassau-Suffolk Counties Regional Planning Board.

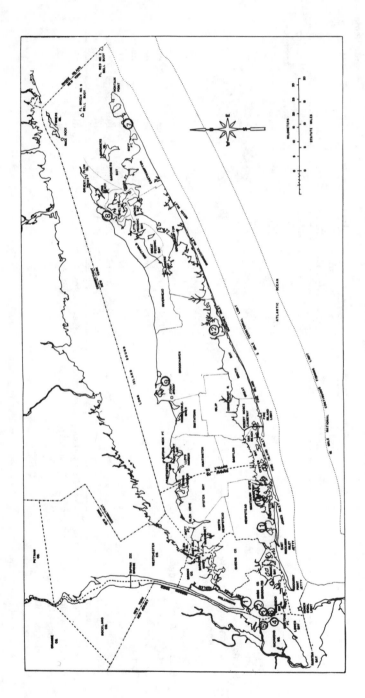

FIGURE 15 Possible sites for support facilities for outer continental shelf oil exploration.

REFERENCES

1. H. G. M. Jones, H. Bronheim, and P F. Palmedo, *Electricity Generating and Oil Refining,* MESA New York Bight Atlas Monograph 25, New York Sea Grant Institute, Albany, N.Y., July 1975, pp. 12-13.
2. Ibid., p. 13.
3. Ibid.
4. N.Y. Public Service Law, Sec. 5 (1) (b), 1970.
5. Ibid., Sec. 140, 141.
6. Chapter 385, Laws of 1972, Sec. 1.
7. N.Y. Public Service Law, Sec. 142(6), 1977.
8. Interview with Robert D. Vessels, Director, Office of Environmental Planning, Department of Public Service, November 2, 1978.
9. Information in this section was obtained from Theodore J. Nagel, "Operating a Major Utility Today," *Science,* 201 (15 September 1978) 985-993.
10. Ibid., p. 990.
11. NYS Environment, October 1978, p. 6.
12. Nagel, "Operating a Major Utility Today," p. 991.
13. Ibid.
14. Ibid.
15. N.Y. State Department of Environmental Conservation, *New York State and Outer Continental Shelf Development: An Assessment of Impacts,* Albany, N.Y., October 1977.
16. Ibid., p. 10.
17. Ibid., p. 12.
18. Ibid., p. 157.

CHAPTER 9

THE NEW YORK STATE APPROACH TO
COASTAL PROGRAM DEVELOPMENT

Congress enacted the Coastal Zone Management Act to encourage coastal states to develop resources management programs. In return for grants to develop and administer such programs, the states were required to conform what they did to the rules and regulations promulgated by the Secretary of Commerce. Only if the state programs were found to comply with the regulations, would grants be made available to implement them.

The Coastal Zone Management Act became law in 1972, but this was not the beginning of coastal resources management in the United States. Many states had enacted laws and established programs to manage coastal resources before 1972. New York was one of those states. The major objective of this study was to identify some of the New York State laws and the agencies responsible for implementing them that are concerned with coastal resources management. It is not enough, however, to pass laws; coastal resources management does not become reality until the laws are implemented and enforced. The effectiveness of resources management will depend to a large extent on the way in which responsibilities are assigned to governmental organizations and on how well they respond.

ALTERNATIVE MANAGEMENT TECHNIQUES

One way to look at management structure is to consider what it is supposed to do. The federal act suggests three alternative management techniques that could be used alone or in combination. Design of the management structure would presumably depend, at least partly, on the management techniques to be used. The alternatives have been listed in Chapter 1, but they are worth repeating:

1. state criteria and standards for local implementation, subject to state administrative review and enforcement of compliance,

185

2. direct state land and water use planning and regulation, and
3. state administrative review for consistency with the management program of all development plans, projects or land and water use regulations proposed by any state or local authority or private developer, with power to approve or disapprove after public notice and an opportunity for hearings.

For all of these alternatives, a state coastal resources management program is requisite. The differences between them are with regard to responsibility for program implementation. Direct state land and water use planning and regulation involves a state agency in promulgating detailed regulations by which it would evaluate applications received for use permits in the coastal zone. By making permit decisions itself, the state agency would preempt local government in the traditional zoning process for the coastal zone [1].

If a state were to use the alternate technique of establishing criteria or standards for local implementation of the state plan, then the local governments would adopt their own coastal zoning ordinances and regulations. They would recieve and decide on use permit applications and also enforce the regulations ro prevent unauthorized uses or development. State administrative review would be for consistency of local regulation and enforcement with state criteria and standards. The state agency would not intervene in individual permit decisions. Nevertheless "in the event of deficiencies either in regulation or local enforcement, state enforcement of compliance would require either appropriate changes in local regulation or enforcement or direct state intervention" [2].

The third alternative involves state coastal management agency review of all development regulations and project proposals by other state agencies, by local governments, and by private interests to see that they are consistent with the state coastal management program.

This option leaves the local unit of government free to adopt zoning ordinances or regulations without state criteria and standards other than the program itself, but subjects certain actions by the local unit of government to automatic state review, including public notice and a hearing when requested by a party. . . .

It should be noted that state review is for consistency with the management program, not of the merits or of the facts on which the local decision is based [3].

STATE MANAGEMENT NETWORK

Coastal resources management in New York is not confined to any one of these techniques. All of them are already in use and will continue. Some state departments exercise direct operating and regulating responsibilities for particular coastal resources. Regional, county and municipal agencies are also involved in planning, managing publicly owned resources, and regulating private activities. Regional and local agencies sometimes operate under general state enabling laws, sometimes they follow state guidelines, and sometimes their decisions are subject to state administrative review.

Coastal resources are far from being managed by a monolithic structure in New York. This state has a highly decentralized government within which an interagency network must be established to coordinate coastal management activities. At the center of this network is the lead agency. Figure 16 shows that the network really consists of subsidiary networks. Interagency coordination is required at the federal level, for sometimes federal agencies work at cross purposes in their coastal zone activities. The same is true of state agencies. Coordination of regional and local agencies requires its own network. These three networks must be tied together by a more comprehensive network for federal-state coordination, intrastate coordination, and state-local coordination. Operating this network is a complex and demanding task for the lead agency.

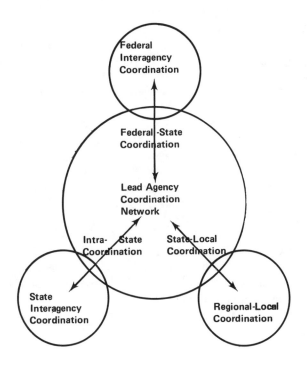

FIGURE 16 Interagency and Intergovernmental Coordination Networks.

Governor Malcolm Wilson had designated the Office of Planning Services, which was in the Executive Department, to be the lead agency for coastal program development. The State Legislature abolished the Office of Planning Services in 1975, and transferred the lead agency responsibility to the Department of State (DOS). The Division of State Planning (DSP) had operating responsibility for the program within DOS. In its role as lead agency, the Department of State was at the center of the coastal management coordination network. It had been designated to take this role only during the program development or planning stage. One of the products of this activity would be a proposal for a coastal resources management structure that may have a different lead agency.

The Division of State Planning (DSP) was responsible within DOS for producing a complete coastal resources management program that would be acceptable to the federal authorities. DSP was not preparing the program entirely inhouse, however, using its own staff resources. Instead, some plan-making activities had been contracted out partly to regional and county planning agencies, and partly to the Department of Environmental Conservation. DSP did have responsibility for integrating these plan segments into a comprehensive, unified state program.

The DSP role in coastal management program development was not simply that of a powerless communicator making sure that each participating agency knew what the others were doing. According to the federal act, the lead agency receives and distributes grant funds for program planning, and it is accountable to the governor and the Office of Coastal Zone Management for the final product.

It has already been noted that New York State was not waiting until a management program had been accepted in Washington before doing anything about its coastal resources. The Department of Environmental Conservation was already operating its own management programs and regulating private activities. The Office of Parks and Recreation had many facilities in coastal areas, and programs of the state departments of Health, Transportation and Commerce vitally affected conservation and utilization of coastal resources. Local governments have long regulated land use through zoning and subdivision controls. Counties also have planning responsibilities and provide a variety of public services. Coastal zone management existed, but it was not yet a coherent and unified state program in New York. It was the responsibility of the Division of State Planning, within the Department of State, to make it so.

REORGANIZATION OF COASTAL
MANAGEMENT PLANNING

The election of Governor Hugh Carey and a critical need to reduce state expenditures combined to cause the abolition of the Office of Planning Services in 1975. There was a hiatus of several months in coastal program development until the state legislature designated the Department of State as the new lead agency for coastal zone management. Budget resources were also then made available for a new Division of State Planning to carry out this responsibility.

The Office of Planning Services, which first assumed the role of lead agency, divided the first federal grant equally between the state and regional or local agencies that had contracted to perform part of the planning work. The Office of Planning Services and the Department of Environmental Conservation used most of the state share. The substate contractors, as they were called, included seven regional planning organizations, three county planning agencies, and three city agencies—among them the New York City Planning Board.

The first year of the New York State Coastal Zone Management Program was directed at determining the need, desirability, and feasibility of coastal zone management approaches and methods. It was decided to concentrate a substantial portion of the program at the regional and local levels. Contracts were developed between the State and Regional, County, and Municipal Agencies having planning responsibilities along New York State's Marine, Great Lakes, and major river coast lines. As the program approached the second year, increased regional and local community interest in coastal management became apparent and additional planning agencies and municipalities requested an opportunity to participate in the development of a coastal management program. This reaction was positive and indicated a growing awareness of coastal zone management and an interest in helping to formulate the second year coastal management work program for New York State. . . . New York shares with most other states a strong allegiance to home rule powers, especially for the control of land use. As the Coastal Zone Management Program unfolds, its provisions will be seen by some as an infringement on the home rule concept despite strong local government participation in the program in many areas of the State. It will be a challenge to devise a management program to reflect these concerns while at the same time providing for the achievement of program objectives. Inherent in this challenge, of course, is a need for a high level of public involvement in designing an acceptable management program [4].

Relying on regional and local planning agencies for data collection, analysis and planning had its costs. Work performed was not likely to be uniform in quality and somewhat different planning emphases emerged. Coastal management planning got off to a slow start because the first lead agency was abolished and another one designated early in the program. Further delays resulted from deficiencies in the work of the substate contractors. Sometimes work called for in the contracts was incomplete or of poor quality. The Division of State Planning carefully reviewed the reports of the contractors and required revisions where necessary. Sometimes the work had to be done over more than once, so review and revision was a slow process. One of the substate contractors, the Genesee-Finger Lakes Regional Planning Board, went out of business just when its first year contract was to have been completed. The work of another regional agency, the Black River-St. Lawrence Regional Planning Board, was disrupted by the loss of the director of its coastal zone work and further delay was caused by deficiencies in the information provided by one of its county subcontractors. From this experience it became evident to the Division of State Planning that local and regional planning staffs were unfamiliar with the technical requirements of coastal resources management and had to be educated along with the general public [5].

The Division of State Planning recognized that costs were involved in bringing regional and local planning bodies into the process of developing a state coastal management program. Nevertheless, it stuck to its guns and defended the New York approach when the Office of Coastal Zone Management in Washington expressed concern with progress in the first year program:

> From the outset it was recognized that to build a viable [Coastal Zone Management] Program in New York State, local support would have to be developed through close contacts with sub-state agencies. Additionally, largely because of the extensive coastline which includes three somewhat dissimilar coastal areas . . . it was decided that much of the basic information upon which the ultimate CZM Program will be based could best be collected and analyzed at the local level or at least on a level much closer to the individual citizen than that of the state agencies. Hence, we are embarked on a program that maximizes local input and which we hope will continue to ensure meaningful participation by citizens in the planning and subsequent management process. We have steadfastly championed this philosophy in meetings with the public, public and private interest groups, agencies at the municipal, county and regional levels, as well as state and federal agencies [6].

The federal Office of Coastal Zone Management eventually became impatient with the slow progress New York State was making in developing its coastal management program. Representatives of OCZM went to Albany for a complete review and evaluation of the state's program development activities. As the result of this visit, a new organization was created, personnel were changed and a new planning approach was introduced.

The State Planning Division was relieved of its responsibility for developing the coastal management plan. A new Coastal Management Program was created whose Manager, Robert Hansen, reported directly to the Office of the

Secretary of State. The staff was considerably enlarged and the Coastal Management Program itself assumed major responsibility for producing the state coastal program. Grants to most regional and county "contractors" were reduced to small amounts that would maintain their interest and participation in the program.

THE DRAFT NEW YORK COASTAL MANAGEMENT PROPOSAL

At this time it is possible only to sketch the outlines of the New York coastal zone management program, for it is still in the developing stage. In draft form it has been presented at a series of public meetings to provide an opportunity for citizens and local officials to participate in policy making. The draft program was revised to reflect the information received at these meetings and was open to public consideration again at formal hearings during April 1979. Final revisions will prepare the plan for submission to the Governor by July 1979. The timetable for implementation calls for the State legislature to enact necessary legislation in June 1979 and for submission of the final program to the U.S. Department of Commerce for review by mid-year.

The Coastal Management Program in the New York Department of State devised a strategic approach to developing its program that was based on four principal concepts. The first was to establish a partnership between state and local governments. The State already had several statewide programs to protect air, water and land resources, some of which have been described here. At the same time, decisions affecting the lands and waters of the coastal zone are regularly made by local elected officials, planning boards, zoning appeals boards and other agencies. The State coastal program would have to recognize these existing state and local authorized activities and find a way of coordinating them into a working partnership.

The second premise of the state approach was to use the existing legislative foundation for making and implementing state resource management and development policy. It would also use existing state and local powers to regulate private sector development and activities that impact on the coastal zone. New state legislation would be sought only to assure state agency and local government adherence to state coastal zone policies and to satisfy the requirements of the federal Department of Commerce regulations.

The third premise was that the state management program would not attempt to specify permissible uses and activities on every square yard of the coastal zone or the location of all major public and private facilities. Instead, the state program would formulate performance standards and criteria to guide state and local agency management decisions.

Fourth, the state coastal program would aim to balance needs and objectives for both economic growth and protection of coastal resources. Areas of particular environmental concern or fragile ecosystems would be protected, but suitable provision would be made for economic activities that require waterfront locations, such as port and related transportation facilities as well as docks and processing plants for the fishing industry.

Preparation of a state coastal management program that would satisfy federal requirements involves these major tasks:

1. delineation of the coastal zone boundary,
2. delineation of geographic areas of particular concern for resources conservation and protection as well as for economic development,
3. determination of the technical content of the management program, particularly the identification of the coastal management problems to be addressed and techniques for regulating land and water uses,
4. design of a state institutional structure for coastal management that would determine these features:
   a. Its responsibility and authority
   b. Its relation to state agencies that have prior legislative mandates for managing and regulating the use of coastal resources
   c. Its relation to local governments, which have been delegated by the state legislature powers to regulate land use and development as well as authority over local waterways and their resources, and
5. drafting of state legislation to establish the coastal management structure, to enunciate state coastal policies and to authorize implementation of the state coastal management program.

Delineation of the Coastal Zone Boundary

The long narrow coastal zone strip extends on land from the New York boundary with New Jersey on the western bank of the Hudson River northward up the river to the federal dam at Troy, then down the eastern bank and around Westchester and Bronx counties to the state boundary with Connecticut on Long Island Sound. The entire shore of New York City and Long Island are included. Along the Great Lakes and St. Lawrence River, the coastal zone extends from the state boundary with Pennsylvania on the west to the state boundary with Canada on the east. New York coastal managers discussed boundary locations with neighboring coastal states so that shoreland resources programs would be compatible and to avoid conflicting land uses at the state lines.

The coastal zone strip has a landward boundary and a seaward boundary. The seaward boundary is simply described by federal requirements. In the Great Lakes and St. Lawrence River, the line extends along the international boundary with Canada. In the Hudson River, the Kill van Kull and Arthur Kill around Staten Island, the boundary is congruent with the state line between New York and New Jersey. In Long Island Sound, the seaward side of the coastal zone is the state boundary with Connecticut and Rhode Island. In the Atlantic Ocean, the coastal boundary is the 3-mile limit of the state's legal jurisdiction.

Determining the landward boundary of the coastal zone is a much more complicated task. The New York coastal program managers decided on two basic principles for tracing this boundary. The first was that there would be only one tier between the shoreline and the coastal zone boundary, and that the management and regulatory process would be carried out uniformly within it. The Long Island Planning Board decided that for Nassau and Suffolk counties local planning and management would find useful a line that followed the contour line 10 feet above the water level or extending 1000 feet inland from the shoreline, depending on the shore configuration. The coastal tier defined by this line would be managed according to county or regional rather than state guidelines.

The second principle was that the landward coastal zone boundary would follow cultural features or political boundaries, such as roads, railroads, utility rights-of-way or municipal boundaries. These features are readily identified and make it easy to determine if a parcel of land lies inside the coastal zone or outside of it. This official state coastal zone boundary was delineated mainly on the basis of local identification of shorelands where land and water uses would have a "direct and significant impact" on the coastal waters described earlier. All areas designated as "geographic areas of particular concern" were included within the coastal zone boundary. The drainage basins of rivers that empty into the coastal zone may extend many miles inland. Only those portions of riverine estuaries that can be considered significantly related to coastal ecosystems or where land and water uses would significantly affect coastal waters have been included.

Definition of "Direct and Significant Impact." This phrase is encountered over and over again in the Coastal Zone Management Act, the federal regulations and coastal management literature. The reason for this is that these words are the basic criterion established for defining the landward limits of the coastal zone. The location of the boundary affects land values and imposes extra regulatory constraints on property inside the boundary; the width of the coastal zone determines in part the scale and scope of the management process. The New York Coastal Management Program developed this operational definition as a basis for defining coastal zone boundaries:

"Direct and Significant Impact" is that impact [on coastal waters] resulting from land and water uses, which changes the physical, chemical, biological, littoral, aesthetic characteristics or socio-economic values of coastal waters to the extent that the character, use or availability of its resources and/or the environmental quality standards of the coastal waters are so adversely affected that they can only be maintained or restored at high cost to society [7].

Within the general definition, the following more specific criteria were used to identify coastal lands that should be included as part of the coastal zone:

1. Fish and Wildlife Habitats: coastal waters and the waters of tributaries upstream to the first barrier to fish migration;
2. Agricultural Lands: where agriculture is dependent on coastal locations, where it is very intensive and covers a large contiguous area, and where there is a clear inland boundary;
3. Visual Access Points: places where there is visual access to the shore from accessible locations, such as roads and public recreation areas;
4. Power Plant Sites: include all existing steam-electric generating facilities of 50 megawatts or more, all sites for which applications to construct such facilities have been submitted to the State Siting Board and all hydroelectric facilities that use coastal waters for cooling or generating electricity;
5. Historic Sites: those which have a close association with New York State history and historic coastal villages;
6. Industrial Areas: where industries are dependent on coastal locations and areas especially suitable for such use, particularly areas zoned for industry that are located adjacent to existing coastal-dependent industries;
7. 100-Year Flood Line: flood hazard areas identified by the Department of Housing and Urban Development under the National Flood Insurance Program; and
8. Coastal Recreation Areas: the entire area of state, county and municipal parks and beaches, fishing and boating access sites and campgrounds.

Lands owned, leased, held in trust or otherwise controlled exclusively by the federal government are not included in the state coastal zone and are not covered by the coastal management program. The Coastal Zone Management Act provides, however, that federal agencies are to carry out their activities "in a manner which is, to the maximum extent practical, consistent with approved state management programs."

Geographic Areas of Particular Concern

A requirement of the Coastal Zone Management Act in that the state must designate geographic areas that are considered to be of particular environmental or economic concern. Two kinds of geographic areas of particular concern (GAPC) have been identified: (1) "site-specific areas" are characterized by some unique values in those places that are of statewide concern; all GAPC have statewide rather than local significance; (2) "generic areas" refer to the areas that fit within the classes of tidal and freshwater wetlands, historic sites and structures, state parks, and existing and potential power plant sites [8].

Criteria for identifying GAPC were based on federal rules and regulations. County planning agencies and the State Department of Environmental Conservation made the initial nominations for more than 400 site-specific GAPC. A reduced list of 70 areas was circulated to local and state agencies. As the result of this review some areas were eliminated and others were added. Private groups and individual persons also nominated areas. The Coastal Management Program lists 97 designated site-specific GAPC. More will probably be added. The generic GAPC are described briefly in the following paragraphs.

Tidal and Freshwater Wetlands. This class of GAPC includes all wetlands that come under the jurisdiction of the state Tidal Wetlands and Freshwater Wetlands Acts. Management objectives are to protect the wetlands and prevent permitted development from altering their natural benefits. The Coastal Management Program will rely on the state legislation to attain these objectives.

Historic Sites. Although there are various kinds of federal, state and local government incentives for preservation, there are no state laws that prohibit the owner of a historic structure from altering or even destroying it. Many historic treasures have already been lost. The Coastal Management Program has therefore designated as GAPC all historic sites of coastal significance that are on the National Register of Historic Places. Existing state property acquisition programs and local laws and ordinances will be relied on for management implementation.

State Parks. Because public access to the New York shoreline is limited by extensive private ownership in residential, commercial, industrial and transportation development, state parks offer important water-based recreational opportunities. The State Office of Parks and Recreation will continue to manage these GAPC. The regulatory powers of local governments will be relied upon to prohibit or minimize incompatible development around these parks.

Existing and Potential Power Plant Sites. Electric power generating facilities are necessary, but thermal pollution, air pollution and negative visual effects produce serious environmental impacts. Existing power plant sites are designated as GAPC, but so are sites for future plants for which state certification is being sought. Management objectives for mitigating adverse environmental impacts will be realized by application of the review procedures established by Article VIII of the State Public Service Law.

Coastal Management Issues and Policies

The draft State Coastal Management program grew out of an inventory and analysis of New York's most significant coastal land and water activities. Eleven issues or concerns were identified as having the greatest importance for the management of coastal resources. It is around these issues that the technical elements of the program were developed. They are intended to recommend state coastal policies, identify the basic legislative authority for implementing them and provide guidelines for management techniques and performance standards for both state and local agencies. These are the eleven policy/management elements:

1. *Protection of Aesthetic Resources:* preserve coastal landscapes and water vistas, cultural and historic values, and enhance them to develop recreational opportunities and the tourist industry.
2. *Recreation Resources to Meet Increasing Demands:* develop New York's coastal areas to provide facilities to meet increasing demands for recreation resulting from urban population growth in the region and increasing leisure time, and to promote the contribution of tourism to local and state economies.
3. *Public Access to the Shore:* improve opportunities for public access where they are cut off by private ownership and development of shorelands and waterfronts; concern for visual as well as physical access.
4. *Economic Development:* stimulate economic enterprises in manufacturing, transportation, fishing, and recreation that require coastal or waterfront sites, in suitable locations and without unreasonable environmental degradation.
5. *Petroleum Exploration on the Outer Continental Shelf:* prepare for the onshore impacts of exploration, extraction, transportation, storage, and industrial processing of oil and gas that may be discovered.
6. *Energy Production to Meet Increasing Demand:* resolve issues of location and design characteristics of electricity generating facilities and the production and marketing of fuels, particularly petroleum products.
7. *Protection of Agricultural Resources:* support New York's largest single industry, which depends to a great extent on the tempering influence of coastal climates, by protecting agricultural lands against the competing demands of residential and recreational development.
8. *Protection Against Coastal Erosion and Flooding:* avoid loss of life and property values by regulating development to avoid hazardous areass and by restoring beaches and dunes.
9. *Protecting Fish and Wildlife and Their Habitats:* protection of breeding and nursery areas, migration, rest and feeding areas, and other habitats from pollution and adverse development.
10. *Water Quality:* manage municipal waste and wastewaters and regulate individual residential, industrial, and other discharges to maintain the quality of water resources for drinking, recreation, fishing, and other purposes.
11. *Air Quality:* abate and prevent air pollution to meet state standards, provide a health living environment, and avoid obstacles to economic development [9].

The New York Coastal Management Program contains extensive and detailed elaborations of each of these issues. The issues and related problems are described, and suggested New York State policies are formally stated for each one. Particular attention is paid to identifying the legislative authority and the state agencies that would have some part of the responsibility for implementing these policies. A wide range of state laws and state programs are available, some of which have been described in the preceding chapters. The Department of Environmental Conservation manages most of these programs, but important contributions will be made by the Departments of Health, Transportation, Commerce, and Agriculture and Markets. Other state agencies with vital roles are the Office of Parks and Recreation, the State Energy Office and the Public Service Commission.

County and municipal governments already use their considerable regulatory powers over land use and local waterways and their own public service programs, especially recreation, in ways that are effective in coastal management. These programs have also been noted earlier. The New York Coastal Management Program will expect local governments to become stronger partners in the joint coastal resources management enterprise. Details of their proposed role will be presented later in the chapter.

Federal government agencies also play an important part in coastal management by means of their regulatory powers and operating programs. The Departments of Commerce, Defense, Interior, Transportation, and Housing and Urban Development are the obvious major agencies. The National Park Service, the Army Corps of Engineers, the National Insurance Administration, the Coast Guard, and the Fish and Wildlife Service are particularly involved. These federal agencies control extensive tracts of land and large installations along the New York coast. These are excluded from the state definition of the coastal zone and federal activities are not subject to state supervision. Nevertheless, federal agencies are enjoined by the Coastal Zone Management Act to conform their activities as much as possible to the State Coastal Management Program.

Given the complex array of federal, state and local laws, regulations and agencies that overlap and interact in coastal resources management, a key element in the New York Coastal Management Program is its proposal for the institutional structure that would have responsibility for integrating all of these powers and activities into a coherent program. This will be a tremendous management task. The structure and functions of this agency and the draft legislation to establish it are described in the next section. Legislation has also been drafted to focus state responsibility for implementing state coastal policies concerning shore erosion and regulating water-dependent industrial and other land uses.

Institutional Structure and Legislative Foundation

The federal Coastal Zone Management Act established a two-stage coastal management process. The first stage involved program development, or planning, and it was called the "305" stage after the section in the federal act that authorized grants to states to carry out this work. Normally, the federal Office of Coastal Zone Management will offer up to four annual grants to cover 80% of program development costs. During its 4-year "305" stage, New York received a total of almost $3.96 million in federal grants. The state contributed $1.53 million as its share.

If the Secretary of Commerce finally approves a state's coastal management program, it enters the program administration, or implementation stage. This is the "306" stage, for federal grants are authorized under this section of the act to finance part of the program implementation costs. The New York Department of State was the "305" lead agency to develop the state coastal program. It has already been noted that one of the key planning decisions that had to be made was on the institutional structure for the "306" lead agency.

The draft coastal management program presented to the people of the state, the Governor and the legislature for their consideration calls for a three-member Coastal Management Board to be housed in the Department of State. Local governments would be invited to participate on a voluntary basis in the preparation of detailed coastal programs for the shores within their jurisdictions. Should particular local governments prefer not to assume this responsibility, especially with regard to the implementation of state policies on the location of water-dependent economic activities and the protection of erosion hazard areas, then the counties or the state itself would take over. These proposals have been formulated in three draft pieces of legislation.

The Proposed Coastal Management Board. The first draft legislative proposal was for an act to amend the Executive Law, which governs the state executive branch, to add a new article to be called the "Coastal Management Act." The act would create a Coastal Management Board of three members. They would be appointed by the governor with the advice and consent of the Senate. The governor would designate the chairman, the members would be chosen to represent "the public" rather than special interests, and they would serve terms concurrent with the governor's incumbency. The Board would receive administrative support from the Department of State but it would not be supervised or take policy direction from the Secretary [10].

The draft legislation proposed the formal adoption of the coastal zone map and the coastal policies on the eleven management issues described earlier. Some of these policies would apply to the entire coastal zone. Others would apply only to specific areas, but in these instances the Board would first seek approval of the Governor and then identify them on the coastal zone map. The draft act also prescribed the criteria to be used by the Board in designating "geographic areas of particular concern" and the procedure to be followed, including public hearings, and in making amendments and additional designations.

The Coastal Management Board would have to develop special relationships with the various state agencies that have prior powers and responsibilities for coastal resources management that were delegated by the state legislature. The sensitive task of the Board would be to assure that the permitting, financing, capital construction and planning functions of these agencies, as they are carried out in the coastal zone, would be consistent with the adopted state policies. One way to do this would be by a memorandum of understanding between the Board and each state agency that they would take primary responsibility for assuring consistency of their actions with state coastal policies; but the Board would be informed of such actions and have the opportunity to discuss any problems of consistency with the agencies.

The other way to assure consistency, as provided for in the draft act, would be by preparing a different kind of memorandum of understanding under which the Board would have authority for reviewing proposed state actions in the coastal zone to determine consistency before agency action could proceed. Under this alternate procedure, the Board would not be able to require an agency to take action contrary to its legislated mandate or responsibility; but the Board could issue an order restraining the agency from acting in a way that would be inconsistent with adopted state coastal policies. The Governor would settle disagreements and would reverse or modify the Board's determination. It should be emphasized that the draft legislation would authorize either procedure for interagency coordination. The choice between the two alternatives would be made by agreement between the Board and each state agency.

The Coastal Management Board would also have the task of eliciting local government cooperation in implementing the state coastal management program. Cities, towns and villages would be encouraged, but not required, to prepare their own coastal management programs consistent with state policies. The local programs would be implemented by the traditional land use planning and regulatory powers of local governments and their own resource management and public service programs. Local coastal management programs that had been approved by the Board would be incorporated into the State Coastal Management Program. The Board would also monitor the administration of local programs for consistency with state policies. Local governments that chose to cooperate in coastal management would receive technical and financial assistance from state and federal sources.

Location of Water-Dependent Economic Activity. The second legislative proposal contained in the New York Coastal Management Program was for "an act to amend the executive law, in relation to providing for water-dependent uses" [11]. The purpose of the draft act was to foster economic development by identifying urban coastal areas that are particularly suitable for water-dependent activities, and prevent their being preempted by other uses that prefer, but do not need, waterfront locations. Coastal cities would be required by law to designate such areas and the land uses that would have priority for locating there. Towns and villages would be permitted to take these actions if they wished to.

Certain kinds of industrial, commercial and transportation enterprises require waterfront locations. Coastal cities in New York State, especially the older ones, have such sites that are obsolete, underutilized and underdeveloped. State economic development policy encourages the establishment of new enterprises, and this draft act was intended to assure the availability of waterfront sites for activities that depend on such access. Under its provisions, the Coastal Management Board would be authorized to offer technical help to coastal cities to help them to identify both the areas that should be reserved and the particular water-dependent activities that should be given priority for locating in them. The cities would then prepare their own regulations for "water-dependent uses," which would be subject to approval by the Board. The Board could revoke its approval if the city failed to enforce its regulations, and it would appeal permit decisions with which it disagreed to the local zoning board of appeals or to the state courts.

If a coastal city, except New York City, failed to prepare acceptable "water-dependent use" regulations, counties would be authorized to adopt local laws for this purpose and would be provided by state statute with the necessary powers for implementation. These counties would have the same technical assistance and supervision from the Coastal Management Board as the cities in whose stead they are acting. If the counties also failed to take appropriate action, the Coastal Management Board would itself prepare and enforce the necessary regulations.

A city could retrieve its authority for regulating areas for water-dependent activities by preparing and obtaining approval for its regulations from the Board. In addition to offering state technical assistance to cities and counties for preparing and administering the appropriate regulations, there would be another inducement. These regulations would become part of the New York Coastal Management Program. Federal and state agency projects and operations would then have to be consistent with land use reservations and priorities established by the regulations.

Development in Coastal Erosion Hazard Areas. Coastal erosion is considered by the New York Coastal Management Program to be a serious enough problem to warrant special regulatory legislation. The third draft act would amend the Environmental Conservation Law to provide a legal basis for state requirements on the regulation of development in coastal erosion hazard areas. This draft law differs significantly from those previously described in that it amends the state Environmental Conservation Law rather than the Executive Law, and it gives administrative responsibility for implementation to the Department of Environmental Conservation rather than to the Coastal Management Board [12].

The proposed act recognizes that erosion caused by storm and long-term actions of coastal waters results in loss of economic values in property and threatens human life. At the same time, building construction in areas subject to erosion hazards may aggravate the erosion process and add to potential property losses. Building on dunes causes their destruction, and erecting structures such as groins and bulkheads that are intended to stabilize particular property shorelines, may actually accelerate erosion damage to other properties.

Under authority of the draft legislation, the State Department of Environmental Conservation, together with local governments, would identify and map shorelines that are eroding at the rate of one foot or more per year, and that would be expected to erode at that rate for another 40 years. Also identified would be areas where alteration of the shoreline by buildings or stabilization structures could increase the exposure of other areas to erosion hazards. Cities, towns, and villages with identified coastal erosion hazard areas would have six months, and technical assistance from DEC, to prepare local development regulations to control development there. The regulations would have to meet with DEC approval.

If the municipality, other than New York City, failed to adopt satisfactory regulations, the counties would have the option of doing so. The counties would also be given the statutory powers to implement the regulations. If the counties failed to act, DEC would itself take action to regulate development in erosion hazard areas. Local governments, however, could retrieve their regulatory powers by complying with the provisions of the proposed act.

The draft legislation contained guidelines for the preparation of erosion hazard area regulations. These would contain building setback lines to avoid erosion damage for at least 30 years. New development that would alter natural erosion protection features, such as dunes and barrier beaches, would be prohibited. Erosion protection structures would not be permitted unless it could be shown that they would have an effective life of at least 30 years and not cause or accelerate erosion of other shorelands.

**Modifications in the Proposed
Management Structure**

After formal public hearings had been held in several cities along the New York coast, the Department of State revised its draft Coastal Management Program to take into account comments and suggestions that had been made by citizen groups and state agencies. The strongest objections had been made to the structure and powers of the proposed Coastal Management Board. Draft state legislation to create such a board was dropped in favor of designating the Secretary of State as the "306" lead agency. Determination of the consistency of proposed public and private actions in the coastal zone with the Coastal Management Program would be determined by the state agencies themselves according to the State Environmental Quality Review Act procedures and provisions of the Uniform Procedures Act for consolidating review of permit applications [13]. Both of these state laws are administered by the Department of Environmental Conservation.

Two substitute bills were proposed by the Department of State to replace the three drafts described earlier. One was a new draft for Article 40 to be added to the Executive Law. This was called the "program bill," and it included the provisions of the former "water-dependent use bill." The other bill was a revision of the "coastal erosion hazard bill," designated to become Article 34 of the Environmental Conservation Law [14].

The Program Bill (proposed Article 40, Executive Law). This bill designates the Secretary of State as the "lead agency" for coastal management. The Secretary would receive and administer federal grants made available under the Coastal Zone Management Act for program implementation. He would not have power to override decisions made by other state agencies with respect to either their own projects or to permit decisions on proposed private activities. Consistency of these proposals with the Coastal Management Program guidelines would be determined by the state agencies themselves according to the State Environmental Quality Review process. This process is similar at the state level to federal requirements for environmental impact analysis under the Environmental Protection Act.

The Secretary of State would be assisted by an Advisory Committee. It would have representation from 10 fields of technical expertise in coastal management and representatives of eight designated geographic coastal areas. Seven ex-officio members would represent state agencies that have major responsibilities for implementing the Coastal Management Program.

Where two or more state agencies have jurisdiction over a particular project and differ as to its consistency with the Coastal Management Program, either agency or the applicant for a permit for the project may ask the

Secretary of State to resolve the differences. The 'Secretary could consult with the Advisory Committee in resolving such disputes.

The Coastal Erosion Hazard Areas Bill (preposed Article 34, Environmental Conservation Law). Several changes were made to the original bill. Coastal erosion hazard areas would be designated only after the Department of Environmental Conservation had adopted regulations defining such areas. They could include dunes, beaches and other natural areas in locations where they provide protection for upland and other coastal areas against erosion. DEC would also promulgate standards and criteria for the design and construction of protective structures so that they would have a reasonable probability of controlling erosion for at least 30 years.

Benefits of the Coastal Management Program

The draft New York Coastal Management Program has been four years in the making, but it will not become operational until it has been accepted, with or without significant modifications, by concerned citizens, the Governor, the legislature and the federal Secretary of Commerce. The state's coastal management staff in the Department of State has tried to satisfy federal law and regulations and anticipate New York State policy response to the issues of coastal resources management. The program is therefore expected to bring these benefits to the state:

1. The program will balance the need for continued economic growth with the objective of protecting coastal ecologies as well as cultural and recreational resources.
2. Designation of geographic areas of particular concern will help to focus management programs on those areas that should have priority for economic investment and those that should have priority for protection of environmental and cultural values.
3. Federal approval of a New York Coastal Management Program will assure that projects and actions carried out or supported by federal agencies will be consistent with the objectives and policies set forth in the state program.
4. An institutional structure will be available to ensure consistency of state agency activities with approved coastal policies.
5. Federal financial grants will be made available to help state and local governments achieve the coastal development and conservation objectives set out in the state program.

STATE-LOCAL MANAGEMENT
PARTNERSHIP

Early federal coastal management law and regulations appear to have visualized strong centralized authority in a state agency. Section 302 of the Coastal Zone Management Act states that, "the key to more effective protection and use of land and water resources of the coastal zone is to encourage the states to exercise their full authority." Many states have avoided centralized management, however, in favor of a "networking" structure, which includes participating state agencies and local governments.

Jens Sorensen has studied examples of the decentralized form in nine coastal states. He calls it "state-local collaborative planning," and identified 10 common procedural components:

1. Development of state-level objectives, policies and guidelines.
2. Preparation of local programs.
3. State review and evaluation of local programs.
4. Negotiation to resolve conflicts and program approval or denial.
5. Sanctions imposed by the state if an acceptable local program has not been prepared.
6. Local implementation of programs.
7. State monitoring of local program implementation.
8. Appeals to the state of local actions or permit decisions deemed to be inconsistent with local programs.
9. State review of proposed amendments to local programs.
10. State sanctions imposed if local programs are not adequately implemented [15].

The management structure proposed in the New York Coastal Management Program contains variations on most of these elements. Nevertheless, it may be anticipated that some local governments, and even citizen organizations, will oppose the coastal management program in general and the state role in particular. They will see a new state bureaucracy threatening local autonomy and home rule. In practice, there may be more state authority than state-local collaboration in the coastal management process. Sorenson notes from his field studies that:

> If the arrangement is to work, both parties must participate and be willing to negotiate, bargain and make trade-offs. . . . Local governments will enter into this mutual adjustment process because they anticipate they will gain more than they will lose from the outcome. . . . They will be attracted by the incentives and avoidance of sanctions plus the willingness of the state administrative agency to work out differences with local government in order to minimize confrontation and its attendant political reverberations [16].

It may be taken for granted that the state-local partnership proposed in the New York Coastal Management Program will not work perfectly at first, even if it is approved by the Governor and legislature. Local governments may have to add to their planning staffs, and there will likely be some problems of communication and mutual understanding between local and state staffs and officials. The state program and local governments may even have conflicting policies and goals. If the state agency demands too much from the municipalities, they may in fact accept the state's offer and dump program preparation in the lap of the state lead agency. This could happen if state administrators do not understand the capabilities of and constraints on local operations. On the other hand, if state requirements are not demanding enough, local programs may fail to achieve state objectives.

The state coastal management agency will have to be sensitive to the problems of establishing effective program collaboration with local governments and with other state agencies that have statutory responsibility for coastal resources management. Some of the difficulties of dealing with local governments may be ameliorated by taking these measures: (1) state appropriations and distributions of federal funds should be adequate to cover state administrative expenses but also grants to local governments for preparation and implementation of their programs; (2) the coastal management agency should have some staff committed to administering grants, providing technical assistance and serving as a communications link between local governments and the various state and federal agencies involved in coastal management; and (3) an informal advisory task force of local planners and officials could be helpful to the agency in fostering the integration of coastal planning, and in assessing the appropriateness of state policies in light of local capabilities and political constraints. These measures are promised in the draft legislation described earlier. Success of the New York Coastal Management Program will depend in considerable measure on the state's ability to deliver on these promises.

REFERENCES

1. 40 *Federal Register* 1691, Sec. 923.26(b) (2), January 9, 1975.
2. 40 *Federal Register* 1691, Sec. 923.26(b) (1), January 9, 1975.
3. 40 *Federal Register* 1691, Sec. 923.26(b) (3), January 9, 1975.
4. New York State, Department of State, "Coastal Zone Management Program Second Year Grant Application," Albany, New York, revised March 19, 1976, pp. 1 and 5.
5. Letter from D. E. Buerle, New York Department of State to W. Matuszeski, Office of Coastal Zone Management, January 20, 1977.

6. Ibid.
7. New York State, Department of State, *Coastal Management Program,* Vol. 1, Albany, New York, March 1979, p. III-3. (Processed)
8. Ibid., pp. VII-1 to VII-3.
9. Ibid., Chapter IV, pp. IV-2 to IV-138.
10. Ibid., Vol. II, Appendix B, pp. 1-38.
11. Ibid., Appendix B, Article G-6, pp. 1-21.
12. Ibid., Appendix B, Article 34, pp. 1-16.
13. State Environmental Quality Review Act, *Environmental Conservation Law,* Article 8, September 1, 1976; Uniform Procedures Act, *Environmental Conservation Law,* Article 70, November 1, 1977.
14. Memorandum by Robert Hansen, Coastal Program Manager, dated May 18, 1979.
15. Jens Sorenson, *State-Local Collaborative Planning: A Growing Trend in Coastal Zone Management,* Office of Coastal Zone Management and Office of Sea Grant, NOAA, U.S. Department of Commerce, pre-publication draft, July 1978, pp. 1-9. Final publication will be by the University of California Sea Grant College Program, La Jolla.
16. Ibid., pp. 2-10.

207